Round about Industrial Britain, 1830-1860

HERE is a description of a lively and unusual tour of industrial Britain in the period which reached its public climax in the Great Exhibition of 1851. Professor Fay sets his tour in the heart of the "stream of industrial invention" in the fields of metals, machinery, transportation, and industrial arts such as spinning, weaving, and paper-making. We travel with him through the industrial sections of Britain, observing conditions in the steel industries of Sheffield, the mines of Merthyr Tydfil, the shipyards of the Clyde, and the factories of Bradford. We see social, economic, and financial conditions in these areas, presented often through contemporary documents, and meet such significant, colourful figures as Adam Smith, Faraday, and Robert Owen.

C. R. FAY is Reader Emeritus in Economic History, Cambridge, and formerly Professor of Economics at the University of Toronto. He is the author of many notable volumes in political economy.

General view of the British Isles

THE TORONTO LECTURES

Round about Industrial Britain
1830-1860

By

C. R. FAY

UNIVERSITY OF TORONTO PRESS
Toronto, 1952

Copyright, Canada, 1952
University of Toronto Press
Reprinted 2017
London: Geoffrey Cumberlege
Oxford University Press
ISBN 978-1-4875-9848-8 (paper)

THE

Preface

NOT strong myself on the technical side I have long desired to offer a course of lectures in which the emphasis should be on technique. For in the words of Dr. Charles Singer, "technology is the skeleton on which economics is the flesh." This I have accomplished by the help of friends who responded freely (I think of the phrase "free and gratuitous coinage") to my request. And I give here their names and the portions for which they are responsible.

It might seem that I should have put their names under their respective contributions, but with their permission I made adjustments in their text to conform with the general ideas. If one section is briefer than another (e.g. Manchester than the Clyde) it is because I asked that it should be so, having regard to the wealth of literature in the one and the paucity of it in the other. I prefer therefore to accept a formal responsibility for the whole. Chapters marked ——— are my own work.

1. Adam Smith and the Stream of Social Education	———
(Factory Note by Mrs. C. D. Rackham)	
2. The Stream of Industrial Invention	*E. I. Lewis*
3. Patent Law and Commodity Study	———
4. Birmingham	*Asa Briggs*
Sheffield	*G. P. Jones*
5. Merthyr Tydfil	*T. M. Hodges*
Birkenhead	*J. E. Allison*
6. Manchester	*W. O. Henderson*
Bradford	*E. M. Sigsworth*
Dundee–St. Andrews	*J. W. Nisbet*
7. The Clyde	*W. S. Cormack*
8. Ireland	*James Meenan*
American Finance	———
9. With Faraday in London	———
10. Tasks Ahead	———

Any one familiar with the pace of lecturing will know that in ten lectures I could not speak all these words. I merely adverted to the matter of chapter three, and to Manchester (chapter six): and I curtailed considerably the material on Merthyr Tydfil, Bradford, and Ireland. Chapters one, nine, and ten are as I spoke them.

I trust that after this explanation I shall not recall the title of that novel of Sir Walter Scott which is set in the Orkney and Shetland Islands.

These lectures were given in October 1950. It is now 1952 and another reign. I recall with pride that after World War I Prince Albert and Prince Henry attended, in Christ's College, Cambridge, some of the lectures which later became *Life and Labour in the Nineteenth Century*.

C. R. Fay

TABLE OF

Contents

LIST OF

Maps and Illustrations

Round about Industrial Britain, 1830-1860

CHAPTER ONE

Adam Smith and the Stream of Social Education

"A MAN commonly saunters a little in turning his hand from one sort of employment to another. When he first begins the new work he is seldom very keen and hearty."

Most true; furthermore, when a man is suddenly transported by air from one continent to another to revisit old scenes and meet old friends and partake of unrationed food, the disinclination to work is colossal.

The Wealth of Nations starts in a pin factory and ends in institutions for the education of youth, since only thus could the dulness of mind, caused by division of labour, be repaired by civic sense and martial ardour. It was in Scotland that the treatise was written, in the little town of Kirkcaldy, where, so legend says, there once were visible in his house the grease marks on the mantelpiece where he rubbed against it with his wig in the absent-minded agony of authorship.

Were I that Dodo of the British economy, a rich man, I would hire a plane and take you with me from Prestwick to St. Andrews by way of New Lanark, Edinburgh, and Kirkcaldy, alighting for a while at each. (John Lowe, Oxford's very reverend Vice-Chancellor, does it, but then he is a Canadian, or else he charges it to decanal expenses.) At New Lanark we should call on Robert Owen; at Edinburgh on Leonard Horner; at Kirkcaldy on the Master himself; in St. Andrews on Andrew Bell; and at the end we should have a satisfying view of the stream of social education 1770-1870—from the time that Adam Smith was compiling his *magnum opus* to the year of the first National Education Act for England and Wales. We should learn much at each place, but most, I think, at New Lanark. In March 1913, improbable as it may seem, I talked with an old man of 84, John Hepburn by name, who had known Robert Owen. He took me to the shady path where Owen used to walk beside the Falls of Clyde at Cora Linn, a few yards below the cave into which, tradition has it, Wallace sprang for safety. Nearby was the water-wheel, still in use, which drove the cotton mills built by Richard Arkwright and David Dale and made immortal by their next proprietor, Robert Owen, the son-in-law of Dale.

Immortal because its owner, after a decade or more of high success, stepped down from his entrepreneurial throne to announce first to his own countrymen and then to the world a New View of Society. Stripped of non-essentials it was a gospel of social education for children, juveniles, and adults; and as this could not be provided without limiting the hours of factory work, he gave his testimony twice over, first before the Factory Committee of 1816 (Chairman, Peel Senior) and then before Brougham's Education Committee of the same year (Education of the Lower Orders in the Metropolis). The first is fuller, and so good that I will give the central piece verbatim:

What reason have you to suppose it is injurious to the children to be employed in regular manufactories at an earlier age?—The evidence of very strong facts.

What are those facts?—Seventeen years ago, a number of individuals, with myself, purchased the New Lanark establishment from the late Mr. Dale, of Glasgow. At that period I found there were 500 children, who had been taken from poorhouses, chiefly in Edinburgh, and those children were generally from the age of five and six, to seven and eight; they were so taken because Mr. Dale could not, I learned afterwards, obtain them at a more advanced period of life; if he did not take them at those ages, he could not obtain them at all. The hours of work at this time were thirteen, inclusive of meal times, and an hour and a half was allowed for meals. I very soon discovered that, although those children were extremely well fed, well clothed, well lodged, and very great care taken of them when out of the mills, their growth and their minds were materially injured by being employed at those ages within the cotton mills for eleven hours and a half per day. It is true that those children, in consequence of being so well fed and clothed and lodged, looked fresh, and, to a superficial observer, healthy in their countenances; yet their limbs were very generally deformed, their growth was stunted, and, although one of the best schoolmasters upon the old plan was engaged to instruct those children regularly every night, in general they made but a very slow progress, even in learning the common alphabet. Those appearances strongly impressed themselves upon my mind to proceed solely from the number of hours they were employed in those mills during the day, because in every other respect they were as well taken care of, and as well looked after, as any children could be. Those were some, and perhaps they may be considered by the Committee sufficient, facts to induce me to suppose that the

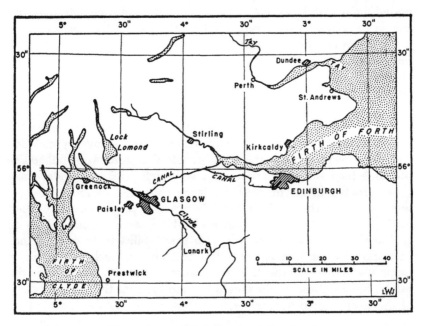

The industrial Lowlands of Scotland

children were injured by being taken into the mills at this early age, and employed for so many hours; therefore, as soon as I had it in my power, I adopted regulations to put an end to a system which appeared to me to be so injurious.

The 1st of January last to the time I left the establishment, about a week ago, out of two hundred and about twenty children, who are in school in the day, and three hundred and eighty or ninety, who are in school at night, there has not been occasion to punish one single individual; and as the school is arranged upon such principles as are calculated to give the children a good deal of exercise and some amusement, the children are more willing and more desirous of attending the school, and the occupations which they are engaged in there, than of going to their ordinary play: the most unpleasant time they have in the week is the Saturday afternoon, which is necessarily a holiday, in consequence of the schools, in which they are taught, being washed and cleaned on that day.

And further:

Will you state who supports the schools?—The schools are supported immediately at the expense of the establishment; they are indeed literally and truly supported by the people themselves.

Will you explain how that is?—New Lanark was a new settlement formed by Mr. Dale; the part of the country in which these works were erected was very thinly inhabited, and the Scotch peasantry generally were disinclined to work in cotton mills; it was necessary that great efforts should therefore be made to collect a new population in such a situation, and such population was collected before the usual and customary means for conveniently supplying a population with food were formed, the work people therefore were obliged to buy their food and other articles at a very high price, and under many great disadvantages; to counterbalance this inconvenience, a store was opened at the establishment, into which provisions of the best quality, and clothes of the most useful kind, were introduced, to be sold at the option of the people, at a price sufficient to cover prime-cost and charges, and to cover the accidents of such a business, it being understood at the time that whatever profits arose from this establishment, those profits should be employed for the general benefit of the work people themselves; and these school establishments have been supported, as well as other things, by the surplus profits, because in consequence of the pretty general moral habits of the people, there have been very few losses by bad debts, and although they have been supplied considerably under the price of provisions in the neighbourhood, yet the surplus profits have in all cases been sufficient to bear the expense of these school establishments; therefore, they have literally been supported by the people themselves.

"The people themselves"—that was the seed from which our consumers' co-operative movement sprang—"that store over yonder" to which old John directed me. Years later, on a tea estate in Ceylon belonging to the Co-operative Wholesale Society, I addressed a group of Indian estate coolies. I told them of Rochdale and the consumers' dividend: they told me how they had set up a store for themselves and out of the profits built a school which their own children and those on the adjoining estate attended *gratis*. They with their school were more faithful to the fountain head than I with my purchase dividend. Owen, in fact, conceived of society as a co-operative school where education never ceases; and it was the greatest single concept in the protective armoury of the new industrialism. Recalled by the Committee, he demolished in advance the supreme nonsense of Nassau Senior about all profits coming from the last hour:

You say you have tried the experiment, since the first of January, of only ten hours and three quarters per day; what was the result of these experiments?—The result of the experiment with regard to the persons employed has been most favourable in every way; the result to the proprietors is much less unfavourable, under the most unfavourable circumstances in which it could be tried, than could be supposed. The difference between our former time of working and the present is an hour per day; . . . since the first of January last the hours of work [at New Lanark] have been ten and three quarters; and I find . . . that the difference to the proprietors will not be more than one farthing per yard upon the goods manufactured from the yarn spun at that manufactory; and I have reason to believe, from the progressive increase in the quantity which has taken place every month since this change took place, that before the end of the year, the yarn will be manufactured as cheap, working ten hours and three quarters per day, as ever we manufactured it, working eleven hours and three quarters per day.

You have expressed your opinion, that before the end of the year the loss of a farthing in twenty-pence, which you mentioned as accruing from the alteration in the hours of work, would vanish; from what did you form that opinion?—On the increased strength and activity, and improved spirits, of the individuals, in consequence of being employed a shorter time in the day.

Have you made any alteration in your wages?—The wages are precisely the same as they were before the alteration of the time. Part of the people are paid by the day, but perhaps the greater part are paid by the quantity they produce.

Those that work by the piece will be losers by the change?—They will sustain some diminution but not a diminution equal to the time, because the produce has been increased beyond the difference of time.

And now on to Edinburgh. For piety we shall visit first the Church of the Burg of Canongate, to bend in reverence before the Master's grave. (I remember in 1938 seeing two gold-spectacled Japanese wandering in the street outside, peering here and there, whereupon I went up and asked them if they were looking for Adam Smith's grave. Their joy when I took them to it was the best service I have rendered to Anglo-Japanese under-standing.) This duty done you will expect me, perhaps, to take you to the Scottish Customs Office in Edinburgh to peruse the Minutes of Adam Smith's day, signed in his school-boy hand, when he was a Commissioner of Customs. But I cannot, because London has become possessed of them, and therefore I have written of them elsewhere in the company of Huskisson and Deacon Hume.

Instead, I will take you to two educational foundations, associated, as a memorial stone tells us, with the name of England's greatest factory inspector, Leonard Horner, the younger brother of Francis Horner of Bullion Committee fame:

17 January 1785—5 March 1864
Founded 1822 Edinburgh School of Art for Mechanics
One of the two founders of Edinburgh Academy
Twenty-four years Government Inspector of Factories.

The Edinburgh Academy, as everyone knows, is one of Edin-burgh's famous schools. Its co-founder was Sir Walter Scott; and the brilliant dux of Horner's time was his young friend Archie Tait, who became Archbishop of Canterbury.

The School of Art for Mechanics has been merged with other institutions in the present Edinburgh College of Art, which is the federal descendant of the School of the Board of Manufac-turers that dates back to the Union and was called "The Trustees Academy"; of the Royal Scottish Academy Life School; of the School of Applied Art; and of the Art Department of the Heriot-Watt College. This Colleges adjoins the University, and Horner's statue is over the doorway.

I am not about to suggest that England in some impossible way owes to Scotland her art and classical culture. That reverses truth. If we are to do it by epigram, it must be "England brought to Scotland capital and culture, which Scotland repaid in enterprise and greed"—yes, indeed, greed for advancement and for education. The Aberdonian and his sixpence: the old chestnut, "I don't know what like of folk they are, for I only talked with heads of departments": or the, to me, newer titbit, "I come frae Dundee, I took ma degree at Glasgey, but it was at Oxford University that I lost ma Scortish ahccent"—all these are part of the saga. Adam Smith was at Balliol. Whether he left his Scottish accent in its library I cannot say. But we do know that he returned to Glasgow to lecture there in the English tongue, following the example of his teacher Hutcheson, and this educationally was as revolutionary a change as the introduction of laboratory work into science teaching at the instance of T. H. Huxley. When Lyon Playfair, grandson of Principal Playfair of St. Andrews, was a candidate for the coveted chair of Chemistry at Edinburgh in 1858, Michael Faraday sent a testimonial, commending his power to expound experimental science "in a clear, logical, audible, and, to me, satisfactory manner"; and Faraday by long practice had equipped himself, the bookbinder's apprentice, with the qualities which he now commended in another. But the mention of Faraday takes me back to New Lanark. What manner of man had done it and with what material? An imaginative Welshman in a cotton mill equipped with English machinery and served by a native population drawn at the outset from the poor-houses of Edinburgh. The key of Owen's doctrine was the influence of environment. I wish I knew enough of electricity to introduce the metaphors of induced current and magnetic field. For that is the sort of response which his workers made to the environment he provided for them—invisible, yet intensely real, a stream of force, *inducing* social life.

But we are bound for Kirkcaldy and St. Andrews. I still believe that sometime somewhere I shall stumble on unpublished minutes or letters, or local press notices, which will throw new light on the author of *The Wealth of Nations*. It may be in Edinburgh, in Glasgow, in St. Andrews, or in distant Aberdeen; it may be in the library of some Scottish country house. The pursuit of economic history is as exciting as any fox chase. At St. Andrews, where our flight is to end, I believe that pleasant surprises are in store for us. I believe that St. Andrews is going *inter alia* to tell us more about Andrew Bell and the quite preposterous origin of English elementary education: in writing upon the sand at Madras, the cheapest and most enduring of all exercise books, in slates and slate pencils that were nearly as cheap, in the cheapness of the single teacher who from one book read out the lesson which pupil teachers, "monitors," repeated along the line—all an anticipation of the final perfection of Children's Hour over the B.B.C., when one voice can reach the whole of Great Britain, and be recorded, if need be, for the English-speaking world! Bell, I understand, was a shrewder man than Lancaster; and St. Andrews, I understand, benefited by his shrewdness. Thus England gave to Scotland capital and culture which Scotland repaid in enterprise—and Bell.

The second best thing that ever happened to England was the Scottish invasion of industrial (and agricultural) England, the first best thing the earlier invasion of Huguenots, in which my ancestors, on the male side, had a share. The most meritorious of the Scottish invaders established himself at Manchester, as chief inspector of factories for Lancashire, part of Yorkshire, and the four northern counties—to wit the afore-mentioned Leonard Horner.[1]

He was of that gifted Edinburgh circle who made the *Edinburgh Review*—Jeffrey, Brougham, Cockburn, Francis Horner. They and their London friends, Francis Baring, Sydney Smith, Henry Labouchere, Dr. and Mrs. Marcet, were so long in political opposition that their opponents in office—Liverpool, Canning, Huskisson, Peel—put on the statute book the fiscal and legal reforms which should have come from them. But their chance came in 1832; and among other things Melbourne in November, 1833, at the instance of Francis Jeffrey, the Lord Advocate of Scotland, had the good sense to secure Horner for the post of Inspector under the Factory Act of 1833. His first

---

[1]For an intimate study of Horner see the *Memoir* by his daughter Katherine M. Lyell, 2 vols. (London, privately printed, 1890).

district was Scotland, his second Lancashire, the factory region *par excellence*. When the Factory Act was under examination before the Committee on the Operation of the Act for the Regulation of Mills and Factories (1840) his was the principal evidence. One answer is revealing:

—Did you find the children in the factories in Scotland attending the parochial schools?

—The mills in Scotland have almost excluded all children under 13.

There was no difficulty over the age limit in Scotland. The parents were greedy for education for their children. And the parents were the factor which counted. For, as Horner went on to say:

The Committee must bear in mind that the larger proportion of the children under 13 years of age employed in both cotton and woollen mills, especially in cotton, are employed, hired and paid by the operatives and not by the masters.

This is a point which, I confess, I had not appreciated before. From 1840 onwards Horner's stature grew. On April 21, 1842, "Thomas Tooke Esq., Thomas Southwood Smith Esq., Doctor of Medicine together with Leonard Horner and Robert John Saunders Two of Our Inspectors of Factories" signed the most dramatic social document of the century—the report of the Royal Commission on the Employment and Condition of Children and Young Persons, *First Report: Mines and Collieries*—and one Commissioner at least knew his mines at first hand! The *Second Report: Trades and Manufactures,* a more diffuse document, followed the next year. Horner was no fanatic. There were occasions when the Short-Time Committees wanted his blood, as well as Shaftesbury's. His approach was that of a travelled scholar with liberal leanings and a specialist's knowledge of geology. For he was President of the Geological Society in 1846 and in his presidential review he drew attention to the work of W. E. Logan on the coal measures in the Canadian Maritimes.[2] He was the father-in-law of the great Sir Charles Lyell, and Darwin was the intimate friend of both. As an inspector Horner

[2] *Journal of the Geological Society,* II, 1846, 145 *et seq.*

insisted on knowing and seeing the facts; for, as Faraday said, you can question facts. He made friends with enlightened mill-owners, and having won their confidence found the reasonable standard to which all could be required to conform. But he was by no means in the mill-owners' pocket. Here is a printed reply to Nassau Senior's *Letters on the Factory Act* (1837), and it is forthright enough:

The law was not passed for such mills as those of Messrs. Greg & Co. at Bollington, Messrs. Ashworths, at Turton, and Mr. Thomas Ashton, at Hyde: had all factories been conducted as theirs are, and as many others I could name are, there would probably have been no legislative interference at any time. But there are very many mill-owners whose standard of morality is low, whose feelings are very obtuse, whose governing principle is to make money, and who care not a straw for the children, so as they turn them well to money account. These men cannot be controlled by any other force than the strong arm of the law; and the Gregs, the Ashworths, and Ashtons, and others like them, must consider that the Act, and the rules and regulations issued under its authority, have been framed to check the evil practices of those who have brought discredit upon the trade; and they must submit to some inconveniences in order that their less scrupulous neighbours may be controlled.

The masters complain bitterly, you say, of the machinery of the Act. They know perfectly well that without other machinery than what is contained in the Act itself, the law could not be enforced; and so, doubtless, Parliament was aware, and they gave the inspectors the power of making such regulations as, in the working of the Act, might be proved to be necessary; a power which has been represented as novel, and as being unknown to the constitution; whereas there are precedents without number. The principle upon which the inspectors have all along acted has been, to endeavour to discover in what way the law could be carried into effect with the least possible inconvenience to the mill-owner or his work-people. To those mill-owners who have complained of the machinery, I have said again and again—"You see what the law requires as well as I do; and if you will point out a mode by which it can be carried into execution, with less trouble to you than attends compliance without regulations, we shall give it our best attention, and will gladly adopt it if we can." *Nothing practicable has been suggested.* Objections have been made in abundance by some mill-owners, but they have proposed no substitute; the demand is, "Do away with your troublesome machinery"; which is another way of saying, "Do not put the law in force."

It is greatly to the advantage of a social service when its first big man has a long span of office. By 1860 the Factory Inspectorate was firmly rooted in the English tradition; the Mining Inspectorate was modelled on it; and the educational system leaned on it to an extent that was unreasonable in principle, but justifiable for historical reasons.

Let us now bring our tributary channels—Adam Smith, Robert Owen, Leonard Horner—into one main stream. Just as no invention is indisputably the first of itself, so there is a pre-Smithian economics, a pre-Owenite socialism (though called by other names), a pre-Horner attack on the problem of child labour not merely at New Lanark but also in the eighteenth-century Quaker lead mines of the North of England.

Now, the high merit of *The Wealth of Nations* was this, that it went along with things: it was not dynamic in the stilted form of Part I Static Part II Dynamic. The two are subtly integrated by a unique literary device—the long digression on silver, which in any but the most skilled hands would have thrown the book out of shape. *The Wealth of Nations* is primarily a book of policy: in fine, the case for Free Trade; and this, I think, explains why it only won general acclamation when, after the great ministry of Peel, 1841-6, England in its heart (and in the pages of Mr. Punch) went full free trade. In the interval between 1776 and 1846 other economists made distinctive contributions, some good and some bad, the worst of the bad being the conversion of political economy into a dismal science and the next worst the obscuration of it by jargon. In Adam Smith there is neither pessimism nor jargon. He rejoiced in high wages, put landlords and capitalists where they belonged, believed in education with a Scotsman's zeal for it, and had a vision of empire (which forms the finale of his book) at once liberal and constructive. The whole way he could not go. For his Britain is pre–Industrial Revolution Britain without railways or steamships, without great factories or urban aggregations. Owen, coming later, supplied the spirit of association, strengthening the side on which Adam Smith was weak; and Horner, combining the liberalism of Smith with the reformism of Owen, brought strength and distinction to a service which was the pathway to another and greater service, the education of the country's youth.

I began with the title "Adam Smith and the Stream of Social Education"; and I must end by justifying it. Why stream? why social? why education? why Adam Smith?

Why stream? Because, with the concurrent progress in physics and biology, any treatment of the social sciences which lacked the idea of evolution was *démodé* from the start. Malthus had the idea. As they themselves acknowledged, he inspired both Darwin and Russell Wallace; and this gives him a key position in the progress of socio-economic thought. I have still to be convinced that Ricardo and Mill were aware of their short-comings here. And because of his eye for evolution Karl Marx (who lies in Highgate cemetery on the other side from Michael Faraday, both graves tended with discipular care), though he was a harsher and less constructive character than Owen, had a deeper influence on the intellect of posterity.

Why social? We may, I think, say that until 1830 the tender spot of the British economy was commercial and fiscal; after 1830, industrial and social. The great unfolding of the social scene, if you prefer the lifting of the lid from the seething social cauldron, took place from 1832 to 1862, from the Royal Commission on the Poor Laws to the Royal Commission on Education, with Mines, Factories, and Handloom Weavers in the middle ground. Up to 1830 the economists kept level with progressive fiscal thought. After 1830, until Marshall came on the scene, they trailed sullenly after social reform—I think of McCulloch with his hidebound Ricardianism and mental muddle over absentee landlordism, of Nassau Senior, Jevons, and many another in their unscholarly war on trade unionism; of John Stuart Mill in his pedantic opposition to the protection of female labour. There was not much depth in Charles Kingsley and the Christian Socialists, still less in John Ruskin, but in the social field they had more worth-while things to say than their coevals in the camp of political economy.

Why education? Because education is the only adequate makeweight for the ravage of world war, the only practicable substitute for fear of starvation as an incentive to industrial effort. Defence, indeed, is of more importance than opulence, but education is more important than either. For war is the off-spring of ignorance and fear, and the world's hope lies principally in this, that the light of knowledge will drive out fear.

Why Adam Smith? In the whole fruit store of economic science *The Wealth of Nations* is the best keeper. I cannot say why in a sentence or two, but I can perhaps throw out a helpful thought. Ricardo, perhaps, had a keener mind, Mill a greater humanity. But Adam Smith had the two supreme gifts of a great historian—the gift of illustration which corresponds with the scientist's gift of experiment, and the gift of synthesis which equates with discovery in natural experimental science. It is an incidental advantage that he possessed a felicity of style, only approached by Walter Bagehot, which makes his masterpiece a joy to read.

NOTE ON THE GROWTH AND EVOLUTION OF THE FACTORY INSPECTORATE, 1833–1860

There is no more important event in the history of the Factory Acts than the appointment of paid inspectors by the Home Office in 1833. This was the result of the passing of the Factory Act of that year. An earlier act in 1802 had provided for the appointment of voluntary unpaid persons to visit the factories, but this provision had been a complete failure. In many districts no visitors were appointed and in others the visitors had little time or inclination for the work. The failure was fully recognized by 1833 and the great turning-point in factory legislation was effected. The inspectorate was placed on a sound foundation from the first in that it was put under central control and thus freed from local opposition and prejudice. The country was divided into four divisions with an inspector in charge of each, and very large powers were placed in their hands. They had the right of entry into the factories and they could make rules and regulations for the carrying out of the Acts. At the same time the total of four inspectors was far too few to cover the number of factories, over four thousand, to be inspected. This led to the appointment of superintendents, of whom there were eight, to assist the inspectors. But these were not at first empowered to enter the factories except by courtesy of the employers. Their numbers grew rapidly, far more rapidly than the number of inspectors; their title was changed in 1844 to sub-inspectors; their office was not finally abolished until 1878.

The progress of factory inspection was largely a matter of trial and error. The powers of the inspector underwent great changes from time to time. The power to make rules and regulations was taken from them. In 1844 they were forbidden to act as magistrates; under the 1833 Act an inspector sitting alone had been entitled to adjudicate on breaches of factory law but the objections to this were obvious and the inspectors themselves welcomed the change. Of ever increasing importance were the reports which were furnished by the inspectors to the Home Office. It was on these that successive Factory Acts were based. It was at first difficult to secure unanimity among the inspectors on the subject-matter of their reports. The early inspectors were men of strong character and each was working independently in his own division. There was an inevitable difference of opinion on many points. This was specially noticeable in the number of prosecutions for infringements of the law which were initiated in the different divisions, varying from 8 between 1833 and 1836 in the Northern Division and 117 in the Lancashire Division in the same period.[1] These figures indicated a real difference of opinion as to whether it was the duty of an inspector to prosecute when he found a breach of the law or whether he should try to get the matter set right before leaving the factory and only take proceedings in extreme cases. The latter view has prevailed in succeeding years and prosecutions, though essential in the last resort, are very few indeed in comparison with the number of inspectors. Minor breaches of the law are now dealt with by admonition and warning. The differences of opinion among the inspectors were bound to cause difficulty, but the opposition to further centralization was continuous until in 1878 a Chief Inspector was appointed to be responsible for the consistent administration of factory law.

[1]See Maurice Walter Thomas, *The Early Factory Legislation* (Leigh-on-Sea, 1948).

The sphere of the inspectors was continually widening as new industries were brought under the control of the Factory Acts. At first only textile mills were included, but in course of time print, dye, lace, and other works were added. Not only did the actual scope of the inspectors' work increase but it became increasingly complicated. The hours of labour of women and young persons were restricted by successive Acts to a certain number each day, but the working hours might be spread over the whole of the day. Different workers or groups of workers could be employed for different periods and it was impossible to detect for how many hours any particular worker had been employed. "If there were twenty inspectors," said the manager of a Manchester mill, "we could defy them all if working by relays were allowed." It was not until 1853 that the normal working day was established by law and the labours of the factory inspectors were thus considerably lightened.

The employment of large numbers of children in factories presented another problem to the inspectors. Parliament might lay it down that a child was not to be employed under the age of nine but as there was no registration of births at that time there was no means of ascertaining the age of children. The inspectors made every effort to find some test on which they could rely and the inspection of the children's teeth to see how far the second teeth had come through was actually suggested and tried. In addition to the problem of age there was also the provision of schools. The early Factory Acts laid it down that a child under a certain age must attend school for a certain number of hours in the day or in the week and the inspector had to see that this was done. But in many places there were no schools for the children to attend while in others the schools were so inefficient as to be of no educational value to the children. It was not until 1860 that the inspection of schools was taken over by the Committee of the Privy Council on Education.

It must be remembered that for the greater part of the century the efforts of the inspectors met with bitter hostility from many quarters. There were opponents in Parliament who for ideological reasons disliked any government interference between employers and their work-people and feared that its effect would be harmful to the industry of the country. Employers naturally resented both the Acts themselves and the visits of the inspectors to their factories. Parents in too many cases looked with fear at the prospect of being deprived of the earnings of their children if the inspectors discovered that their employment was illegal. Through all these difficulties and opposition the inspectors made their way and established the system of factory inspection in Great Britain, generally acknowledged to be the best in the world. On the foundations laid in 1833 it has been possible to build up an inspectorate that has the confidence of employers and work-people alike and is competent to grapple with the ever increasing complications of modern industrial life.

CHAPTER TWO

The Stream of Industrial Invention

It is not easy for us today to realize the conditions under which mechanical invention was prosecuted and the difficulties with which the inventors had to contend only a century ago, but one cannot do justice to them unless these conditions are remembered. Nowadays research is a profession: education and training for it are organized for, and made accessible to, those in whom the urge is strong, as well as to some who have little aptitude for it or are without the personal qualities required. It was a hazardous business then, with punishment for non-success.

Materials were less varied in those days. The properties and suitability of the various kinds of timber and the best way to handle and mature them had been well known for centuries. New importations were not numerous. The wheelwright, builder, and cabinet-maker were highly skilled, their tools though few were adequate. Apart from the use and care of carpentry machines, they would have little to learn from, but something to teach to, their successors today: it is the older, skilled woodworker who will thank you now for the loan of Bourne's *Wheelwright's Shop* or Rose's *Village Carpenter*.

As regards metals the tale is different. The mechanic of today knows metals and alloys of which the early nineteenth-century artisan never dreamed. The latter chose between the few available to him. There were malleable (or wrought) iron, and steel. How one could be changed into the other he knew well enough; the higher carbon steels for cutlery he could harden, soften, and temper; and he knew also how to cast both iron and steel. But since their composition would vary in spite of him, their behaviour was not entirely predictable. With native metals—the noble metals gold and silver, the easily worked copper, tin, and lead, and even the brittle antimony and bismuth—he had a specialist's acquaintance. Indeed by 1750 the alloys of long standing, too, those discovered because their ores occur in association or in the same locality, and could be mixed, or those whose components could be melted together—bronze and its varieties (bell metal and gun metal), pewter, Britannia metal, type-metal, solder, and a few others—were in daily use. Brass under the name of latten, much used for inscribed plates over tombs, had been imported for centuries, but for a long time its composition remained a puzzle. Its component zinc was not isolated in England until halfway through the 1700's.

If a craftsman needed an alloy with properties other than those possessed by the above-named, he found himself nearly or quite at a standstill. It is hardly too much to say that today the metallurgist, given a list of desired properties reasonably flexible in an alloy unknown to the inquirer, could in many instances, even if it is novel, construct a recipe for it, indicate the proper treatment for it, and come very near to success. It is likely now that the engineer rather than the metallurgist is the backward party and that the latter has already made such an alloy, examined it, and proclaimed its possibilities.

Progress with the steels alone has been astounding—the very definition has expanded and, to some extent, changed. Today we have the silicon steels, brittle but hot-acid resisting; the even more successful and welcome stainless steels with their 12 per cent or so of chromium, which have been increasing ever since 1913 when Brearley, in a first-rate piece of work, discovered the first of them, and which are important not only to the cutler but to every industrial chemist in the land; the tough manganese and nickel steels of the armourer and shipbuilder; the amazing "self-hardening" or "high-speed" steels of Mushet (1868) and Taylor and White (1900), containing tungsten, chromium, and other once unobtainable metals, which have revolutionized nearly every operation in engineering everywhere.

It was during the twenty years preceding the Great Exhibition of 1851 that the foundations of this, and the following, development were laid. The outstanding figure of the above advances was R. F. Mushet (1811-91) whose experiments with manganese in 1848 were the starting-point for the alloy steels of today. The work on aluminium during the same period was hardly less important in their development. Hence we have now light metals and light metal alloys thought hardly possible when Davy in 1808 obtained molten beads of some of them. Although it was not seen by him, the most important so far is aluminium, not only pure and in its more prominent alloys—aluminium bronzes and magnalium, for instance—but as a re-agent in powder form in the new aluminothermy or so-called thermite process, developed by Foster and Meyer (London patent 1891) and by Goldschmidt of Essen in 1895, by which a number of recalcitrant heavy metals—chromium, molybdenum, vanadium, tantalum, and others—have been obtained molten, and boron and silicon as powders that can be melted in the electric furnace.

The story of aluminium, so important to the aircraft industry, occupies no inconsiderable portion of the history of invention in the nineteenth and twentieth centuries, particularly in the field of mechanical engineering. The metal, not much more than seen by the Dane, Oersted, in 1825, was isolated by Wöhler in 1827, and produced on a large scale by a chemical process in France by Delville in 1851. As in all such cases the plant itself was the occasion of many inventions and discoveries, a statement even truer perhaps of the electrolytic method (supplanter of Delville's process), discovered by his fellow-countryman Hérault in France, and independently by Hall in the United States, *circa* 1889, within a short time of each other: that is, the electrolysis of molten aluminium compounds, particularly bauxite, with cryolite (calcium fluoride). Before Delville's success the price of aluminium was nearly £6 per pound. By 1864 it had fallen below £2 per pound. Then rapid cheapening, bringing it by steps out of the semi-precious metal class, took place: 10s. per pound by 1889, 1s. 6d. in 1900, and, temporarily, even 6d. per pound a few years later; for with this metal the metallurgists stole a march on the engineers, who were unprepared to make use of it in the available quantities. The challenge did not long remain unaccepted; by 1944, as a consequence of the prodigious demands of the fighting forces and especially of the air arm, and the consequent frenzy of invention, the capacity of the

United States and Canada alone had reached over a million tons, and German industry under Max Haas's directorship was producing enormous quantities too. Its importance during the war is indicated by the subtitle of R. Pitavel's *Histoire de l'aluminium: Métal de la victoire* (1946).

Engineers who practised before 1780 were, compared with their fellows of the following decades, greatly handicapped as regards the production and transmission of power. In earlier days the source of power, whether men or animals, air or water, determined the site. It might be a wind-swept height, catching the breeze for a windmill; it might be a stream flowing through a valley, serving the machinery of a textile mill or the hammers, grinding or boring gear of a metal workshop. Later, water-power became subsidiary, and mills arose where it was otherwise convenient, provided the requisite boiler was installed and its fuel assured. Then, with overshaft or undershaft transmission, the power could be supplied from greater distances with less loss to operate either a few large machines—a rolling mill or carding machine perhaps—or a whole roomful of lathes, frames, or looms, arranged more conveniently than was possible before; or alternatively the precision watchmaker's lathes, etc., of a small experimental workshop.

From 1785 onwards cotton mills, particularly in Lancashire, were being equipped with Watt's rotary-motion steam-engine. England, said he, was becoming steam-engine mad. The prospect of obtaining power so conveniently and uninterruptedly stimulated inventors to devise machines for many hand-worked industries. In 1779 William Sellars of Bristol, with his fast and loose pulleys, brought quieter and more economical conditions into many a factory. Perhaps the most dramatic development before 1851 was the steam hammer devised by Nasmyth in 1838 and patented by him in 1841. Its performance struck the imagination of the visitors to the Exhibition of 1851 more forcibly than that of any other piece of mechanism.

But even before our chosen central period of thirty years had ended the internal combustion engine was occupying the thoughts of many a fertile brain; the monopoly of the steam-engine was threatened. The challenge was taken up in 1860 by

Lenoir's gas engine. In 1867 Otto, profiting by the teaching of de Rochas, produced the very successful, and in some ways more convenient, four-stroke engine. Soon larger and larger engines of this type were being built for all manner of purposes. Nor, in steam itself, was the powerful improved triple and quadruple expansion reciprocating engine of 1878, so well suited for ship propulsion, immune: by 1884 Parsons's steam turbine—especially convenient, directly coupled, for the rapid rotation of dynamic armatures—was competing with it. The grid system of distribution became worth while and offered industry, some kinds more than others, an opportunity to return to a modified form of cottage industry, where the single machine actuated by a small electric motor can be set going or stopped at will. Little advantage has yet been taken of this chance, possibly because of the preference of women for the gregarious factory. One step at least has been made where, in a factory, each machine is directly driven by an individual small motor. The next step has already been made in Lyons where, even fifteen years ago, you might have found the two or three pedal silk looms in a moderate sized workshop attached to the home replaced by one or two electrically driven looms. Should a type of domestic system come, the sewing-machine makers at least will be ready with their easily handled machines, which have only to be "plugged in."

In the early 1700's most inventors were craftsmen with ideas and the manipulative skill to carry them out. Their common task was some daily productive work upon which their imagination had full play, either to improve a hand process or to mechanize it, or to improve the machine which they were operating, or to replace it by a better. Or they might be mechanics with like qualities in charge of machines which they tended or helped to construct. A rare member of the latter type was William Murdock (1754–1839), whose original outlook, insight, and competence amount to genius. But usually these craftsmen were of the first type. When success crowned their efforts nearly all of them were content to improve and to exploit their invention for their personal profit, either by producing it for sale or by using it as manufacturers. Those of steady character with a flair for business might become wealthy factory owners. Such, amongst many, was John Heathcoat (1783-1861) of lace-machine fame, a cultured man and considerate employer, to whom his industry, his adopted borough and county, and his country owed much. Not many grew into what we today should term mechanical engineers and salute as inventors and pioneers, but the few who did were very notable men. Chemistry, for instance, could hardly be said to have emerged before the rise of some of their contemporaries, such as Watt's friend John Roebuck (1718–94). It happened then, as it has happened more than once in history, that there arose a brilliant band of men more or less well known to one another who adorned the title of inventor. Their interests were concentrated upon the machines as machines. Among them were Boulton and Watt themselves, Wilkinson the ironmaster, the Stephensons, George and Robert, and James Nasmyth of Patricroft, Lancs.[1]

An offshoot from these was a type we may roughly designate as the engineers' engineers. They devised machines not so much to make goods as to make better machines to make goods better, and, especially, their business was to design and improve machines to make machines—engineering tools as distinct from loose tools for hand and machine use. It is almost impossible to exaggerate the importance of their work. There was no clear distinction between the main group and the offshoot; any member of either group would, more or less temporarily, shift his interest. Thus James Watt and Matthew Boulton, for instance, had to create tools with which to carry out their greater purposes since these did not exist before. In such work Murdock was in no way behind. In the same way Bramah (1790) prepared for his hydraulic press, but, as the teacher of Maudslay, he was of the inner circle. Henry Maudslay (1771-1831) was essentially of that smaller set. His additions to the lathe made it a precision instrument with which he accomplished the necessary prelimin-

[1]In the Faraday papers there is a delightful letter from Nasmyth to Faraday describing the beauty of his new pile driver: "Such pile driving the world never saw before. From three to seven minutes was the time required to drive a pile of fifty feet thirty-five feet into the ground—against twenty-four to thirty hours by the old process, the apparatus sitting on the pile and going down with it." It was used, he said, on the Newcastle Railway Bridge, on the Nile Dam, in Russia, and in the United States. To both of them it was the poetry of power.

ary work for improving and standardizing the screw, which following his example first Clement and then Whitworth brought to near perfection.

An important change in engineering was effected as the result of the efforts of Roberts and Whitworth to obtain a true plane. Whitworth's plane table was almost the *sine qua non* of accurate physical measurement and of precision tools: all measurements start from it. One is to be found, usually centrally placed, in all high-standard engineering and some other shops for the use of the artisans. Trustworthy screws are the basis of most measurements of high accuracy and especially of minute differences. A perfect screw would have an unvarying pitch from one end to the other so that the distance the end advances is everywhere accurately related to the angle turned. So perfect a spiral is probably unattainable. Each improvement, however, begets another, the results being cumulative. When the limit is reached, calibration must correct small variations. The pitch of the screw being exactly known, 1/10" say, the advance of the end for a complete turn will be 1/10". If the circumference of the head is divided and marked off into 100 equal parts, then the screw will advance 1/1000" for a turn of one mark to the next. That is the principle of the micrometer screw gauge which nearly all fitters will read and work to with certainty; some will work comfortably to a quarter thousand. Microscopes, telescopes, and many other scientific instruments, especially those whose movements are operated and controlled by screws, are constructed to read changes of position upon the same principle. For greater accuracy, especially for the smaller movements, they are provided with verniers,[2] which may be magnified by lenses. Science has been indebted for many of its spectacular achievements to the patient and painstaking work of Maudslay, Clement, and Whitworth, and when optical methods were employed to enlarge the field of research, they were standardized against the most refined instruments of their time.

Bramah lived from 1748 to 1814; Maudslay from 1771 to 1831; Clement from 1779 to 1844; Whitworth from 1803 to

[2]After Paul Vernier (1580-1637)—a short moveable scale by which more minute measurements may be obtained.

1887; Nasmyth from 1808 to 1890—an overlapping, unbroken line. Various standards and gauges were fixed by them, especially by Whitworth. Their followers were provided with just the right metal for distributing copies of the legal linear standards in Guillaume's invar (1897), a rust-resisting steel alloy of 36 per cent nickel and 2 per cent carbon which has a maximum co-efficient of expansion (for 1° C.) of .0000008, i.e. about 5 inches per 100 miles. Individual ingots have yielded samples with practically no change whatever in length for 1° rise.

Technical training two centuries ago was almost unavoidably confined to actual experience with the cottage or factory machine. Fortunately in those days of serious general apprenticeship youths who might attain to it were not given to that shrinking from the responsibilities of skill which some fear in the youth of today. Amongst publications scientific "literature" was the exception. Books were few and expensive (there was a tax on paper) and Kempe's *Engineers' Year Book*, 570 pages, was first published in 1894 at 8s. It is much bulkier now. In the 1830's and 1840's, though there were many popular journals of science and technology such as the *Mechanics' Magazine*, technical journals were relatively few and general rather than specialized. Today they proliferate and contain particularly full records of patents applied for and granted. The magnificent technical college or school of today was then barely contemplated. Though the seed was sown in the Mechanics' Institutes of the 1820's and 1830's, these soon lost their original function. Technical education, as we have it, was the fruit of the 1851 Exhibition.

A man no sooner made a new tool or machine than jealous and acquisitive rivals sought to steal the fruits of it both before and after it was patented, and fearful workmen were ready to smash and burn it. The inexperienced were commonly unable so to word their specifications that the patent was of any value to them. Kay, Boulton and Watt, Heathcoat, and many others suffered from these difficulties. Many an inventor showed greater wisdom by silence concerning his plans and secrecy in using his machine, and if he did take out a patent he made the specification deliberately vague. That work can today be safely left to one of the many experienced patent agents.

The twenty years preceding the Great Exhibition saw considerable technical progress in many leading British industries. In 1834–5 came the wire rope and the two-decker cage, which stimulated the mining of coal and other minerals. William Fairbairn was busy building the new iron steam-boats, first at Manchester and later at Millwall, and in 1846 the Thames Iron Works was established, which, seven years after the Exhibition, produced the first naval ironclad. Cooke and Wheatstone obtained their patent for the electric telegraph in 1837 and the Electric Telegraph Company was formed in 1846. It was not long before the Atlantic was spanned by a cable. The Morse (U.S.A.) Code had been available since 1837.

These developments in means of transport and communication were of less moment only than the spread of the railways—itself dependent on inventions too numerous to detail—which transformed Britain from a land of farmers and craftsmen into an industrial power. The wars and threats of wars have of late shown us the other side of the shield, and farmers like George Henderson (*Farming Progress*, 1950) have pointed to the desirability and way of retracing more or less some of these steps, to improve at any rate the future of farming. Nevertheless farming itself, especially in England, has become mechanized. Even before our period Patrick Bell (1826) had made his reaper, which McCormick (U.S.A.) bettered in 1834. Croskell's roller came out in 1841. The first binder (steel wire) followed as early as 1849. Philip Pusey, who wrote the official report on agricultural machinery of the Great Exhibition, paid tribute to the "two good American reaping machines by McCormick and Hussey."

Neither has the office been neglected, nor mathematical calculation. In the 1820's Charles Babbage, a Cambridge professor of mat ematics, conceived his "difference engine" to produce mathematical functions by building them up from their finite differences. He induced the government to sponsor his machine but the construction proceeded slowly, and Peel, losing patience, refused further support in 1842. "At that moment En land had the chance of securing the leading calculating machines. But the chance was lost, thrown away, and never recovered." Babbage's slowness was partly due to lack of machine tools and mass production methods. He came before Whitworth and the others. The American inventors grasped the opportunity, together with certain Germans. A positive result of the same men's work, which England again failed to exploit, was the making of small precision tools. The typewriter, for instance, is overwhelmingly American—it came (1867-73, Sholes) from a sewing-machine factory. Yet the Englishman Henry Mill had made a sort of typewriter as far back as January 1714. One wonders how he could do it in those days.

In textiles the record was different, for textiles were Britain's industrial specialty, and cotton was the spearhead of the manufacturing revolution. The nineteenth century continued the triumphs of the eighteenth, and the achievements of 1830-60 emphasize the continuity of the progress in technique.

Weaving

Although Cartwright had invented a power loom by 1787, powered looms made little headway in the mills before 1813 when the improved crank loom of William Horrocks appeared; even in 1818 only one-third of the looms were power driven. Nevertheless most of the great inventions for the weaving loom were in general use by the end of the twenties; this decade indeed was distinguished by the introduction to England of the "pattern-controlling" equipment of Jacquard.[3] The way for automatic looms was to open soon after 1850, although Northrop, who left England for America, did not develop his inventions until 1889. Meanwhile, avoiding the use of both Jacquard and Dobby, the patent Axminster carpet loom, with its previously prepared chenille weft, appeared in 1839, followed in 1852 by the complementary so-called tapestry carpet of Whytock in which the warp, contributing the pattern, was "printed" on a drum before beaming.

Spinning

In spinning and the pre-spinning processes activity was to concentrate upon certain important developments. Roberts's

---

[3]In James II's reign Joseph Mason, a man before his time, invented the "fill over" loom, a forerunner of the Jacquard (much used from 1802 on in making fashionable shawls).

self-acting mule had already appeared in 1825. The method of "lag," as exemplified in the single-pulley flier spinning-wheel and Arkwright's mechanized application of it, was to be further exploited in America. In 1828 Charles Danforth had introduced the cap machine, the extreme expression of it. In 1829 Addison and Stevens had produced the traveller of the more famous and valuable ring machine. Some ring machines were placed on the market as early as 1831 by Sharp and Roberts, but neither in America nor in England was their value then recognized. For thirty years they suffered comparative neglect, indeed until 1868, when Brookes and Doxey brought them to the front. Soon flier machines were being rapidly replaced by ring machines everywhere.

Even more impressive were the combing machines, so difficult to perfect, so complicated, that they came a century later than carding machines—that is, apart from Cartwright's attempt *c.* 1790. The first to appear was that of Heilman (an Alsatian) in 1845, followed within the next decade, but quite independent of it, by the machines of the Englishmen Holden, Lister (Lord Masham), and Noble, all three assisted by Donnisthorpe. Although differing fairly widely amongst themselves, all four were mechanical interpretations of the hand-combs, themselves tools based on the manner in which women order their tresses. Victoria saw Donnisthorpe's machine at the Crystal Palace in 1851.

Knitting and Lace

During the forty years from 1775, feverish energy was expended in England by a number of inventors upon the improved and adapted models of the English-invented "warp knitting frame" in attempts to reproduce the beautiful and dainty designs of hand-wrought laces, both needle-point and pillow-made. Their largely frustrated efforts reluctantly died down as Heathcoat's traverse lace-net machine (1808-9) and the great machines it inspired gathered proof of their superior fitness. Only one or two English textile engineers, still well known, remained faithful to the warp frame and its offshoot the Milanese frame; otherwise its development, especially in respect of greater speed, was left to Germans and Americans, who gradually worked up to a rate of 400 to 500 courses per minute until, in 1935-45, a brilliant

comeback by the English FNF warp frame knitted 1,000 courses
per minute. There was, however, an important incidental English
adaptation in 1839, namely the application to the warp frame,
and subsequently to the lace machines, of the Dawson wheel
which very simply controlled the pattern end and, in particular,
encouraged lacelike designs in machine-knitted wear. Invented
in 1790, well before either the Jacquard or Dobby appeared on
weaving looms, this simple effective device did similar service
for knitting and lace making.

The circular knitting machine had been started in 1798 by
the Frenchman, Delacroix. M. I. Brunel, in 1806, among others,
tried his hand in making it more practical. Complete success,
however, awaited F. Clausen's improvements in 1845, when power
drive also was applied to knitting machines generally.

Soon after, in 1849, Matthew Townsend invented his latch
needle—the third great event, following the warp frame and the
circular, in machine knitting. Quite recently, at the end of 1949,
his priority has been disputed. An American textile journal discovered, and rightly published, details of an 1806 French patent
(Jeandeau's) which described a needle dependent upon the latch
idea, and of an American needle (Hibbert's) of similar construction, patented in the United States in 1849, only a month or
two before that of Townsend in England. The first remained
unknown even in France: there is no evidence that it ever came
into use. The American needle was a tool to aid the hand-knitter
(as there are nowadays adaptations of the Townsend needle for
deladdering stockings and for hand-work carpet making): even
so it appears to have had little if any vogue even at home. On
the other hand Townsend not only invented his needle but made
it a practical success in the knitting frame and, in addition, produced the undoubtedly original double-ended form. Considering
the conditions prevailing 100 and 150 years ago; his social status
and narrow contacts; the relatively slow distribution of news in
circles such as his; the paucity of trade journals providing such
information; the comparative neglect of his predecessors' needles;
the fact that neither at the time nor during the fifty years after
Jeandeau's patent had any writer or engineer in any country concerned with or engaged upon knitting frames thrown the slightest

doubt upon Townsend's claims, it seems most unlikely that he had heard of either inventor or knew of their needles. Nevertheless they must be accorded priority.

There had been outstanding British developments of Heathcoat's traverse lace-net machine. The first was Lever's of 1803. To this, as improved by Beebe and Biddle in 1823, Draper in 1834 had adapted the Jacquard harness which, with the subsidiary Dawson's wheel, enabled it to achieve designs of extreme complexity. Further expansion by Livesay in 1846 led to the construction of the present-day elephantine Nottingham lace-curtain machine, improved by Tillotson about 1870, which may be provided with upwards of 27,000 miles of reeled yarns before beginning a piece of work. In contrast, the small circular lace machine of the Frenchman Malhère (a developed braiding machine) came about 1872.

The Sewing Machine

In 1798 T. Saint of London had designed a single-thread (chain-stitch) sewing machine. Abroad the problem was taken up more seriously by Thimmonier, who by 1832 was both making and selling chain-stitch machines in France. Exhibiting his improved model at the 1851 Exhibition brought him neither recognition nor reward. From the time of his patent, initiative passed almost entirely to the United States. Hunt, in 1832, had conceived the sub-plate shuttle, which, with the vertical needle above it, contrives the lock-stitch, but it was a fellow-countryman, Elias Howe, who, in 1844, so mastered all the early difficulties that he has been generally thought of as the inventor of the lock-stitch machine. Failing to obtain support in his own country Howe crossed to London and there licensed W. F. Thomas as the English maker. Apparently Thomas did not treat him too well, but when, soon after, he returned to New England, he fared far worse at the hands of American rivals, trade-union leaders, and hand workers. Organized sabotage by his opponents culminated in the "sewing-machine riots." It was so long before his claims were legally established and admitted in the United States that he and his family survived only at near-starvation level.

In 1849 A. B. Wilson of the United States invented the rotary hook, an alternative to the torpedo-shaped shuttle, and made a number of important additions and improvements. In 1851 I. M. Singer brought out his first model and did much to popularize sewing machines. Bonnaz brought out an embroidery machine, improved by Cornély in 1863, both of France, and both using the chain-stitch. Heilmann, as far back as 1834, had constructed a multiple sewing machine. Such efforts led by stages to the giant Schiffli (German or Swiss) so-called "lace machine," but in fact a lock-stitch sewing machine with its hundreds of two-tiered needles and shuttles. Later the weft of certain types of Axminster carpet was secured at the edge by a very large lock-stitch shuttle and needle.

In 1802 Robert Brown of Nottingham had shown how, by a method all but anticipating Hunt's needle and shuttle, a machine could tie true knots in taut threads fixed at both ends. This was an incidental invention in adapting the warp knitting frame to lace manufacture. It forestalled the fishing-net machines. About the same time Jacquard in France was busy upon the latter problem, for which he won an English award. By 1820 Patterson of Musselburgh, Scotland, with more or less help from Ritchie, and also Robertson of Edinburgh, proceeding along rather different lines, had overcome the difficulties of the machine and begun to make fishing nets. By 1840 Pequer of France also had produced a practical machine. Both Scottish and French types are still in use in various parts of Britain. The models differ in detail, but, since most makers of the nets are the engineers of their machines, these details are not usually disclosed. The knotting—each knot involving two cords—is quite different from that tied in a single cord by Appleby's "binder" of 1874, an intriguing device. By 1844 Barnard of Norwich had invented a machine—a rather noisy one—for making wire netting. It employs the hexagonal mesh of certain kinds of lace and of Heathcoat's textile net machine, differing in that the zig-zags are roughly vertical, not slanting. There is no knotting, but the twisted wires differ in appearance as well as in process from the older wire cloth woven in the loom. The twists are given extra security by immersion in molten spelter.

Attendant Processes Affecting Fabrics

About 1845 John Mercer followed up his observation that fibres of cotton when immersed in caustic soda solution lose almost one-fifth of their length while they gain strength half as great again and are more easily dyed. By keeping the yarn under stretch in the caustic soda solution he found that the fibres untwist, become approximately straight tubules, swell up, and acquire smooth ridges. In this new physical condition they take on a lustrous silk-like sheen. Flax fibres can be made to undergo the same changes, although not so conveniently. Textile experts and chemists alike almost entirely ignored this extremely important discovery for thirty years—some authorities say fifty; today the transformation is the *raison d'être* of a great specialized industry.

In 1836 J. Gibson and J. G. Gordon (of Glasgow) introduced their improved process of "long spinning" for long fibres (silk, worsted, and flax). In 1857 S. C. Lister worked out details for spinning into yarn what we now call "spun silk."

In 1856 Sir William Henry Perkin discovered the aniline dye which he called mauve. He promptly began to exploit it, but the Germans, by their energy and adroitness, did better and gained a stranglehold on the British industry.

Paper Making

Closely allied to the machine textile industries is that of modern paper making, in which a vast amount of work was undertaken towards the end of the eighteenth century and during the next half-century, especially the first twenty-five years of it. The hand process which had remained almost undisturbed for seventeen centuries had had a foretaste of a major change when, a century earlier, the old beetling hammers were displaced by the "Hollander" beater. But the hand-mould was not displaced and the industry settled down again. At the very end of the eighteenth century (about 1795) Nicholas Robert, superintendent at the Essones paper mill of the Didots, exasperated and wearied by the pettiness of the workmen, thought out a machine such that no workmen or only a few would be needed. After only partial success the Didots, in 1801, called upon their English relative John Gamble for help. He engaged an energetic and skilful engineer named Brian Donkin as well as the interest of the brothers Fourdrinier (naturalized Huguenot stationers of London). In the incredible time of five years this brilliant engineer, with practical help from both the Fourdriniers and Didot, erected the first working Fourdrinier in Hertfordshire. By 1820 a model entirely successful was running. Brunel said of the invention, "it is one of the most splendid of the present age," but the promoters—the Fourdriniers—were ruined, partly through hard luck, partly through the stupidity of the government (ably supported by the Excise) and the ignorance of a chief justice. It was a stupendous, though not a deliberate, gift to this country. It saved the government stationery account alone several times more in a few years than the reluctant compensation made to the Fourdriniers, a paltry £7,000. It was not yet full grown but quickly became so by such additions as T. B. Crumpton's drying bowls in 1821, improved by Ranson in 1839. To keep pace with it came the König cylinder printing machine of 1814, followed in 1851 (at the Great Exhibition) by Nelson's rotary machine.

That was not all that happened in paper making, for meanwhile Dickinson had been elaborating a different though related conception which, known as the circular mould machine, he patented in 1809. One model of this was in operation up to 1935 at the Croxley Mill of his successors. The essential difference between the two machines is that in the Fourdrinier the pulp drains on a travelling endless bronze-mesh belt, while in the Dickinson machine it is deposited on the revolving curved wire-mesh surface of an otherwise hollow cylinder. The latter machine in particular was quickly copied by Gilpin (United States) and recopied, also in the United States, in 1831. Dickinson had other inventions to his name, amongst them his "thread paper" of 1829, one example of which is the narrow metallic strip buried in the substance of ten-shilling and twenty-shilling currency notes, introduced to discourage forgers in the early years of World War II. The largest Fourdrinier today delivers upwards of 1,200 feet of newsprint 26½ inches wide per minute.

Both machines, but especially the Fourdrinier, are partly fed by the cheap and plentiful ground-wood pulp. In 1800 M. Koops published a book in London (appealing to George III for his interest) of which several pages were furnished by wood pulp of his own manufacture. English engineers and paper makers turned blind eyes and deaf ears to both his example and his farseeing prophecies (which some of them afterwards, but too late, made true) leaving the highly profitable exploitation to Germany. It was a Saxon weaver, F. G. Keller, who in 1840 made the first wet-wood grinding engine, anticipating by a year the Canadian Fenerty. Burgess and Watt, in England, made soda pulp from wood in 1851. Frozen out in their own country they went over to America to develop and patent their process in 1854. The way to sulphite pulp was first shown by the American Tilghmann in 1857-8. The investigation was carried on by G. Fry in Arundel and Ekerman, a Swede, at Northfleet; there Fry soon joined him. Together they succeeded by 1872 in making the sulphite pulp. In 1874 the German Professor Mitscherlich devised an excellent process whose product is especially suitable for viscose manufacture. Lastly, in 1884, the sulphate process, which provides the brown Kraft type of wrapping paper, was achieved by C. F. Dahl. Meanwhile by 1860 Routledge at the Eynsham paper mills near Oxford showed the suitability of esparto grass as a furnish alternative to rags.

Other important discoveries in paper making come within the first half of the eighteenth century, such as the addition of rosin as sizing to the Hollander beating machine—"engine sizing" —by Illig of Germany (1800). In 1831 Hall of Dartford added screens to the Hollander to improve the washing of the furnish. In 1821 Marshall added the dandy roll to the Fourdrinier. In 1845 the Englishman W. H. Smith introduced the light and shade method of producing watermarks, a beautiful example of the portrait type of which may be seen within the clear circles of currency notes. He did not patent the idea.

As an indication of the astonishing growth of machine paper making in Great Britain consider that during 1805, when all paper was still made by hand, there were 760 vats in operation whose known average gave a total output of 16,500 tons. Today the yearly figures for the Kemsley mill alone—which, though the largest, is only one of scores of paper mills in Great Britain, only two of them being still solely concerned with hand-made papers —is over twice as great as the 1805 figure for the whole country. The only comparable example of rapid growth in an industry with immense machine output is that of plastics since 1916, when Baekeland produced the first synthetic resin moulding powder. Today, however, by North American standards the British output in both is exiguous.

Plastics

It may seem a far cry from machine-made paper to machine-made plastics except that ground-wood meal is an important furnish to the one and the chief filler to the synthetic powders of the other but, in fact, these two industries, not far apart in their early beginnings, touch here and there.

In 1839 Hancock and Goodyear in the United States discovered the important ordinary hot method of vulcanizing rubber. Rubber was not the only plastic of that day. Asphalt had many uses as had other materials of that nature. One can still trace the methods used with them in the great engines of today.

Within a few years, in 1846, Alexander Parkes of lead desilverizing fame put forward the "cold cure" method of vulcanizing thin pieces and layers. This was quickly adapted to making rain-proof fabric which has been treated with rubber solution, and a few years afterwards was sold to Charles Mackintosh by whose name it has since been known. Parkes had had to devise methods of preparing carbon disulphide and sulphur chloride. He was a man of many parts; he was probably the first to make nitro-cellulose and he was certainly the first to make the plastic celluloid (which he named Parkesine), a discovery once attributed to Hyatt of the United States, whose work came about 1872. Parkes was electrometallurgist to Messrs. Elkington, the well-known and long-established electro-plate specialists, who had begun that work in 1838. In 1844, according to Sir Robert Hadfield, Siemens sold his electro-plating patents to the Elkingtons, who promptly ordered from Prime & Son an electro-magnetic induction machine, designed by J. S. Woolrich, to supply the current. Faraday's immensely important researches on electro-magnetic induction appeared in 1831, and his papers on the laws of electrolysis in 1833. In 1844 he visited Messrs. Primes' factory to examine the first actual machine embodying his ideas, the forerunner of all dynamos. He was delighted with it. For many years the Elkingtons used that machine. It now rests for all to admire in Aston Hall, Birmingham. On this triumphant note we may conclude this summary review of the "Stream of Invention" during the twenty years before 1851 and some of its more important post-Exhibition consequences.

CHAPTER THREE

Patent Law and Commodity Study

1849   Commons Committee on the Signet and Privy Seal
        Signed by Minto (Ld Privy Seal)
                G. Cornewall Lewis (Under Secretary,
                  Home Office)
                H. Rich

Report

Recommends abolition of the Signet Office, and the transfer of its duties to the Home Office—its business was the passing of Letters Patent, so called because not sealed up.

Patents were of two classes:

    (i) appointment of officers under the Crown, pensions, honours, etc.[1]

    (ii) grants to inventors of sole use of their invention.

Main points under (ii):

1. No statute is to be found relating to grants for the sole use of inventions prior to the statute of 21 Jas. I. c. 3 called the Statute of Monopolies. That statute was passed for the purpose of restraining the Crown from making extravagant and illegal grants of monopolies. It declared all monopolies whatsoever to be contrary to law and void except "Letters Patent and grants of privilege of the sole working or making of any new manufacture to the first inventor thereof." The only other public Acts relating generally to patents are the 5 and 6 Will. 4 c. 83 (Letters Patent for Inventions), 2 and 3 Vict. c. 67 (Patents), and 7 and 8 Vict. c. 69 (Judicial Committee), which provide remedies for deficiencies in the old law.

[1]As in the noble phrase "he derives his patent of gentility direct from God."

2. Every patent for a new invention contains a proviso that the patentee shall describe his invention by an instrument in writing, under his hand and seal, termed a specification, and the specification must be enrolled in Chancery within a given time after the date of the patent. In default of which the patent becomes void. It was enacted by 11 & 12 Vict. c. 94 (Court of Chancery offices) that all specifications shall be enrolled in this Enrolment Office.

3. The object of granting a patent for an invention is not merely to secure to an inventor the fair reward of his labour and ingenuity but also to benefit the public by encouraging such invention.

4. "We are of opinion that these [specifications] should be issued in book-form in a common hand, that proper indexes should be made of them. They would then become very valuable references to the public."

Evidence of Different Patent Agents (stated to be not more than ten in all in London)

Mr. A. "I am of opinion that a man with a good general knowledge such as I apprehend the Attorney or Solicitor General usually possesses, and mathematics likewise, is just as well calculated to judge of these things as any scientific men. I find that some scientific men argue one side, and some on the other and frequently lead people into great confusion.

Is there at present any complete register of patents?—There is said to be one at the Great Seal Office, with the Lord Chancellor's Principal Secretary, but it is a register merely arranged chronologically, and that is about as much use as if it was not there at all, because with such a multiplicity of patents as now exists, it is impossible for us to sit down before a register and wade through them and try to ascertain, e.g. what patents have been granted for steam-engines. What we want is a register."

[*Mr. B.*—Thomas Webster, special pleader and author of a treatise on the Law of Patents.

Another name worth preserving is Moses Poole, Clerk of Inventions, 1817 to 1849, following his father who held the office 1776-1817—between the two of them a case of "From Adam Smith to the Present Day."]

Mr. C. "If I were to bring the Committee a list of all the patents that have been granted for improvements in navigation, I could find you perhaps two scores of patents granted for the same thing." The patent agents are "none of them acquainted with a tithe of the patents that have been granted."

Searching to see whether there is already a patent for an invention is "a terribly difficult thing."

"If there be a previous patent in existence for the same invention, the second patent is void?—It is, because the contract by the Crown is that after fourteen years' monopoly, it becomes public property, and the public are entitled to the invention."

As to taking out a patent where one already exists, "Nothing is more frequent, and all the money expended on it lost. . . . It is not the fees alone I complain of, but the great time lost by the inventor in going from one office to another."

Mr. D. "It happens very often that an invention is patented which by itself is good for nothing, but which if it had something altered in it, or added to it, would be extremely valuable. No one, however, is at liberty during the subsistence of the patent to supply what may be wanted without the leave and licence of the patentee; and, knowing this, many [patent holders] who could do so readily, are deterred from making the grant."

Hence "the course of improvement in the particular department of arts or manufactures to which an invention relates is wholly stopped till the patent expires, which may be close on half a generation. It is settled law, to be sure, that if an invention is, in point of fact, good for nothing, the patent for it is also good for nothing; but there must be a process of law to have that declared, a process of *scire facias* which even in the plainest cases is one attended with great expense."[2]

But on the other hand if patents could be had for a nominal sum "everyone who fancied he could make anything by a patent would have one; and so in the end we should have Sir Robert Peel's imaginary case more than realised,—'every journeyman in every manufactory in the Kingdom with his patent, and every manufactory crippled, if not stopped, by a host of unfortunate claimants, two or three of them perhaps the authors of inventions

[2]See below, p. 41.

of real utility, but the majority, most certainly, of the class of mere dreamers and obstructives.' "

To reduce their expense, without incurring the above drawback, each patent should be limited to one substantive matter as in France. "The practice at present is to crowd as many things into one patent as the words of the title can carry, and to make these words as vague, large and comprehensive as possible: a practice arising, no doubt, out of a general feeling that the cost of a patent is too high, and that where so much is exacted, it is but fair to get as much as people can for their money. Were this done [i.e., were there limitation as in France] even though the cost were reduced to one third, the aggregate receipts would not be diminished."

1851   COMMISSION ON THE PROCESS, PRACTICE, AND SYSTEM OF PLEADING IN THE SUPERIOR COURTS OF COMMON LAW
First Report
(*Re* getting rid of formalities and fictions)

"Failing the issue of a writ of execution, a writ called a *scire facias quare executionem non* is issued to the sheriff of the county, commanding that it be made known to defendant to shew cause why execution should not issue."

The functions of our old friends Richard Roe and John Doe are then explained (Dickens published *Bleak House* 1852-3), and the Report ends:

"If these suggestions are carried into effect, suitors will be relieved from a tax most grievously complained of [i.e. Court fees], the emoluments of the officers will cease to be uncertain and liable to the fluctuation of business, and the establishment of the Court will be rendered more uniform and effective."

"CONTAINING THE WHOLE SCIENCE OF GOVERNMENT"*

"He spoke in that quite deliberate manner, and in that undertone, which is often observable in mechanics who consider and adjust with great nicety. It belonged to him like his suppleness

*Charles Dickens, *Little Dorrit*, chap. x.

of thumb, or his peculiar way of tilting up his hat at the back every now and then, as if he were contemplating some half-finished work of his hand, and thinking about it.

'Disappointed?' he went on, as he walked between them under the trees, 'Yes. No doubt I am disappointed. Hurt? Yes. No doubt I am hurt. That's only natural. But what I mean, when I say that people who put themselves in the same position, are mostly used in the same way——'

'In England,' said Mr. Meagles.

'Oh! of course I mean in England. When they take their inventions into foreign countries, that's quite different. And that's the reason why so many go there.'

Mr. Meagles very hot indeed again.

'What I mean is, that however this comes to be the regular way of our government, it is its regular way. Have you ever heard of any projector or inventor who failed to find it all but inaccessible, and whom it did not discourage and ill-treat?'

'I cannot say that I ever have.'

'Have you ever known it to be beforehand in the adoption of any useful thing? Ever known it to set an example of any useful kind?'

'I am a good deal older than my friend here,' said Mr. Meagles, 'and I'll answer that. Never.'

'But we all three have known, I expect,' said the inventor, 'a pretty many cases of its fixed determination to be miles upon miles, and years upon years, behind the rest of us; and of its being found out persisting in the use of things long superseded, even after the better things were well known and generally taken up?'

They all agreed upon that.

'Well then,' said Doyce with a sigh, 'as I know what such a metal will do at such a temperature, and such a body under such a pressure, so I may know (if I will only consider), how these great lords and gentlemen will certainly deal with such a matter as mine. I have no right to be surprised, with a head upon my shoulders, and memory in it, that I fall into the ranks with all who came before me. I ought to have let it alone. I have had warning enough, I am sure.' "

1948   A COMMODITY STUDY DE LUXE: ALUM, THE EARLIEST
         CHEMICAL INDUSTRY*

Alum owes its commercial, industrial and historic importance
chiefly to its affinity for fibres of wool, silk, cotton and linen.
These, or fabrics woven from then, when impregnated with
alum, will absorb certain natural dyestuffs more freely and
develop colours that are brighter and more fast than if not so
treated. Alum is thus a fixer of dyes, or *mordant*. . . .

The central event in the history of [alum] was the discovery,
about the middle of the fifteenth century, of the existence and
workability of vast quantities of alunite near Rome. Soon after
(and perhaps before), a way was invented of making alum from
urine and aluminous shale, a formation that is widely distributed.
This method was to prove a rival to that based on alunite. Later
it was found that yet other rocks could be used in the production
of alum.

Alum depends for its value on its purity. Of impurities the
most deleterious for dyeing are soluble salts of iron. Crystallisa-
tion, often repeated, is a recognized way of purifying salts, and
the ease with which alum crystallises makes the removal of its
impurities relatively simple. The chemical properties of a substance can hardly be investigated until it is obtained pure, and
alum has historical significance as the only chemically pure
substance (except perhaps gold) known in antiquity. Its general
chemical nature, however, did not become apparent until after
the middle of the eighteenth century. By the end of the first
third of the nineteenth its general constitution had become well
recognised and the nature of its metallic bases, aluminium and
potassium, had been revealed. . . .

In the sixth and seventh decades of the fifteenth century
several . . . sources of alum were found . . . in Italy. . . . At
the same time workmen came west from the disintegrating Eastern Empire and brought with them their dyeing secrets. . . .

In 1461 alunite in large quantities was found in papal terri-

*The Earliest Chemical Industry: An Essay in the Historical Relations of
Economics & Technology Illustrated from the Alum Trade.* By Charles Singer.
With a Preface by Derek Spence, Managing Director of Peter Spence & Sons,
Ltd. (A centenary memorial.) London: The Folio Society. 1948. Extracts by
courtesy of Dr. Singer.

tory at Tolfa [northeast of Civita Vecchia]. . . . This the Papacy sought to control . . . by the creation of an alum cartel, trust or syndicate, which should corner the market to its own advantage. . . .

By the spring of 1463 the production of alum at Tolfa had developed to an industrial scale, with four mines and 8,000 workmen. . . .

By the dawn of the sixteenth century competitive production outside the Papal States had stimulated general resistance to papal claims of monopoly. The production of alum in Central Europe was rising, and alum was also reaching transalpine Europe from the Orient, surreptitiously but in bulk. . . .

Alunite is a comparatively rare mineral, found only in volcanic regions and usually in association with actual or extinct volcanoes. . . . But the chief industrial supplies of alum were to come from a very different source and by a technical method which involved the use of pyrites or pyritic rock. . . .

Alum in England

"Alum is made of a Stone digged out of a Mine, of a Seaweed, and of Urine. The Stone is found in most of the Hills between Scarborough and the River Tees in the County of York. . . ." [Account of 1678.]

Except for the Scottish factories nearly the whole British output of alum until 1847 came from the Yorkshire coast. [But note Alum Bay, near the Needles, Isle of Wight.] The methods there changed little and the last was closed in 1871. . . .

Millions of tons of shale have been removed from the Yorkshire cliffs. Notably in Kettleness and Boulby [south of Saltburn] the whole profile of the headlands has been thus remodelled. The coast is still reddened by iron oxide where the burnt shale was dumped over the cliffs. . . . The enormous excavations of Lias [blue limestone] revealed numerous striking marine fossils. . . . The museums of the world were long provided with specimens from this source. . . . The life of the Yorkshire alum works was prolonged by the opening of the Whitby railway in the [1830's] by George Stephenson.

The introduction of coal-tar dye-stuffs, beginning with the commercial preparation of mauve (1858) by W. H. Perkin . . .

has completely revolutionised dyeing. From about 1880 the "natural" dyes rapidly went out of use, and with them the chief application of alum which was unnecessary for the new dye-stuffs. . . .

Along with the growth in knowledge of the chemical nature of alum [Lavoisier, Gay-Lussac, Dalton], there developed two processes which determined its method of manufacture while they deeply influenced many other industries. One was the commercial production of sulphuric acid. The other was the spread of the use of coal-gas. . . .

About 1820 the price of gas was 15 to 20 shillings per 1000 cubic feet and its cost for equal lighting power was one-third that of oil lamps. By 1829 there were over 200 gas-works in the United Kingdom, and the price in London had fallen to about 12 shillings.

The main hope of improvement was by raising the temperature of carbonisation. The resulting wear on the retorts necessitated the replacement of cast iron by cheaper and more enduring fireclay. The yield per ton of coal was thus raised while the composition of the gas was changed with the formation of the profitable benzene hydro-carbons due to "cracking" of the paraffins. Thus the price of gas could be halved. But the critical event in the gas industry came in 1856 when the chemist, W. H. Perkin (1838–1907) discovered the first "coal-tar dye," *mauveine,* when seeking to synthetise quinine from aniline. This provided a use for the waste product coal-tar, since aniline is made from benzene, a constituent of tar. As is well known, a vast industrial development dates from this discovery.

The older methods of making alum consisted essentially of adding a potassium or ammonium salt or both to a crude solution of aluminium sulphate. So far as the English trade was concerned the potassium was derived either from the lixiviation[3] of wood ash or, locally, from kelp. On the Yorkshire coast kelp was also produced largely for use in soap-making and in glass-manufacture. From the last two industries it was displaced by the introduction of the soda made from salt by Nicholas Leblanc (1742-1806) in France (1791) and by James Muspratt (1791-

[3]I.e., separating a soluble from an insoluble substance by the percolation of water.

1823) in England (1823). Thus kelp-burning became less profitable. The normal source of ammonia until the nineteenth century was stale urine. . . . A regular service of boats brought it in quantity from London to the Yorkshire coast expressly for the alum industry. With the rise of gas-lighting there became available a much cheaper and more convenient source of ammonia, namely the washings from coal-gas. . . .

The Yorkshire shale-deposits were relatively poor in sulphur content. Thus it was necessary to calcine large quantities to obtain small amounts of alum. Approximately 100 parts of shale yielded 3 of the commercial alum product. [Not so the rich carboniferous shale of Scotland.] The extraction of alum from [this] suggested itself to the fertile brain of Charles Mackintosh (1706-1843), inventor of the waterproof fabric that bears his name. . . . The alum yield of the Scottish shales was far higher than those of Yorkshire.

[We reach now our period of 1830–60 and the firm which has sponsored the book.]

A revolution in alum manufacture was introduced by Peter Spence (1806-1883) of Brechin. . . . In 1845 [he] obtained a patent which covered the production of alum from hot freshly calcined shales by treating them with hot and fairly concentrated sulphuric acid. . . . Spence was possessed by the thought of conserving heat. . . .

Spence saw that for his purpose the Manchester area offered advantages. Coal shale and coals were abundant there and markets for alum were in easy reach. In 1846, with Henry Dixon as partner, he established alum works at Pendleton,[4] using sulphuric acid. . . . The shale waste was used for making cement. . . . In 1858, having dissolved partnership with Dixon, he moved his works into Manchester. There they earned a reputation as a model chemical organisation.

Production by this process rapidly developed. In 1850, . . . about twenty tons of alum were made per week; in 1860 110 tons; in 1870, 250 tons per week. Most of this was ammonium alum. Spence contracted for the gas liquor from the Manchester and Salford Gas Works for some thirty years, using over five

[4]On the western fringe of Manchester, north of Salford.

million gallons per annum. The surplus was converted into ammonium sulphate for fertiliser. . . .

Spence found that the shale from the Pendleton coal pits, with which he started, carried far too much iron. In 1853 he contracted for supplies from farther afield to be brought by the canal which ran alongside his works. . . . By the late seventies he was recognised as the chief alum manufacturer in the world. In 1882 he disclosed that his yearly output of alum exceeded 10,000 tons. . . .

Spence also realised that a pure aluminium sulphate, free from iron, could largely replace alum for many industrial purposes. . . . With better grade shale he produced fairly pure aluminium sulphate. . . .

In 1855 Spence started an alum manufactory at Goole.[5] . . . The works . . . still operate. In 1856 Spence developed at Goole processes in connection with the smelting of ores of copper pyrites. These, derived chiefly from Cornwall, were customarily used only as a source of metal, the sulphurous fumes escaping. Spence planned a continuous process of calcining so as to convert the sulphur oxides into sulphuric acid for use in alum manufacture on the spot. Goole is on the canal system and its railway communications were developing. It was thus a favourable centre for adding the metallurgical to the alum venture.

In 1881 Spence stated before a Parliamentary Committee that, apart from his own works at Goole and Manchester, the only considerable manufacture of alum in Britain was at Wakefield, near Leeds. Alum was then probably cheaper than it had ever been. France, Italy and Britain were now all competing for the markets of the Near and Middle East, which in earlier centuries had supplied the West. Spence himself and his alum trade were factors in the development of the Manchester Ship Canal projected in 1882, opened in 1894. He was granted fifty-six patents. In the earlier years the most important of these have to do with alum. Later they refer largely to the making of sulphate of alumina carrying a small amount of iron sulphate. From about 1880 his output of various forms of this substance exceeded that of alum, both in bulk and value.

[5] On the Humber at the confluence of the Ouse and Don.

Certain chemical advances that were first put into operation in 1880 made it possible to prepare, from coal tar, dyes that needed no mordants. . . . Thus certain of the uses of alum have become of more historical than practical interest. Aluminium sulphate can now be prepared on an industrial scale in nearly as pure a state as alum and this pure form, together with those that are less pure, can perform many of the functions of alum. For some purposes, however, alum remains in great demand while its scientific interest [in relation to crystallography, the subject of a special chapter] has increased rather than diminished. Except for the precious metals and perhaps salt there can hardly be a chemical substance that has held attention for so long. Its history of four thousand years illustrates almost every phase of chemical industry and touches every civilisation.

[*This book by a distinguished scientist, on which I have been permitted to draw, is beautifully produced, in respect both of text and illustrations; and the firm at whose instance it has been compiled has nobly subordinated publicity for itself to objective historical technology.*]

CHAPTER FOUR

Birmingham and Sheffield

BIRMINGHAM

MR. PICKWICK, with Sam Weller, Bob Sawyer, and Ben Allen, was journeying to the Midlands to obtain the consent of Mr. Winkle senior to the marriage of Nathaniel with Arabella Allen.

It was quite dark when Mr. Pickwick roused himself sufficiently to look out of the window. The straggling cottages by the road-side, the dingy hue of every object visible, the murky atmosphere, the paths of cinders and brick-dust, the deep-red glow of furnace fires in the distance, the volumes of dense smoke issuing heavily forth from high toppling chimneys, blackening and obscuring everything around; the glare of distant lights, the ponderous waggons which toiled along the road, laden with clashing rods of iron, or piled with heavy goods— all betokened their rapid approach to the great working town of Birmingham.

Birmingham had earned the title of "Toyshop of Europe" in the eighteenth century. It was not until the late nineteenth century that it laid claim to that of "The Best Governed City in the World." It remained Brummagem throughout, and Birmingham products and Birmingham men were clearly distinguishable not only from Manchester products and Manchester men, but also from the more immediate products and men of the adjacent Black Country.

Birmingham's economic importance was based on the finishing trades, which were famous as early as 1830 for their variety and skills. Their range always impressed foreigners. J. G. Bodmer, the German engineer, who visited the city in 1816-17, found time to visit a papier-mâché works, a gun-lock maker, a gun-barrel forger, a copper-roller, a wire-drawer, a button factory, a factory for cast-iron hinges, a plated-goods maker, a hammer-

and-anvil maker, a file-maker, a comb-maker, glassworks, the Eagle Foundry, and the gun-makers' proof house. Joshua Field told the same story of industrial versatility in 1821; Léon Faucher in the 1840's: "Nous approchons du seul district où l'industrie en Angleterre puisse prétendre à un certain caractère d'universalité . . . les applications de l'industrie y sont innombrables. A l'exemple de Paris, cette ville fait un peu de tout, le fait bien, et au plus bas prix. Seulement Paris recherche d'avantage le beau, et Birmingham l'utile." The physicist James Clerk Maxwell had similar things to say in the fifties.

Birmingham men were proud of the fact that they could impress the visitor. They sang their own merits loudly—not only the variety of products, but also the men. When Thomas Attwood (of currency fame) led a deputation of Birmingham men to London in 1812 to protest against the Orders-in-Council, he could not resist writing back to his wife: "Such a foolish set of mortals as the members of both Houses are, I did never expect to meet with in this world. The best among them are scarce equal to the worst in Birmingham."

Economic versatility was accompanied by smallness of enterprise. There were few big factories in the city. The characteristic economic unit in Birmingham was the small workshop or warehouse, where the independent small master, and not the industrial capitalist, reigned supreme, and where there would be anywhere from six to thirty skilled workers. The economic developments of 1830–60 and particularly the increasing use of steam multiplied the number of producing units instead of provoking spectacular growth in existing enterprises. As late as 1914 "the small man system" was still the rule.

The social repercussions of this economic structure were of great importance in English history. There was no hard and fast line in Birmingham between employer and employed. There was often an intimate link between masters and men, which was stressed by all local politicians. Thomas Attwood, as founder of the Birmingham Political Union, made the most of this relationship in formulating his propaganda. "The interests of masters and men are, in fact, one. If the masters flourish, the men are certain to flourish with them, and if the masters suffer difficulties, their difficulties must shortly affect the workmen in a threefold degree. The masters, therefore, ought not to say to the workmen, 'give us your wages,' but take their workmen by the hand, and knock at the gates of government and demand the redress of their common grievances." There was thus an obvious basis for a common front, and it was this common front which Attwood built within the Birmingham Political Union, instituted in December 1829. The object was parliamentary reform, and so active was Birmingham's share in the struggle for the Reform Bill that Daniel O'Connell said that "it was not Grey and Althorp, who carried it, but the brave and determined men of Birmingham." Lord Durham maintained that "the country owed Reform to Birmingham, and its salvation from Revolution."

But why parliamentary reform? It was not an end so much as a means to an end; and the end, as envisaged by Attwood and the "Birmingham School" which gathered round him, was currency reform. Reform of the currency, it was believed, would save Birmingham from fluctuations in trade and periodic bouts of distress. The cause of distress did not lie with finishers, nor with ironmasters, nor with bankers—Attwood was a country banker— but with the government. "It was a question of under-production of money and not of over-production of iron." By a system of controlled circulation, based not on gold but on the level of employment—difficult to tell how—"the country might always be preserved in a high degree of prosperity. The prices of bullion would be left to find their own level and would accommodate themselves, like all other things, to the wants and demands of men. The fluctuations of prices to which gold, like other things, is naturally subject, would act upon insensible masses of metal instead of being forced to act upon life, and flesh, and blood." This was Birmingham economics; it clashed sharply with the rising orthodoxies of the City and of Manchester. It led away, too, from laissez-faire. It is said that laissez-faire is a bad word to use about trends in England; it was anathema in Birmingham, long before Joseph Chamberlain dabbled in "municipal socialism."

For a time, the economic philosophy of the currency reformers captured all sections of Birmingham opinion. Then, after a series of disappointments, men ceased to believe in it. From 1832 onwards working-class radicals in Birmingham put forward their own theory of distress, and for a time they had Bronterre O'Brien living with them—always the most thoughtful of the Chartists. He thought Attwood "a paper-money schemer." Similarly Feargus O'Connor called currency talk "rag botheration"—it was one of the few points on which he and Francis Place agreed. By 1838 there was open disagreement in Birmingham between middle-class leaders, still wedded to currency reform, and working-class Chartists, seeking militant social action. In November 1838, O'Connor was cheered inside the holy of holies itself, the Council of the Political Union. With the split, Birmingham lost its position of primacy in the radical movement, and despite attempts by Joseph Sturge to build up understanding between the working class and the middle class on new foundations—repeal of the corn laws and an extension of the suffrage—local confidence had gone. There was working-class drilling in the back streets in 1840, and an increasing contact between the politically active skilled workers in Birmingham itself and the impoverished and more militant metal workers in the Black Country just outside.

But this was the political trough. Economic conditions were good in the fifties, and not only social peace but also social cooperation was restored. When Bright became member for Birmingham after being defeated at Manchester in 1857, Cobden wrote: "The former state of society [that of Birmingham] is more healthy and natural in a moral and political sense. There is a freer intercourse between all classes than in the Lancashire town, where a great and impassable gulf separates the workman from his employer. . . . If Bright should be able to lead a party for parliamentary reform, in my opinion, Birmingham will be a better home than Manchester." Both the analysis and the prophecy proved true in the fight for the Second Reform Bill of 1867.

In the 1860's Birmingham evinced a growing interest in politics. It was during those years, too, that the foundations were laid for the civic gospel of Joseph Chamberlain, particularly by Nonconformist ministers like Dawson and Dale. They reacted

against the domination of the Council by the "economy party,"
and 1828, their powers were extended and consolidated. They lit
always had been a desire for social improvement in Birmingham
—at least from the 1820's onwards. It never was the "insensate
industrial town" of Mumford's myths. The Birmingham Street
Commissioners, beginning their work in 1769 and ending it in
1851, saw to that. By three important local acts in 1801, 1812,
and pleaded for wider horizons in local government. There
the streets, first with oil lamps, then more effectively with gas.
They organized the watch. They took from the unskilled hands
of the parish surveyors the construction and care of the roads,
so that the streets of Birmingham became known as among the
best constructed and best maintained in England. They made
provision for the railways; for a large market hall, "the finest market hall in England," with a wide flight of steps, massive Doric
façades, and an arched roof 500 feet long; for Hansom and
Welsh's classical town hall (they rejected a plan by Barry); and
not least for a far more efficient system of drainage than existed
in many towns. They were indeed more enterprising and successful than the Town Council in its first fifteen years of "Old Woodman" rule after 1852.[1]

While the Commissioners were at work, Birmingham was
growing in size and importance. The population in 1831 was
147,000: it had only been 73,000 in 1801. By 1861 it had almost
reached the 300,000 mark. The growth of the first suburbs was
changing the face of the surrounding countryside and finally
obliterating the memories of "the great market town." Perhaps
more important in the expansion of the city than the granting of
a charter in 1838 was the arrival of the Liverpool and Birmingham Railway a year before. In October 1838 the Birmingham
and London Railway was opened. Because of fare policy, a
second-class passenger from London to Liverpool had to stop at
Birmingham for the night or else change his ticket to first class.
This policy lasted until 1872. Birmingham was of great importance in the construction of a national railway system. In 1844,
at the pinnacle of the railway mania, seventeen proposals were

[1]The Councillors met in the Old Woodman Tavern in Easy Row before the
debates. They enjoyed little dignity and gave little service at that period.

put forward for lines running there. Snow Hill and New Street supplanted Curzon Street, and with their growth, Birmingham moved slightly west, while passengers cursed the frequently necessary short journey past what was eventually to become the Cathedral.

It was growing in industrial importance, too. The Great Exhibition had already been anticipated by industrial exhibitions in Birmingham. On his subsequent visit to the city to lay the foundation stone of the Midland Institute, Prince Albert admitted that the example of Birmingham had helped the Executive Committee of the greater undertaking to carry that work to a successful issue. Birmingham exhibitors in 1851 sent a greater number of classes of exhibits and occupied more space than any other town in the world, "the Metropolis alone excepted," and they proudly celebrated their part in that festival with a *fête champêtre* in the Botanic Gardens and a lunch for 300 at the Queen's Hotel. In a sense the founding of the Midland Institute (1855) was a sequel to the Exhibition. "As Birmingham was thus foremost in giving a practical stimulus to the works of art and industry, so she is now one of the first in the field to encourage a scientific study of the principles on which these works depend for success."

When Timmins in 1886 edited *The Resources, Products and Industrial History of Birmingham and the Midland Hardware District*, he could trace the process whereby Birmingham had been transformed from a "hardware village" into the capital of the Midlands and a great exporting centre to all parts of the world. The big difficulty he found in compiling the work was compression. "The volume may fail in giving an adequate idea of the extent and variety of our local trades, but it will have done something to show that within a radius of thirty miles of Birmingham nearly the whole of the hardware wants of the world are practically supplied. The coal and iron of Staffordshire —the chemical products, glass and alkalis and soap of Smethwick —the metal works in infinite variety which Birmingham produces, from the costliest plate and jewellery down to the commonest gilt toys—the engines and machinery of every description exported to all parts of the world—every class of articles being produced, from the very cheapest to the very best—can be only imperfectly described even in the seven hundred pages of this work." Seven hundred pages, and that was merely to describe. Timmins was writing in boom years. The boom broke. Before 1875, the industrial development of the Black Country and indirectly of Birmingham had depended on the natural resources of the region. After 1875 the men and the skills were to become more important than the materials. In this new story, Birmingham was to occupy the centre of the picture, just as in politics it was to catch much of the national limelight. The *Illustrated London News* in 1873 furnished a part of the explanation when it said: "Birmingham, as well as Manchester, which has latterly become rather inert, contains perhaps a larger amount of social energy in proportion to its size, than exists in the huge bulk of London."

SHEFFIELD

Here are ten facets of Sheffield life and work, taken in each case from contemporary sources.

1. *Making Knives**

By repeated heatings and hammerings, the steel is drawn into narrow strings of from one to two yards in length and in that state sent to the blade-maker.

The blade-maker's first operation is to heat the end of one of the strings of steel red hot and to mould or fashion the blade rudely on the anvil with his hammer. He then places it on the hag-iron attached to the anvil, to which is affixed a gauge; and with a stroke of the hammer cuts it off; and so on till he has moulded the number required. He next takes the point of the blade in his tongs, heats the other end, and forms the tang or square end of the blade that serves for the joint. The next process is the *smithing*, which requires the blade to be heated again, when the maker gives it its proper shape with back and edge; and

*From the *Sheffield Mechanics' Exhibition Magazine*, no. 15, Sept. 12, 1840, pp. 188-90.

strikes the nail-mark with a punch, set in the grove of his anvil; these processes complete the forging of the blade. It is now passed into other hands, to be filed and fitted to a pattern-blade, in order to ensure of its being of a proper size and form; after which it is sent to the grinding-wheel, to have the shale or oxide ground off, which clears the tang ready for the maker's name etc. to be struck; and this is sometimes done while the blade is cold, at other times when heated to a warm red. After the marking, the blade is *hardened* by heating it red, and immersing it in water. In this state, it is too hard for use, and requires *tempering.* The blade is now rubbed bright on one side with sand-stone, in order that the progress of the tempering may be seen. It is then placed with the back downward on a plate of sheet-iron, which is put on the fire, and the workman very attentively watches the changes of colour in the blade, till they attain to a straw colour approaching a brown, which is the test of the proper degree of temper; he then slacks it to arrest further change. It is again sent to the grinder, to be slightly ground or *scorched,* as it is technically called; and after that, goes to the *setter-in,* or knife maker, who fits it by a *fitting tang* for insertion into the haft. He next *dresses,* or in other words, smooth files and burnishes the edges of the tang, and afterwards glazes, by a wheel dressed with emery, the flat sides, to clear away the fash raised by dressing. A round-ended knife is sent to the wheel again, to have the tang polished, which process is as follows: it is *glazed* on a wheel dressed with emery cake, which is composed of bees'-wax, suet, and flower emery; with this glazer, the polisher erases all the scratches, and gets the tang to a fine bottom. For the second glazing he rubs a little bees'-wax and soft charcoal on the face of his wheel, and holds a pebble on for a short time, which brings it to the proper face for polishing or giving the last glaze; sometimes it is further polished on another wheel, covered with leather and dressed with crocus (a preparation of the oxide of iron), which gives a rich lustre to the steel. The blade is again returned to the setter-in, who inserts it into the haft, which he finishes. The haft is then wrapped in paper, to keep it clean; and the knife is sent to the wheel to have the blade finished, which is ground on a stone to a thin edge, so as to ply the finger nail when laid to it; it is next taken to be *lapped*. The *lap* is a wheel faced with lead, and dressed with flour emery and sweet oil. This process takes out all the marks left by the grindstone, and produces a smooth surface; it is fined still further after a piece of flint has been held in contact with the face of the lap, while running. It is now ready for the last polishing, which is similar to that described above,—the wheel is dressed with crocus, and the polisher occasionally dips a piece of wool hat in crocus, and holds it to the wheel; this gives a finishing lustre to the blade. The knife is then returned to the setter-in, or some competent person, to be *whetted*, which operation completes the penknife blade, and is generally performed on a Turkey hone.

[Here surely is a poetry of process with words in it which would have delighted Keats.]

2. *Craftsmanship and Design**

Many of these articles are wonderful achievements of skill, exhibiting the most exquisite workmanship, and the greatest ingenuity in their contrivance, but they are frequently at variance with good taste, and rendered altogether useless by the extravagant forms they assume. Our mechanics pride themselves too much on making the largest, the most diminutive, the most costly, or the most complex articles. This is a false idea of excellence, and is injurious insomuch as there is a great expenditure of time and labour and mechanical skill without an equivalent result. A first rate workman may have been employed for several months on a very complex piece of cutlery, worked in the most costly materials and the workmanship may be perfect of its kind; but after all, if the article is useless, it must necessarily fail of giving the pleasure that an union of the *useful* with the *beautiful* always affords. A simple one-bladed knife made of the best materials, both as regards the steel and the covering of the haft, and neither more nor less of either than is actually required, having an elegant form, and one that will at the same time sit easy in the hand, with all the filing and fitting perfectly true, the steel well ground and polished, and the whetting, which fits the

*From the *Sheffield Mechanics' Exhibition Magazine*, no. 9, Aug. 1, 1840, pp. 99-100.

article for its ultimate purpose of cutting, properly accomplished, is in our opinion, a more legitimate specimen of excellence in cutlery than all the wonderfully complex and many-hundred-bladed knives that were ever made, and a truer test of the superior skill and taste of the workman.

[The knife with the 1851 blades was on show again in the Victoria and Albert Museum in 1951.]

3. *The End of Monopoly**

This Act of the 21st of James I . . . enacted, that all persons engaged in those manufactures, within the aforesaid limits shall form one body politic, perpetual, and incorporate . . . the said *Company of Cutlers of the lordship of Hallamshire*. . . . Immediately after the passing of this act, 300 persons enrolled themselves members of the company, and by their proper officers proceeded to enact such *bye-laws* etc. as at that time appeared necessary for the better regulation of their trade and for the punishment of fraudulent artificers. To the *six searchers* power was given to enter dwelling-houses where they had reason to suppose that deceitful wares were concealed. The restrictions on taking apprentices, already sufficiently rigid, were made yet more so. . . . An act passed in 1791 introduced several changes . . . that any number of freemen's sons might be taken as apprentices, but of the children of non-freemen no person should take another apprentice until his youngest had served his third year; that no person should be allowed to exercise any of the incorporated trades who was not a freeman . . . and that any person might obtain his *freedom by paying* £20 *to the Corporation Funds*. . . . Many of the clauses in this act were, however, still too restrictive and so ill-adapted to the rapid growth of the manufactures of the town that a slight relaxation of them was made by statute in 1801; but in 1814 they had become so unpopular that they were altogether swept away by an *act of the 54th of George III.*, which extended the liberty of engaging in any of the incorporated trades, either as masters or journeymen, to all persons, whether freemen or strangers, whether they had

*William White, *History and General Directory of the Borough of Sheffield*, etc. (Sheffield, 1833), pp. 37–9.

served an apprenticeship or no, and whether they had a mark assigned them by the company or not, any where within the limits of Hallamshire; so that though the corporate body still exists, has a hall and regularly appoints a master cutler and other officers, it has now no restrictive or controlling power, except that of protecting from infringement the *marks* which have been granted to the freemen, provided they continue to pay the yearly mark rent of 6d. at the feast of Pentecost. Marks are also granted to non-freemen, on the payment of certain premiums. Some of the oldest of these marks are of considerable value to their owners, as in many countries they are taken as an unquestionable warranty of the excellence of the articles impressed therewith.

4. *Bessemer Steel**

The Bessemer process has been in use in Sheffield for the last two or three years. It is the invention of Mr. Henry Bessemer, who has a manufactory here for making steel upon his own method. The plan is exceedingly simple but very remarkable in its results. The time required for making bar steel, reckoning from the period when it is put into the furnace till it is cool enough to take out, is from fifteen to twenty days; and then three hours and a half more are required to change the bars into cast steel. Looking at these facts it seems hardly credible that by the Bessemer process crude iron can be changed into steel within thirty minutes. Yet such is the fact. The vessel in which the steel conversion takes place upon Mr. Bessemer's plan is made of strong boiler plate, the interior being preserved with a lining of powdered stone called "ganister" found in the neighbourhood of the town. The vessel is oval, with an aperture at the top for pouring the metal in and out. At the bottom there are inserted seven tuyeres of fireclay, each having seven holes in it; and through these a blast from the engine enters. Though the converting vessel is made large enough to hold several tons of metal, it is constructed so that it will readily swing about in any direction required. In the commencement of the process the vessel is thoroughly heated with coke. A sufficient quantity of

*From *Pawson & Brailsford's Illustrated Guide to Sheffield and Neighbourhood* (c. 1862), p. 114.

pig iron having been melted in an adjoining furnace, the converting vessel is turned on one side, and the iron is poured in at the hole in the top already described. The vessel is then put back into its ordinary position, the blast having been turned on into the interior through the holes mentioned in the bottom. This causes a most powerful combustion to take place. As the fire increases in intensity, it causes a series of miniature explosions of spark and flame, which are interesting to watch; while the place is illuminated with a beautiful white light. The most pleasing part of the process, however, to the visitor is when the vessel is swung down again, at the close of the operation. He has to stand on one side, where he is perfectly secure, while the molten metal sends forth a torrent of large and brilliant sparks, which dart straight ahead with great force. When the practised eye of the workman sees that the metal is ripe for his purpose, the vessel is tilted forward, and he puts in a quantity of charcoal pig iron containing a certain proportion of carbon. The carbon combines with the mass of molten iron, and thus it becomes steel. The vessel is then placed in a position in which the metal will run out, and it is poured into a large ladle, and thence into the ingot moulds. The process of conversion occupies about 28 minutes.

5. Armour Plate*

The rolling of armour plates at the manufactory of Messrs. Brown[1] and Co. is not to be surpassed in interest. The process is commenced by taking about 132 slabs of iron, measuring about 30 inches by 12, and an inch and a half thick. Four of these pieces, after being heated in a furnace, are rolled into a solid plate of about four feet square. In this way the whole of the slabs are by degrees welded together until they form four plates, each 10 feet long by 4 feet 4 inches wide, and 2½ inches thick. These four have to be rolled together to make the armour plate which is used for the protection of the ship. As may well be imagined, it requires peculiar machinery and gigantic appliances to deal with such masses of metal. The four plates are

*From *Pawson & Brailsford's Illustrated Guide to Sheffield and Neighbourhood* (c. 1862), pp. 128–30.
[1]John Brown (1816–96), a pioneer in the production of armour plate for the British Navy. See Sir John Brown in *DNB*.

placed in an enormous furnace, where they are left until they
are red hot all through. And now comes the final and exciting
operation. The huge rollers are at a distance of about 20 yards
in front of the furnace; and along this space the mass of metal
has to be drawn. Seventy men are employed in the work. The
door of the furnace opens, and an iron carriage is pushed up to
its mouth for the conveyance of the red-hot plates. They are
drawn out partly by means of a chain passed round the rolls and
partly with huge pincers, each pair of which is so heavy that the
strength of three men is necessary to lift it. These two forces
are put into action, and the vast mass of metal shoots out and
rests itself on the carriage. The chain is rapidly detached and
the men run the carriage up to the rollers, the huge bulk of red
hot iron sending out a stream of heat which is felt far and near.
It passes between the rollers, and the pliable bulk of the mass
is reduced by the pressure from ten to eight inches. By a mechanical contrivance the action of the rollers is now reversed, so
that the iron passes through backwards; but this time it only
loses half an inch in thickness. Altogether it passes through the
rollers eight times. . . . Whenever there is the appearance of a
blister, or raised lump of metal, on the surface, it has to be
removed. This is effected by placing a sharp punch, at the end
of a long shaft, on the blistered spot. The punch is struck into
the blister with a heavy hammer; and this restores the iron to a
level. The rolling of the plate being now completed, it is conveyed by means of a crane to the place for straightening it. This
is performed by placing it on flat iron plates, where two rollers,
each weighing nine tons, pass over it to make it perfectly straight.
After about twelve hours the plate is sufficiently cool to be conveyed to the planing tables, where the edges are cut square
and grooved, so as to adapt it for being fastened to the sides of
the ship for which it is intended. The plates vary in size; but the
general average is about 20 feet long, 4 feet 4 inches broad, 4½
inches thick, and about six tons in weight.

6. *Steel and Skirts**

The Conference of the Wesleyan Methodists being held at
Sheffield in 1863, Mr. Brown invited the assembled ministers . . .

*From *Sheffield and Its Neighbourhood Photographically Illustrated* by
Theophilus Smith (1865), pp. 53, 55.

and friends to pay a visit to the Atlas works. . . . The presence of
so many ladies, most of them presenting the ample skirtage so
generally prevalent in the dress of almost every individual of
the sex, could hardly fail to recall, at such a time and in such a
place, the immense effect which the manufacture of "Crino-
lines" has had upon our local steel trade. Forty years ago, when
the appearance of our fair countrywomen of the higher classes
was mostly that represented by the common portraits of the
lamented Princess Charlotte, who died in 1817, it was little foreseen that fashion would ever produce such a change in the
direction of the old "hoop petticoat," or that the requirements of
the dressmaker would rival the demands of every other industry
upon the steel trade of Sheffield. Yet such has been the fact; and
it is asserted with more than rhetorical truth, that to the orders
and remuneration accruing from this source the trade has been
carried through crises of collateral depression which otherwise
would have been seriously felt; and no wonder, when it is stated
that the quantity produced on the average was not less than
three hundred tons a week. . . . The steel which ought to be, and
at the commencement of the trade generally was, of good quality,
is rolled in sheets of ten feet long and five feet wide to about
the thinness of writing paper; it is then cut up into narrow strips,
resembling the mainspring of a clock, hardened and tempered to
give it the proper degree of elasticity, and then by means of a
curious machine covered with a twisted envelope of cotton.

7. *Condition of the Workers**

Saw Grinders: The average earnings are from 40s. to 50s.
per week, out of which sum the grinder pays wheel rent and the
cost of stones and other articles required in grinding.

The saw making branch may be regarded as generally healthy.
. . . The men are mostly well formed and strong and live to a
fair average age. . . . The wheels in which they work are mostly
propelled by water, being placed upon the streams in the ex-
quisitely beautiful situation within a few miles of the town. . . .
They have frequently either small farms or plots of ground for
garden purposes. . . . Further, the branch does not admit of the

*From G. Calvert Holland, *The Vital Statistics of Sheffield* (1843), pp. 174–5,
182–3, 184.

employment of boys at a tender age or of delicate constitution, the articles being too heavy for either to hold with advantage. Saw grinding is also entirely done on a wet stone and the position of the grinder when at work is standing, so that the lungs have free play, which is not the case in the other branches of grinding.

The saw grinders are peculiarly liable to accidents, from the breaking of stones and from becoming entangled in the machinery. . . .

Spring Knife Manufacture: A few superior workmen may earn from 30s. to 40s. per week. In the first manufactories of the town the average is from 16s. to 25s. But in many of the inferior manufactories the workmen are receiving no more than 12s. or 16s. . . . The tools of the forger, hafter or putter together are few, simple and easily procured. A few pounds will enable the cutler to commence operations and those parts which it is not his business to execute are performed by others, whose co-operation is always readily obtained. . . . Necessity is . . . constantly converting workmen into petty masters, who not only sink the profit of the manufacturer but even sacrifice a large proportion of the ordinary wages of labour. Their goods are purchased by the merchants, and a numerous class of individuals who have only recently sprung into existence—hardware dealers who travel the country selling them by public auction or dispose of them in immense quantities to hawkers and small shopkeepers. . . . The ease with which workmen become manufacturers is the great curse of this branch. . . . Another disadvantage under which this branch labours is the facility which it offers for the employment of children at an early age. Many of the operations may be performed by them; hence there is an inducement superadded to the necessities of the parents to put them early to work. This indeed is a great evil. It strikes at the root of all improvement. It is keeping up a continuous stream of poor and uneducated workmen.

8. Housing*

During the period of commercial prosperity considerable demand for cottage accommodation existed, especially in districts

*From G. Calvert Holland, *The Vital Statistics of Sheffield* (1843), pp. 56–7.

possessing almost the advantages of the country, so that individuals, who could command only a few hundred pounds, were
induced to erect numerous small houses. The calculation was to
realise from 10 to 12 per cent. and this was frequently accomplished by the exceedingly slight and disgraceful character of
the dwellings. . . . In ordinary buildings, the bond timber which
is inserted into the walls is generally three inches thick but in
these modern structures it is usually an inch. The joists, on which
the floors rest, have only half the substance that is put into common houses, and is so contrived as to give the appearance of
stability. The joists employed by the respectable builder are
three inches thick but the elaborate calculator of expense makes
these into two by sawing them in a diagonal direction, presenting
to the observer who looks from below a piece of timber two
inches thick, when on the upper surface it is only one inch.
The same refined study to save material runs throughout the
whole calculations.

9. Health*

Several of the manufactures carried on in this town produce
to a great extent phthisis, the symptoms of which are frequently
masked by those of asthma. . . . Many of these cases might with
greater propriety be designated consumption. One death is stated
to arise from want of food. The observation of any medical
practitioner must indeed be very limited that has not led him
to the conclusion that the deaths of hundreds in this town are
to be traced to a deficiency of the necessaries of life. They may
die of disease but this is induced by poor living conjoined with
laborious exertion. We speak from a personal and extensive
knowledge of the working classes. . . .

Many of the manufactures of this town are detrimental to
health from the severe bodily exertions which they unceasingly
demand and the varying degrees of temperature to which the
workmen are exposed. There is one circumstance which tends in
an especial manner to produce dissipation and its inevitable
result—a high rate of mortality—viz. the independent position of

*From G. Calvert Holland, *The Vital Statistics of Sheffield* (1843), pp. 111,
116.

an immense number of the workmen. Thousands of them do not
work on the premises of their employers and, therefore, are
under no surveillance or control; and even where such is the
case, they too frequently begin and cease to labour according
to their own whim or pleasure. To this peculiar circumstance in
the position of the workmen may be traced much of the prevailing dissipation in times of good trade. In a period of depression, as at present existing, the wages, in many of the branches,
are miserably low; hence the artisans, to earn what is quite inadequate to the maintenance of their families, are under the
necessity of labouring hard, with constitutions breaking up from
exertion and insufficient nourishment.

10. *Rattening**

Rattening [punishing a rat or blackleg] is a mode of enforcing
payment of contributions to and compliance with the rules of
the union. The wheel-bands, tools and other materials of a
workman are taken and held in pledge until he has satisfied the
society. . . . In the majority of cases, where the demands of the
unions have been complied with, and a payment of a small sum
for the expenses of rattening has been made, the property taken
has been restored. Rattening is always done in the interests of
the union and very commonly by the direction of the secretary.
. . . In some cases a member of the union, without express
authority, rattens another member . . . and takes his chance of
having his act adopted by the union. The practice of rattening
is well known to be illegal, and persons detected . . . have frequently been convicted and punished. The excuse offered by
the unions for this system is, that in the absence of legal powers,
rattening affords the most ready means of enforcing payment of
contributions and obedience to the rules of the union.

The system of rattening has generally proved successful in
effecting its object. If, however, the person rattened continues
refractory he commonly receives an anonymous letter. . . . If this
warning is disregarded, recourse has been had to acts of outrage.
. . . Most of the outrages we have investigated were brought

*From the report presented to the Trade Union Commission, 1867, by the
Examiners appointed to inquire into acts of intimidation etc. in Sheffield.

before the justices . . . the offenders have, with two or three exceptions, remained unknown up to the period of this inquiry. . . . there are about 60 trade unions in Sheffield, of which 12 have promoted or encouraged outrages. . . . there has not occurred within the last ten years any act of intimidation, outrage or wrong promoted, encouraged or connived at by any association of employers. We point to the year 1859 as the one in which outrage was most rife, and we notice with pleasure that it has diminished since that time.

CHAPTER FIVE

Merthyr Tydfil and Birkenhead

MERTHYR TYDFIL

IN THE perfunctory sketches of nineteenth century Merthyr Tydfil, that erstwhile mountain village in the bleak wilds of Glamorgan, much attention has been paid to the few who accumulated fame and fortune from its mineral wealth, and little or none to those who spent their brief lives in misery and squalor, in order that the favoured few might acquire their wealth. Let us, therefore, see, through the eyes of the Health of Towns Commissioners, what Merthyr looked like to them in 1845: "Merthyr Tydfil, with Pen y Daran and Dowlais, may be regarded as chiefly a large cottage town, without any public care for supply of water, drainage, or cleansing; the open character and small height of its straggling buildings and the consequent exposure to sun and air, saving its population from still greater evils than those to which they are now exposed from the filth so abundant in it."[1]

This depressing picture could equally have been applied to many other towns, large and small, which had been thrown up in Britain's wealth-grubbing scramble. In the deep valleys or on the bleak hillsides, coal and iron lay cheek by jowl just below the surface. Where there had been rural solitude and quiet for centuries, a few decades of industrialization had brought pulsating life and clangour, and in the process the face of the countryside had become scarred for eternity. Toiling humans, drawn as by a magnet from the four corners of the kingdom and beyond, spent their waking moments in the bowels of the earth, or amidst the heat of the furnaces, and fell into drugged sleep in the fetid atmosphere of the overcrowded dwellings which debouched around the scenes of toil.

[1]Health of Towns Commission, *Second Report*, vol. I, 1845 (602), p. 328.

The population of this township had been rapidly increasing since the beginning of the century, but a spurt took place between 1831 and 1841, adding over 15,000 to the 22,000 of the former year. Each of the following two decades saw increases almost as great. The Merthyr district, which for census purposes included Aberdare in the neighbouring valley on the southwest, increased in population from 30,409 in 1831 to 107,105 in 1861, the bulk of which—85,077 in 1861—dwelt in the two townships of Merthyr and Aberdare themselves.[2]

This district became the Mecca of the migrants to South Wales during these years. The nearby rural counties naturally provided the most accessible supply of labour, but the rural counties of England contributed a share. Large numbers came, too, from Ireland after the potato famine of 1845-6, reaching Cardiff by returning coal boats, and tramping the twenty-seven miles into the hinterland to their destination. Numbers of Spaniards, finding passage in the boats bringing iron ore to South Wales, settled in Dowlais, forming an exotic element there amongst the native Welsh. As high a proportion as two-thirds of the increased population was attributed in 1844 to immigration from outside.

Merthyr was a cottage town. Except for the large residences occupied by the ironmasters, Crawshay of Cyfarthfa Castle, Guest of Dowlais House, Homfray of Penydaren House, and Hill of Plymouth House, the relatively small number of better-class homes were occupied by the tradespeople, the professional men, and the superintendents of the industrial establishments. The bulk of the houses, however, were small and were occupied by those "employed in the ironworks, either in smelting the iron itself, in the subsequent processes, or in procuring the necessary coal and limestone."[3] The best of these workmen's houses were those erected by the ironmasters for their own workmen. Speculators had also built courts, alleys, and rows of identical tenements, wherever opportunity presented itself, entirely without any preconceived plan or provision for systematic drainage.

[2]T. M. Hodges, "The Peopling of the Hinterland and the Port of Cardiff," *Economic History Review*, vol. XVII, no. 1, 1947, pp. 62-72.

[3]See Health of Towns Commission, *Second Report*, for this and ensuing quotations.

The great majority of these cottages consisted of only two rooms, one up and one down, the upper being the sleeping apartment for the family. "There are generally 3 beds in the sleeping apartment containing 5 or 6 persons. These cottages are often very small, 8' by 10', and 8' by 12', being not uncommon. . . . The average rent of these houses is about 6/- a month."

The proportion which these rents bore to the wages earned may be estimated from the following rates of pay: colliers 17/- per week; miners (i.e., ore miners) 14/- per week; labourers, 12/- per week; masons, 14/- per week; firemen 20/- per week; puddlers, 20/- per week. However, seeing that every house had its complement of lodgers, usually single men, who in turn contributed towards the family income, the problem of rent did not press too heavily on the domestic economy.

The regulation of ordinary sanitation did not become the duty of local authorities until the passing of the Public Health Act of 1848, and until that date the provision of water supply and sewage disposal was scanty. "No town in England or Wales of the extent and wealth of Merthyr Tydfil is so much in want of proper regulation as to cleansing, lighting, paving, and watering, and there is no chance of such being ever accomplished except by some compulsory means enacted by the legislature." So spoke Mr. James, Chairman of the Merthyr Board of Guardians, and an important witness before the Commissioners reporting on the sanitary condition in mining districts in 1845.

The consequences of this lack of the means of ensuring minimum standards of decency in everyday life were appalling. "From the poorer inhabitants who constitute the mass of the population, throwing all slops and refuse into the nearest open gutter before their houses, from the impeded courses of such channels, and the scarcity of privies, some parts of the town are complete networks of filth, emitting noxious exhalations." In other words, certain parts of the town stank to high heaven!

There was no act in force for the needed drainage and cleansing, while the chief lines of road, under the Commissioners of the Turnpikes, came under the Highway Act. The depositories for town refuse were "waste pieces of ground near to the different parts of the town, and the beds of the rivers Taffe and Morlais." The consequences of a long spell of dry weather, giving rise to intolerable stenches, can well be imagined, not to speak of the ever present peril from the spread of such diseases as typhus.

Something was done in certain localities towards the systematic removal of house rubbish. "It would appear that the Dowlais Iron Co. undertake to carry away ashes from the doors of the inhabitants of Dowlais at the rate of 1d. per week for each house." But the practice was not general.

Callous indifference to even the common necessities of a decent life was exhibited by unscrupulous builders and property owners alike, whose sole purpose was to knock up mean tenements as cheaply as possible. The Commissioners were told:

> In some localities a privy was found common to 40 or 50 persons, and even up to 100 persons and more. The cinder heaps, as the lines of refuse slags from the ironworks are termed, and the riversides are frequented by persons of all ages and sexes, who manage the best way they can. This system produced much indifference to personal exposure, and may in some way account for the not uncommon practice of the workmen on their return home from their labours, stripping and being washed and rubbed down, while naked, by the females of the houses, or who ever may be in at the time, usually, it is stated, without much regard to their being married or unmarried.

The effect of the abnegation of common privacy on young children brought up in such atmosphere can be gauged by the fact that "when the schools at Dowlais were first built, holding 150 boys, and 150 girls, the children did not know how to make use of the privies, and were obliged to be taught."

The lack of any public supply of fresh water in the town up to the 1850's caused great inconvenience especially during dry spells, and accounted for much of the dirt and squalor. The Commissioners reported in 1845: "There is no public supply of water, and the only thing approaching it seems a pipe carrying water from a spring to spouts used by some of the Pen y Daran houses, and a spout or two at Dowlais." This, presumably, referred to the poorer dwellings of the town, but the general supply was totally inadequate for a town of close on 40,000 people at the time the observation was made. The matter was the cause of great concern and distress in the locality: "There are a great many complaints as to arrangements for water, and the poorer classes are ill-supplied. Pumps and wells are the chief sources whence that for domestic use is obtained. Most of the wells are fed by surface waters, which are not free from mixture with impurities derived from the house refuse soaking into the ground in all directions."

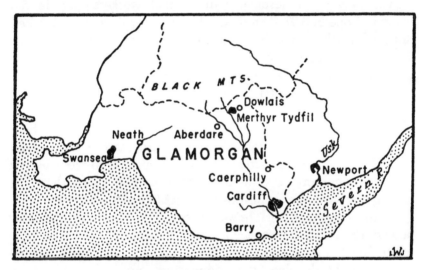

The South Wales coal field

Long distances had to be travelled every day by large numbers of the less fortunate in order to lay in a stock of water from the nearest spout, several gallons being needed by every workman's household for the daily "tub-down" by the male workers of the family. Private individuals, owning wells on their land, were wont to sell water to people in their neighbourhood who had no private supply. The charge, however, was very small for so great a necessity: "There is a well at Merthyr, known as Richard Jones's well, frequented by persons from 7 to 9 a.m., and from 3 to 5 p.m., who pay 6d. per quarter for the water."

It is not surprising that such conditions considerably reduced the rate of survival amongst children below five years of age, and lowered the average expectation of life for males and females to thirty-eight years. Two diseases which took heavy toll of the population in those days were consumption and typhus. "One in six of total deaths is due to consumption." This proportion, though high, was surprisingly less so than that for many other towns in South Wales, such as Brecon, Carmarthen, Haverfordwest, and Swansea, the first three of which were rural and uncontaminated by industry. Furthermore, the disease was higher amongst tradesmen than manual workers, one in 5.3 as against one in 6.07. The dread disease of typhus was a marked cause of death in Merthyr, one in nine dying from it, a higher proportion than anywhere else in South Wales. Its incidence was as great amongst the better classes as amongst the working classes, which substantiates the complaints about the imperfect conditions of the water supply of the town.

The only attempts at centrally controlled provision of bare amenities were those originated by the ironmasters themselves. Indeed, in such communities which had sprung up from barren wastes without any previous tradition of corporate life, these big employers were the mainspring of existence—they it was who gave the community its *raison d'être*. The necessary statutory powers to initiate improvement were lacking, and without adequate local government machinery upon which such responsibility could devolve, the ironmasters were the only local authority who might be expected to promote improvements. Unfortunately the spirit of the age did not believe that public welfare should be a public concern. Remedial measures were little short of dire expediencies. Workers must have shelter somehow, hence dwellings of some sort had to be provided. A minimum standard of health amongst one's workers was also a sensible prerequisite to hard work, hence a medical service had to be provided—at a price. "With regard to medical attendance for the poor, the plan adopted by the four iron companies is that each provides medical attendance for their workmen and their families. In some measure, this removes the want of hospitals and infirmaries, of which there are none, since so large a proportion of the population is employed directly by these companies. Each person employed in the works pays a certain sum, apparently 2d. in the pound, to a sick fund, receiving medical attention when required." It is worth observing that such an arrangement has continued with little basic change down to our own day. To those not belonging to the big works, and too poor to pay for a private doctor, attention was given by the Medical Officer of the Union Workhouse.

In one amenity at least—coal for heating—the inhabitants of the Merthyr district were very favourably placed as compared with many socially superior town-dwellers outside the coalfield. For example, "At the Plymouth works a ton of coal per month is allowed with their cottages at a rate of about 4/- a ton, an arrangement which appears to give great satisfaction." This custom was common to all workers of the four ironworks companies, and accounts for the fact that all witnesses before the 1845 Commission admitted that all houses, however mean and denied other simple needs of sanitation and cleanliness, were at least adequately warm.

II

The year 1839 was marked by disturbances in South Wales which sprang from economic and political frustration. In the West, the counties of Carmarthenshire and Pembrokeshire had been upset by the Rebecca Riots, which had their origin in the resistance to the payment of tolls, and were characterized by the "destruction of gates which began in the Whitland Turnpike Trust, in the confines of the counties of Pembroke and Carmarthen."[4] Merthyr townsfolk did not take part in these riots despite the fact that the varying charges on its four turnpike roads caused public outcries. Merthyr had its canal, however, and the early prospect of the completion of the Taff Vale Railway. The total eclipse of the turnpike roads by the railway was regarded as a *fait accompli* by one witness before the 1844 Committee, who said: "There is now some talk of taking the mail off the road, and coming on to the rail; that shows that there is scarcely any traffic except upon the railway."[5]

[4]Commission on the Present State of the Laws in South Wales as to the Maintenance and Repair of Turnpikes, Highways and Bridges, and on the Causes of the Recent Acts of Violence and Outrage, *Report*, 1844. (Rebecca Riots.)
[5]*Ibid.*, Question 9763.

If Merthyr was not directly concerned in the Rebecca Riots, this was not true of her part in the contemporaneous Chartist movement. Merthyr's connection with Chartism was active and continuous from 1839 to 1846 though not so sensational as that of Newport. The Merthyr Chartists were well organized by their Head Committee and their "Captains of Ten": "All the Chartists of Merthyr and elsewhere are divided into pickets of eleven, and the eleventh man communicates to the other ten the orders from the Head Committee."[6]

The exact number of Chartists in the Merthyr area was unknown, and no doubt changed from time to time according to the fluctuations of popular emotion. Though there was a hard core of loyal Chartists for some years after the disturbances of 1839, there is no doubt that it was just before the march on Newport on November 3, 1839, that the strength of the movement was, numerically, at least, greatest in this area. Throughout the life of the movement the number of known partisans was undoubtedly much smaller than the mass of sympathizers. An observer reporting on the position in 1839 in a letter to the Lord Lieutenant of the County, the Marquess of Bute, wrote: "There may be 1000 Chartists in Dowlais, who are in communication with the Committee, which meets at Cyfarthfa, and who are very particular in excluding common members from their deliberations."[7]

The leaders were "small tradesmen, such as shoemakers, etc.," and the chief was one Morgan Williams, a local woollen manufacturer. There was, however, in the neighbourhood, a Dr. Price, surgeon, who wielded great influence outside Merthyr, and who is reported to have emigrated with a price of £100 on his head for his part in the local disturbances.[8]

The active Chartists had their clubs, or lodges, which met in members' houses, or more frequently at their favourite "local," and there, under the cover of privacy, voiced their most secret hopes and grievances. Members on ceremonial occasions adopted distinctive apparel as public expression of their pride of membership, the men wearing woollen waistcoats and the women a sort

[6]Bute MSS, Bundle XX, no. 2 (Cardiff Library).
[7]*Ibid.*
[8]Bute MSS.

of apron, and all sported membership badges fashioned with a peculiar design.[9]

Red-letter days in the early days of the movement were mass meetings held on the neighbouring mountains, usually on Aberdare Hill, when leading Chartists such as Frost, Vincent, or Feargus O'Connor would address five to six hundred Chartists.[10] Despite the inflammatory speeches which these meetings occasioned, the crowd usually dispersed peacefully. Rumours of forthcoming disturbances were often passed on to the local Justice of the Peace by informers before and after the clash with the military at the Westgate Hotel, Newport, on November 3, 1839, and these guardians of the law came to fear any event likely to attract large numbers of workers. More often than not such rumours were groundless. One such, in May 1839, concerned an organized march from the neighbouring valleys to the annual Whitsun fair, at Llandaff, during which time, it was rumoured, the marchers would destroy the Cardiff Union, and smash up other property in that town. Great alarm amongst property owners and tradespeople was caused, especially as there were about 1,000 men employed in constructing the Taff Vale Railway, and many hundreds also in building the West Bute Dock at Cardiff, both of which undertakings contained large contingents of "irresponsible Irish." A more serious affair took place in Merthyr itself, a little later in the year, when the mob threatened trouble, before it was dispersed by the local militia augmented by special constables: "Had the mob at Merthyr, on Monday 6th June, not been dispersed the labouring classes in the Vale were ripe to rebel." This warning was made to the Lord Lieutenant of the County in a plea to establish military forces in various parts of the County to give protection from such sudden outbreaks. Had the energy displayed in suppressing outbreaks been more profitably utilized in seeking to rectify the causes of these and other manifestations of working-class frustration much misery would have been avoided.

The great mass of Chartists were no doubt entirely ignorant of the political changes contemplated by their leaders, who are

[9]Bute MSS, Bundle XX, no. 69.
[10]This and subsequent citations are from various numbers in the Bute MSS (Cardiff Library).

reported to have promised the rank and file "the removal of taxes that will make every shilling they earn nearly double value, as more than 8d. out of every 1/- is now taken from them by indirect taxation." Recalcitrant people were often moved to join the ranks on threats of having their houses burnt down when the Chartists came into power. Whatever may be thought in retrospect of the sentiments expressed by the Chartists, and whatever criticism may be levelled at the methods adopted to achieve their aims, the fact remains that our final condemnation must fall on the régime which allowed, with callous indifference, the economic and political frustrations to exist.

Despite the fact that most of the Merthyr Chartists, unlike the more violent elements of Monmouthshire, were of the "Moral Force" persuasion, a large contingent marched from there on November 3, 1839, armed with pikes, to take part in the release of Vincent from Newport Gaol, and some became involved in the fighting at the Westgate Hotel.

For some time before this disturbance Merthyr Chartists had become bolder in public by virtue of the apparent ineptitude of the local magistrates and the absence of definite action on the part of the military. They publicly asserted that the overthrow of the existing régime was just a matter of correct timing. Catch phrases such as, "Remember Paris," were bandied about by the more reckless, while *clichés*, such as "The fingers are going to overthrow the thumb," "The rich have ridden over the poor long enough," and "Do not trust men in authority—they are wolves," were on the lips of men who certainly did not wholly comprehend the full implications of their remarks. It was reported that the workers in one Merthyr colliery objected to receiving bank notes in payment, rejecting even those of the Bank of England, on the grounds that they expected a run on the banks in the near future.

The unexpected display of armed force and the consequent bloodshed at Newport thoroughly frightened all but the more ardent of the marchers, and many returned home crestfallen and ashamed, and in some cases with doubtful feelings as to the warmth of their reception. Their brief role as heroes was over, but glory had eluded them. Richard Beaumont, a mine-owner of Gelligaer, wrote to the Marquess of Bute that many of his workmen suffered a humiliating experience on their return home: "They hung about the neighbouring woods for days before showing themselves, being afraid to face their wives who waited for them with rolling pins to belabour them for the part they had played, and the work they had lost."

The fiasco at Newport was a severe set-back to the plans for using its success as a signal for a nation-wide rising; but belief in the righteousness of the cause of Chartism was by no means dead, and the threat of something further brewing in the near future kept local magistrates on their toes. The lack of a Stipendiary Magistrate in Merthyr to punish the wrongdoers, and of a police force to maintain law and order, was deeply deplored. The local magistrates felt that a small force of regular police could do much with the help of special constables in acting as a deterrent.

Prompt action was taken by the Justices of the Peace to prevent a recurrence of the disturbances of the Newport riots, and on November 5 a proclamation forbidding attendance at Chartist meetings was displayed in the public places in Merthyr. Despite the show of authority, however, local spirit was far from cowed. A Fund was organized for the defence of Vincent. One local magistrate writing of this said: "There is not a tradesman shopkeeper scarcely in Merthyr who has not through fear subscribed to a Fund for the defence of Vincent, and the fellows who got up the subscription had the impudence to send a Bellman round the town to thank the shopkeepers."

One of the most potent forces in the spread of Chartist ideas was the distribution of pamphlets and publications. *The Western Vindicator*, which was the work of Vincent, had a regular sale in Merthyr of about 300 to 400 weekly. A magistrate in a letter to Lord Bute asserted that "three-quarters of all Chartist mischief in our District has been generated by that most seditious publication, 'The Western Vindicator.' " Nearly a year after the Newport riots, when it was considered that the danger from further acts of violence had passed, it was noted that unstamped periodicals were still being circulated to a considerable extent, and statements made therein were "highly mischievous and dangerous

to the Public Peace." *Udgorn Cymru,* and its English transla-
tion, *The Advocate,* were the work of the Workingmen's Press
and Publication, and were financed locally. Notice of a meeting
of shareholders to be held "at the School Room, of Mr. David
Evans, George Town, Merthyr Tydfil, on Wednesday, the 14th
October, 1840," gave evidence of a still active membership.

"Moral Force" Chartists seem to have gained the day in
Merthyr during the forties. Black-lists were drawn up of all
Chartists known to have taken part in the Newport disturbance,
and those who were not imprisoned were discharged by their
employers.

By 1846, the situation had much improved, and a changed
temper amongst the working classes towards the forces of law
and order was noted which had more to do with the salutary
effect of imprisonments and dismissals than with the return of
more prosperous times.[11]

<h2 style="text-align:center">III</h2>

Despite the optimistic tone of the 1846 committee of inquiry
employers still found great cause for complaint, not against
subversive political activities, but against the losses entailed by
the high degree of drunkenness amongst employees. Mr. John
Evans, Manager of the Dowlais Iron Works, employing "6,000
workers, and having 18 furnaces in blast," voiced the opinion
of other large employers in his statement to the committee: "We
have about 700 colliers and 1,000 miners, the former earning
from £1. 1s. to £1. 5s. per week, and the latter from 18/- to
£1. per week, *all might earn much more.* Some of our men lose
four days a month, others one week out of four. Their idleness
and irregularity in working puts us to great inconvenience and
expense. We have offered 1d. and 2d. a ton extra to induce them
to work regularly, but cannot succeed."

It was observed in the *Report* that no inconsiderable part
of the temptation and encouragement to these habits of intem-
perance, at least amongst the mining population, was due to

[11]Commissioner Appointed under the Provisions of the Act 5 and 6 Vict.
c. 99, to Inquire into the Operation of That Act, and into the State of the
Population in the Mining Districts, *Report,* 1846.

the practice of contractors in mines and ironworks of paying wages to their men in public houses. This custom relieved the employers of the trouble of finding adequate small change in gold and silver, and also of the extra clerical work entailed in paying every single workman individually.

The larger works employed between twenty and forty contractors, who received the wages due to them and their men from the works' office. These contractors then proceeded to some public house, where change was provided and where the workmen ultimately received their wages. Some employers realized the harmful effects of this practice, not only on grown men but particularly on boys, who were still being employed below the age of ten years despite the act forbidding it. They forbad their contractors to use the public houses for this purpose, but the practice continued.

The manager of Sir John Guest's works at Dowlais reported: "We have about 40 contractors. We supply them with gold and silver sufficient to prevent their taking their men to public-houses under the plea of obtaining change. I have been ordered to discharge any contractor who pays his men in a public-house. Nevertheless, I fear they persist in resorting to them for that purpose."

IV

The Truck Act of 1831 had been in operation for ten years, and its defects were subject to frequent comment during that time. A Select Committee of Inquiry set up by the Commons in 1842 secured (5 & 6 Vict. c. 99) that "In an action brought for wages, no set off shall be allowed for goods supplied by the employers, or by any shops in the profits of which such employer shall have any share or interest." This clause was included to liberate workmen from the thraldom in which unscrupulous masters had previously had the opportunity of placing them. But truck remained in practice in spite of the law.

The arguments used by employers who were in favour of truck shops were twofold. First, they claimed that the "Shops" were beneficial because, "by enabling the wife to obtain all the ordinary supplies for the consumption of the family at 'The

Shop', it prevents the husband, if he is so disposed, from spending the greatest portion of his earnings in drink."[12] This was blatant sophistry, coming as it did from people actuated by no higher motive than exploitation. Secondly, they argued that "the goods in a respectable truck-shop are better and cheaper than those sold by the small retail shopkeeper." What nonsense, in face of the wholesale instances of such goods being higher in price and poorer in quality than comparable articles in any private shops! Moreover, the system gave rise to other iniquitous practices which tied the worker to his employer. For instance, "The most unscrupulous of those employers who practise the truck system, defer the settlement of wages for several weeks in order to oblige their workmen to deal more largely in their shop as they can get credit nowhere else."

As in many other fields of social legislation there were wide discrepancies here and there between legal enactment and the actual implementation of the act, so that abuses which had been made illegal by Parliament were existing evils in many parts where the application of the law was inadequate or where it was connived at. Thus truck, though illegal after 1831, was still practised in South Wales, as elsewhere, for many decades. The Commissioners in their Report of 1852 found, for example, that at that time truck was practised by "twelve of the seventeen iron and coal works on the hills of Monmouthshire and Glamorganshire."

The extent to which private traders in the retail trade suffered by the continued presence of truck shops in their midst must have been considerable, as was emphasized by representatives of the local Anti-Truck Associations:

It is by no means an uncommon case that the earnings in a particular locality amount to £10,000 a week. On the prospect of a weekly demand for ordinary articles of retail, various kinds of business are opened. Suddenly, the proprietors of these works open retail shops on their own account, cause it to be understood in defiance of the law, that they expect their men to receive a certain portion of their wages in goods, and withdraw at once several thousand pounds per week from the business of the independent shopkeepers.

[12]*Ibid.*, 1852 (1525).

The law was flouted even by local Justices of the Peace. In most cases in the Merthyr district such justices were also the chief employers of labour, upon whom the bulk of the population depended for work. An instance of such an employer and local magistrate introducing the truck system into a locality where it had not previously existed for at least twenty years was given by the Aberdare Anti-Truck Association, whose representatives told the Commissioner that £80 had been spent by the Association in getting one conviction:

The population of Aberdare is 15,000. Under the late manager of the Aberdare Iron Works, all wages were paid in money for a period of upwards of twenty years. On the faith of this, in the expectation that it would continue, several persons built houses and others rented them, and established themselves in various branches of business. In November 1850, shortly after the management changed hands, the Truck-system was introduced. An Anti-Truck Association was formed some months afterwards, and cases were brought before the magistrate against the present manager, Mr. Richard Fothergill, who is also one of the proprietors of these large works, consisting of 7 furnaces and rolling mills, and collieries that send down 'steam coal' and other descriptions of coal to Cardiff. They have an extensive work also at Treforest, where there is a truck-shop, managed as the one here. We found that the sums circulating in the town among the tradesmen diminished from the time of the introduction of the Truck System by a sum of at least £3,000 per month in Aberdare alone.

V

Three events, widely spread in time, had contributed towards the economic development of Merthyr Tydfil since the Industrial Revolution. They were: first, the completion of Anthony Bacon's turnpike road in 1767, which linked Merthyr to the Old Quay, at the mouth of the Taff, at Cardiff, and enabled Bacon to export cannon for use in the American War of Independence; second, the completion of the Glamorganshire Canal in 1798, which provided the chief means of transport for the iron products of the Merthyr district for the following forty odd years; and third, the completion of the Taff Vale Railway, on April 28, 1841.[18]

[18]T. M. Hodges, "The Hinterland and Port of Cardiff," MS thesis, 1946, University of London.

The ownership of the Glamorgan Canal had by the thirties passed almost exclusively into the hands of the Crawshay family. The other ironmasters and colliery proprietors, who had provided a share of the initial capital, before being bought out, desired additional transport facilities since the canal was becoming inadequate to cope with the increasing production of iron and coal in the Taff and tributary valleys. They met on October 12, 1835, at the Castle Inn, Merthyr Tydfil, to discuss the construction of a railway line to Cardiff, with branches to the tributary valleys and linking these to the port of Cardiff.[14]

Survey of the area had previously been carried out by the Great Western Railway engineer Isambard K. Brunel who had advised on the practicability of such a line for the carriage of iron, ruling in favour of the standard rather than the broad gauge on account of the frequency of sharp bends to be negotiated in the hilly tract. Strangely enough Brunel is said to have left the vast possibilities of coal exports out of his reckoning. Whether this was so or not, such an oversight was not made by the projectors themselves, as may be seen from the amount of traffic which the railway was expected to carry:

	Tons	*Estimated receipts*
Coal	390,000	£23,288
Iron manufactures	89,000	11,866
Iron ore	51,000	4,462[15]

The requirements of the Cyfarthfa Works, owned by William Crawshay, were not included in this estimate, since their output was being carried by the Glamorgan Canal of which Crawshay was the sole proprietor.

Crawshay was a bitter opponent of the Railway Company from the start, and petitioned against its construction on two counts:

William Crawshay objected that the railway would interfere with the construction of his tinworks being erected in the Vale of Taff (at Treforest) at a cost of £100,000. . . .

The Glamorgan Canal objected that the cost of the line was not justified by the trade of the District. The petition asserted that the

[14]Taff Vale Railway Act, 6 Will. IV c. 82.
[15]T.V.R. Amendment Act (1840), Revised Tariff Receipts, Bute MSS.

Canal tolls had been reduced from 5d. per ton to ¾d. per ton for iron, and from 2d. per ton to ½d. per ton for coal. The Canal it was stated was more than equal to the existing trade and an outlay of £20,000 would render it equal to double the existing trade.[16]

It is true that the Glamorgan Canal had indeed done yeoman service in the development not only of the Merthyr area but of Cardiff itself. In the year of the opening of the Bute Dock, Cardiff, 1839, the Canal carried 132,781 tons of iron and 211,214 tons of coal.[17]

The Railway was Merthyr-inspired, and very largely Merthyr-financed. As a result of the first appeal for £300,000 divided into £100 shares, 2260 shares were taken up at once, local capital being prominent: "Shareholders with direct local interest 88, and capital subscribed by them £115,500; shareholders with indirect local interest 22, and the capital subscribed by them £56,700; shareholders with no local interest 30, and the capital subscribed by them £53,800."[18] Crawshay, the wealthiest of the local industrialists, did not embark in the enterprise for obvious reasons, while the Marquess of Bute was financially extended by the construction of his dock at Cardiff. Bristol financiers provided the bulk of the outside capital, since the Port of Bristol had always had close associations with South Wales, being its main provider of foodstuffs until 1860.

So parlous was the financial position of the T.V.R. in its early years, on account of the heavy price of buying off petitioners, and unforeseen constructional expenses, that the Chairman of the Company, Sir J. John Guest, seriously considered a proposal that the whole of the plant and property should be offered to its creditors in liquidation of their claims, and the situation was saved only by the action of the directors in guaranteeing a loan from the bank.

As the Bute Dock and the Taff Vale Railway Company were intimately bound up, it was suggested to the Marquess of Bute in 1840 that he should take up 200 shares in the Company. This, it was pointed out, would enable him to secure a place on the

---

[16]Merthyr and Cardiff Railway Report, Bute MSS.
[17]Statistical Tables, Bute Docks, Bute MSS.
[18]Merthyr and Cardiff Railway Report, Bute MSS.

directorate, in which capacity he would be able to scotch the Railway Company's threat to build a rival dock at Cogan Pill, near Penarth, at the mouth of the Ely River. At that particular time, Taff Vale Railway shareholders had so little confidence in the success of the venture as to be ready to sell their holdings at a discount of 20 to 25 per cent.[19] There is no evidence that the Marquess of Bute acted on this suggestion then or at any other time, especially since the relations between the two were more or less hostile for many years: "I used to think that the T.V.R. were actuated by the desire to cripple me in dealing with the South Wales Railway Company, but I now think that it is rather from jealousy of that Company than from any ill-will towards me."[20]

The T.V.R. soon got over its teething troubles, and as its traffic increased by leaps and bounds, so that of the Glamorgan Canal dwindled. An attempt was made in 1844 to unite the conflicting interests of the Canal, the Railway, and the Bute Dock interests by amalgamation. The Dock and Railway companies were to take over the Canal in return for £1,636,000 debentures. Crawshay was the prime mover, and this estimate of the value of the Canal's assets was his. Another scheme was proposed by which one-third of the purchase capital amounting to £400,000 should be met by debentures, and the other two-thirds taken up in shares. The scheme came to naught, however, largely owing to Crawshay's obstinacy in not agreeing to pay wharfage dues under the amalgamation.[21]

With the establishment of the heating qualities of the 4' seam steam coal, as demonstrated by John Nixon to the French navy in the forties, the coal export trade of the Taff and tributary valleys was assured. From 1845 onwards the mineral traffic of the T.V.R. expanded far beyond the wildest dreams of its owners, and the prosperity of the company was assured. It remained throughout its existence chiefly a mineral line. By 1855 the amount of minerals and goods passing over its lines had reached

[19]Letter to Marquess of Bute, March 30, 1840, Bute MSS., T.V.R.
[20]Marquess of Bute to T. Collingdon, Manager of Bute Dock (undated), Bute MSS., T.V.R.
[21]Notes on Proposed Amalgamation of T.V.R., Bute Docks, and Glamorgan Canal, 1844, Bute MSS.

1,411,766 tons, of which coal and coke amounted to 1,155,904 tons. In 1913 this figure had reached more than 21,000,000 tons, of which coal and coke accounted for well over 19,000,000 tons.[22]

VI

Iron making and not coal had been the cause of Merthyr's wealth: coal was merely the subsidiary to iron. It was not until the forties that coal usurped the primary position of iron. The expansion of the iron industry in Merthyr had reached its zenith by the thirties, while Merthyr gave way first to Aberdare and then to the Rhondda and Rhymney valleys in coal production.[23]

Merthyr's iron trade had largely developed in the production of iron rails. The works at Cyfarthfa and Dowlais had made these a speciality which gained for Merthyr a high reputation during the railway-building eras of this and other countries. From 1839 to 1849 the Glamorgan Canal and the Bute Dock exported over 737,000 tons, while from that date up to 1860 the Bute Docks alone exported over 1,534,000 tons.[24]

It was at the Dowlais works that the first licence was taken out for the manufacture of Bessemer steel, and the first steel rails made by this process were turned out there. We have the word of Mr. Martin, speaking when he had become one of the foremost steelmasters in the country: "Bessemer Steel was first rolled into rails at the Dowlais Ironworks. I have it on the authority of Sir Henry Bessemer himself that the pig iron from which the ingots were made was grey Blaenavon, and it was converted into soft iron or steel without the addition of spiegel or manganese, the converter being lined with Stourbridge fire-bricks. The rails were rolled from 2 ingots 10″ square."[25]

In 1857 and 1858 further experiments were conducted at the same works in the rolling of steel rails from ingots sent there for experiment by Bessemer. Mr. Martin asserted that as a young man he assisted in these early trials: "I also assisted in getting

[22]T.V.R. Vesting Bill (1909), Statistical Tables, Bute Docks, Bute MSS.
[23]Hodges, "The Hinterland and Port of Cardiff."
[24]Statistical Tables, Bute Docks, Bute MSS.
[25]E. P. Martin's Presidential Address, Iron and Steel Institute, 1897; see *Journal of the Iron and Steel Institute.*

up the blowing and other apparatus for the first experiments on the Bessemer process." During one series of experiments at Dowlais, Bessemer failed to produce steel of uniform quality, and it was suggested at the time that such irregularities were inherent in the process. It was many years after that Mr. Martin, having returned to Merthyr as manager of the Dowlais works, discovered by accident the cause of these early failures. He said to the Institute of Engineers in 1895: "By accident I, some time ago, came upon one of these Bessemer ingots, which had been kept at the Dowlais ever since the first experiments made by Sir Henry Bessemer." He went on to say how he had had them analysed and the result "fully explained the cause of the failure of the process—it not having been ascertained at that time that large quantities of sulphur and phosphorus were detrimental to the manufacture of Bessemer Steel." It also explained, as he asserted, "why, though the Dowlais was one of the first to take up a licence, they did not begin to roll steel rails until 1884."

In fact, the Dowlais works, after the failure of initial trials in steel making, continued to take great pride in the quality of its iron rails and girders, and especially in turning out girders of maximum size. In 1862 an iron flange rail 120 feet long was sent from this works to London for the Exhibition in South Kensington, the Exhibition that was shorn of its promise by the death of the Prince Consort on December 14, 1861.

BIRKENHEAD

At the beginning of the nineteenth century the two shores of the Mersey estuary presented a striking contrast. On the Lancashire side lay Liverpool, a victim of over-rapid growth, perhaps the most congested town in the whole of Britain; on the Cheshire bank there confronted it the agricultural townships of eastern Wirral (the Wirral peninsula between Mersey and Dee being the Monmouthshire of North Wales). These townships were separated from Liverpool by a river whose great width (over 1,000 yards), great depth (45 feet or more), great speed (up to 8 miles an hour), and great tidal range (up to 33 feet) made it a formidable obstacle which few cared to cross "except under pressure of business or of necessity." One of these townships, however, Birkenhead, possessed inherent geographical advantages, which were to ensure for it a new destiny in the age of steam. These were:

(*a*) Its frontage to deep tidal water. This front—about half a mile in length—was characterized by a narrow, shelving, rocky foreshore backed by low sandstone cliffs. In the main, the deep water of the estuary lay on the Cheshire, rather than the Lancashire side, and Tranmere Sloyne, about a mile upstream from Woodside Ferry, Birkenhead, but remote from Liverpool, was regarded as the best Mersey anchorage. Above the Sloyne, however, the shifting sand-flats of the upper Mersey estuary made navigation increasingly difficult.

(*b*) Its possession of two tidal creeks which flanked it respectively to north and south. One of these, Wallasey Pool, was about a mile wide at its entrance between Seacombe Ferry (in Wallasey) and Woodside Ferry; it penetrated inland towards the North Wirral flats for about two miles in a west-northwesterly direction, almost completely cutting off the parish of Wallasey from the rest of the Wirral communities. Tranmere Pool to the south, about 300 yards wide at its mouth, curved inland for about half a mile towards the site of the present Birkenhead Central Station, and served as a boundary between the townships of Birkenhead and Tranmere.

(*c*) Its command of the shortest, and presumably the least dangerous, crossing to central Liverpool, an area which had served as the business heart of Merseyside ever since the Middle Ages. In the early decades of the nineteenth century a number of small, rival ferries linked together the two sides of the estuary. Of these the closest to Liverpool were those of Seacombe and Woodside, the former serving Wallasey Parish only, the latter being of potential importance to the whole of the rest of Wirral. The Woodside district is now not only the site of a ferry terminus and of the terminus of many local motor omnibus routes but also houses the entrances to two trans-estuarine tunnels whose exits are in Liverpool.

(*d*) Its possession of extensive well-drained building sites. Despite the handicap, in Birkenhead, of a marsh near Wallasey Pool, certain localities in and near the township were eminently suited to support a large residential community. The best of such areas were the low ridges of Oxton and Tranmere. These were dry, healthy, and wind-swept, with good view points, and with pleasant, unspoilt countryside and firm, sandy beaches accessible to them. There was also in the district abundance of pure drinking water and good building material—sand, sandstone, and clay.

(*e*) Its relative ease of access, via the Wirral lowlands, to Chester and thence through the Cheshire Gate to the Midlands and London. The choice of a site near Woodside Ferry for the terminus of a main-line railway is one way in which this advantage has been utilized.

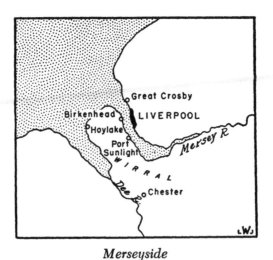

Merseyside

At the end of the Napoleonic era Birkenhead was the most thinly peopled township in Wirral, with the exception of Hoose— a township near Hoylake with little else but marsh and sand dune. By the 1860's it had become the most urbanized and thickly peopled township of the peninsula, functioning partly as a dormitory, partly as a manufacturing town, and partly as a seaport. At the beginning of the century the main obstacle to its growth as a dormitory was the Mersey estuary with its great width, speed, and tidal range; to its growth as a manufacturing town the absence of any supporting group of skilled workpeople; to its growth as a seaport its lack of docking space, its effective distance from an important manufacturing hinterland, and the inefficiency of land transport generally. The period between the years 1820 and 1860, which represents in Birkenhead history the formative period in its urbanism, saw the progressive removal of these obstacles and the utilization of its natural advantages.

The barrier presented by the estuary might perhaps have been overcome at the beginning of the nineteenth century either by bridge, or by under-water tunnel, such as exists both for rail and for motor traffic today, or by some new type of ship more independent of wind and tide than any then existing.

The single-span bridge offered then, however, as it offers now, the maximum of technical difficulty. The multiple-span bridge, whose possibilities in the early years of the century seem hardly to have been considered, would even now be not only extremely costly but would be very liable to interfere with the navigability of the estuary, as it would act as a trap for drifting silt. The under-water tunnel was regarded as a possibility in the 1820's, but its cost would have been prohibitive then.

The mechanically driven vessel, more efficient than the sailing vessel and calling for no expensive track, was in every way better adapted than bridge or tunnel to be—in the early decades of the nineteenth century—the instrument of Birkenhead's new destiny. It was far less costly to construct than either of its possible rivals; its route was less rigid, since the termini could, if need arose, be altered; and the right to operate was already possessed, so far as the journey from Birkenhead to Liverpool was concerned, by Mr. F. R. Price, the Lord of the Manor of Birkenhead. In regard to the crossing in the reverse direction Liverpool had to all intents and purposes forgone her very ancient ferry rights, and these were assumed by Mr. Price without challenge or comment.

The new era began in 1817, when the *Etna* made its first steam journey to North Wirral, crossing between Queen's Dock, Liverpool, and Tranmere. The hopes to which she gave rise were well summed up in a contemporary advertisement: "In crossing the river in a calm or in any state of wind or tide, the passage will always be very short and the inconvenience to passengers and the risk to horses, carriages, etc. which is inseparable from the use of sail boats will be almost entirely removed."

Neither the *Etna* nor her immediate successors which began to ply between Liverpool and Woodside in 1822 gave a very comfortable crossing. The passengers were invariably tossed about and frequently had to choose between being half-drowned on deck or half-suffocated near the boilers below. But in time great improvements were made, notably in the creation of the modern saloon steamer in the 1860's and of the screw steamer which began to replace the paddle boat in the 1890's. Originally ferry passengers had had to wade ashore or be carried on the backs of the boatmen. The first modern landing slipway at Woodside was constructed in 1825. This was considerably improved in 1835, and was replaced in the early 1860's by a landing stage which rose and fell with the tides, the only real solution to the problem of the fluctuating water level of the Mersey. These and parallel improvements on the Liverpool side made the Mersey estuary a link as well as a barrier, and facilitated the creation of new residential communities on its Cheshire bank. Of these dormitories the earliest was Birkenhead.

During the first decades of the nineteenth century, Liverpool, despite the half-century of great prosperity and abnormal expansion, was a highly unattractive place in which to live. Its 100,000 inhabitants were packed into one square mile or so of mean streets and fever-haunted alleys. Not unnaturally, improvements in road building had initiated a process of class segregation, whereby wealthy citizens had begun to take up their residences in surrounding townships, where they could enjoy fresh air and space. The influx into Birkenhead which followed the wake of the first steamship was one aspect of the movement.

It differed, however, from the infiltration into rural Lancashire, not only in regard to the method of transport utilized but also in its magnitude, its foresight, and its will to succeed. It was something like a definite migration, and like all migrations selective of human material. It had its leaders, and these appear to have resolved that the new community should develop into more than a mere appendage of the neighbour. They seem to have been stirred by thoughts not only of a residential area, ordered consciously from its beginnings and avoiding the disasters of that unplanned growth so apparent in Liverpool and elsewhere, but of an industrial town and independent seaport, where social idealism could advance on a business basis and a profitable deal in land was no demerit.

Prominent among these confident newcomers was one William Laird, a native of Greenock and a Liverpool shipbuilder. About 1825, he and others, taking careful stock of Wallasey Pool, whose northern bank was already the site of several minor manufacturing industries, came to believe that by dredging it, building a wall across its mouth, and constructing a connecting canal to Hoylake, they could create a seaport which would rival Liverpool. The ships using this new port would be able to avoid not only the dangerous channels of Liverpool Bay, then a source of grave anxiety to all concerned in navigating them, but also the payment of the heavy Liverpool port dues, since the western entrance of the canal would lie outside the jurisdiction of the Port of Liverpool, and be within that of Chester. A favourable report from their surveyors, Messrs. Telford, Stephenson & Nimmo, was followed in 1828 by the preparations necessary for the grant of parliamentary powers to carry on the work. At this stage, however, the Corporation of Liverpool, getting wind of the business, secretly bought considerable stretches of land near the margins of the Pool and by this means nullified the whole project.

Despite this set-back Laird did not lose faith in the future of Birkenhead. He had already, in 1824, established a boiler-yard and a ship-yard on a site abutting Wallasey Pool, near the head of the present Vittoria Street, induced thereto, report ran, by disagreements with his workmen in Liverpool and necessarily alive to the fact that the river frontage on the Liverpool side was in increasing demand for dock construction. Thence from 1828 he directed his attention to iron shipbuilding, ignoring the whole weight of contemporary technical opinion. In 1829 he built the first, or one of the first, iron ships ever constructed. He had, at the beginning of his venture, great difficulty in obtaining men to bend and fit the plates and frames, and in procuring angle iron and plates of suitable size. In time however he created a new body of skilled workmen and technicians.

The success of iron shipbuilding in this country was almost entirely due to Laird and his son John, who overcame conservatism and fear by sheer force of resolution and technical ability. By 1840 they had constructed thirty-two iron vessels of all kinds, every one in a sense a pioneer. The first iron ships used in India, China, South America, the United States, and Egypt were built by them, sometimes being sent abroad in sections to be reassembled by Birkenhead workmen on the banks of great rivers such as the Euphrates and the Ganges (a very early instance, surely, of prefabrication).[1] Their unquestioned success turned prejudice into advocacy and enlisted the favourable interest of the British Admiralty.

The progress of the new Birkenhead was rapid, and the faith of its pioneers in its destiny amazing. In 1811 its population was 193; by 1821 this had increased to 310; in 1827 it exceeded 1,300, upwards of £100,000 had been expended in two years on buildings and on other improvements, and there was no doubt that the nucleus of a large town had already been formed; since 1818 particular lots of land had risen in value fourfold. In 1831 the inhabitants numbered 2,790; ten years later, in an area originally too poor to support a village, there had been created a vigorous and self-conscious community whose population had grown to 8,769; by the middle forties this population had probably been quadrupled and its achievements had evoked admiration from observers all over Britain. To one, Birkenhead was "a case wholly unparalleled in the annals of this country"; to another "one of the greatest wonders of the age, and indeed one of those by which the character of our age is most strongly expressed."

The main aspects of the achievement of this formative period may be summarized thus:

(1) The acquisition of powers of self-government. The new residents quickly obtained powers of self-government which though modest in scope were more democratic in principle than those then existing in Liverpool. In 1833 an act was passed for "paving, lighting, watching, cleansing and otherwise improving the Township or Chapelry of Birkenhead in the County Palatine

---

[1]Cf. the practice of a Pittsburgh firm in the post-Civil War period. "These steam boats, built by James Rees & Sons Company, were shipped in knocked-down condition to the points of their intended use where they were assembled, in some instances by representatives of the company sent along for the purpose." L. C. Hunter, *Steamboats on the Western Rivers* (Cambridge, Mass., 1949), 63n.

of Chester and for regulating the police thereof and for establishing a market." The provisions of the act were to be carried out by an elected body of representatives to be known as Commissioners. At first these were sixty in number and at least half of them are known to have had business connections with Liverpool. Additional powers followed in due course.

(2) The project of a vast street plan. The relative emptiness of the original township and its lack of physical obstacles were factors favourable to the construction of a comprehensive street grid, in which the optimism of this new immigrant leadership and the dreams of the engineer could find expression. The essential feature of the layout was a series of long, wide, straight streets (running parallel to Wallasey Pool and so directed towards Woodside Ferry), across which a second series of streets ran at right angles. Events were to prove the project over-optimistic and ill-considered: it encouraged sporadic rather than compact building development, and its very vastness had in it the seeds of partial failure.

(3) The establishment of a tradition of good building. Specially noteworthy was Hamilton Square, behind Woodside Ferry, now the administrative and business heart of the borough. Blocks of dignified stone-fronted Georgian buildings are still to be found scattered over the streets of the lower town.

(4) The creation of Birkenhead Park. Work on this park, which is about 126 acres in extent, was begun in 1843 at a time when the great towns of Liverpool, Manchester, Birmingham, and Leeds possessed no public parks. Its creation was thus an exceptionally bold undertaking for a town of approximately 10,000 inhabitants; and as a technical achievement, the credit for which belongs to Sir Joseph Paxton and his assistant Kent, it was noteworthy also, since its lower end, with its ornamental lakes, was carved out of the marsh of the central depression of Birkenhead.[2]

[2]Cf. Board of Health, *Minutes of Information*, 1852: "The mists frequently created on this tract have, since the drains came into operation, disappeared. The expense of that work was 20£ per acre; and the land, which, before the drainage, was worth 1£ per acre is now worth, at the least, 4£ per acre for pasturage; so that the work pays 15% direct profit, besides effecting its main object—the improvement of the neighbourhood in comfort and salubrity."

(5) The purchase of the right of ferry to Liverpool. The Commissioners paid approximately £50,000 for the ferry freehold. The agreement to purchase (1842) was noteworthy in stating that the profits of the ferry undertaking would be applied "in reduction of the rates of the township of Birkenhead." The deal proved a lucrative municipal investment both to the Commissioners and to their successors, the Corporation of Birkenhead, until the profits of the ferry were absorbed, in 1934, into the finances of the Mersey Tunnel Joint Committee.

(6) The construction of the Birkenhead-Chester Railway. This project, first mooted in 1830, was only completed in 1840, mainly owing to disagreement about the route the railway ought to follow. One immediate result of its opening was a decline in coaching traffic. The Birkenhead terminus was at first fixed at Grange Lane; the present terminus at Woodside, half a mile beyond, whose site was chosen to take advantage of superior ferry landing facilities, was only opened in 1878.

A second chance to utilize the great possibilities of Wallasey Pool came in 1843 when the Corporation of Liverpool sold its holdings in small lots to a number of private purchasers. The various transactions having been completed, the purchasers combined and applied to Parliament for a bill to construct a "great floating harbour." The Corporation had sold at a high price knowing dock construction was contemplated, but had not foreseen a scheme of such magnitude. It accordingly opposed the bill, a policy which many in Birkenhead were slow to forgive.

The bill, considerably amended as a result of the opposition of Liverpool, received the Royal Assent in July, 1844. Essentially the scheme was that of the 1820's with the exception of the canal to Deeside. The Township Commissioners, who had been appointed Dock Commissioners, got to work at once, and in October 1844 the foundation stone of the dock wall was laid amidst scenes of great popular rejoicing. Everyone in the township was quite sure that Birkenhead (to use an expression common at that time) was indeed "the City of the Future," and that only a miracle could prevent its continued prosperity. In 1847 two small docks near Woodside, the Morpeth and Egerton

Docks, were opened to shipping; but by this time the universal optimism had given way to apprehension. The year 1847 was one of bank crashes and railway bankruptcies which embarrassed the investing public; and in addition to these financial difficulties there were others—legal, industrial, and technical—which had not been foreseen. As a result, many investors were ruined and great hardship fell upon the labouring folk of the township.

Some indication of the flux of this critical period may be given by statistics. In 1841 the population was 8,223. Five years later it had risen sharply, probably to something like 40,000, but after 1846 collapse set in and thousands left Birkenhead and did not return. The 1851 census enumerated a population of 24,285—a truly remarkable increase of 300 per cent in a decade, but in view of the decline in the second half of that period a misleading total which masks a veritable tragedy of lost endeavour.

The census of 1841 records the existence in Birkenhead township of 1,361 houses, 91 of which (7 per cent) were unoccupied. Three years later, despite the fact that house building had meantime proceeded rapidly, there was such a demand for house room that double the number of working-class dwellings then existing would not have sufficed to solve the problem of congestion. Inevitably there was a decline in the tradition of good building, and as a result the stately houses of the previous decade are now often separated by dwellings of distinctly inferior character. The *Liverpool Standard* of October, 1844, noted that "the number of workpeople employed and immediately to be so, is so great that large houses are taken up for their accommodation where they are necessarily huddled together until cottages can be erected for them." By 1847 there were 3,595 houses in the township, the number thus having almost trebled in six years, but so great had been the exodus that of them 893 were untenanted. One house in four was empty, and grass grew in once busy streets.

During the years 1847 to 1857 there were several spasmodic efforts to complete the docks, and their failure made it abundantly clear that an impossible situation had now developed, and that if the full scheme were ever to be completed some drastic financial and legal rearrangement would have to be carried out. This was accomplished in 1857 when a new public trust, the

The Alabama *telegrams*

THE ELECTRIC AND INTERNATIONAL TELEGRAPH COMPANY.

INCORPORATED 1846.

N.B.—This company does not give or guarantee to the Messenger, and to pay no charges beyond those entered in this sheet.

Charges to Pay.

The following Message forwarded from

and received at *pool* Station *9 July* 186*2*

from Secretary of Customs London

to Collector of Customs *pool*

Seize under foreign enlistment act vessel "two hundred and ninety" If she return or can be met with

No inquiry respecting this Message can be attended to without the production of this Paper.

_____ Clerk.

Please enter Time of delivery, and sign Messenger's Ticket.

The Alabama *telegrams*

Mersey Docks and Harbour Board, was set up to administer the dock estate on both sides of the estuary, and thus to give expression, in one way at least, to the economic unity of all Merseyside.

The period between the first crossing of the *Etna* and the constitution of the Docks and Harbour Board had been one of amazing but unfulfilled promise, and at the end of it Birkenhead, having failed to achieve economic independence, had only narrowly avoided ruin. Her prime need after 1857 was for quiet consolidation. The years which immediately followed were years in which she was ably guided, by men of public spirit, into calmer waters. Thenceforward to the end of the century her growth was steady but unspectacular.

Two visual legacies of the mid-century storm and stress period still remain: the shipyards of the river front, and the branch railway which serves the docks. As a result of dock construction, Lairds found their old yards near Vittoria Street inconvenient for shipbuilding, and in 1853 removed to a site near the head of the Pool. Four years later there followed a second removal, this time to the southern half of the Woodside front, a location which necessitated the quarrying of graving docks and a technique of launching into the Mersey involving the flooding of the dry dock. Though this removal may have been dictated by economic necessity, its consequences were in certain ways unfortunate. In future the populace of Birkenhead was to be denied access to the river front, and the decline of the Hamilton Square district as a good residential area became more or less inevitable.

The extension of the Chester Railway to the dockside was completed in 1850. It cut across the rectangular street grid, and in so doing created a number of awkward triangular patches which have proved very difficult to use well and which to this day disfigure the appearance of the lower town.

The Alabama Case, 1862

In 1861, when the Southern States seceded and set up a Confederate Government, President Lincoln declared a blockade of the Southern ports. The United Kingdom declared the Southern States to be belligerents, and announced its own neutrality.

The United States later alleged against Britain a breach of neutrality during the Civil War, in that Britain permitted in 1862 the Confederate privateer and blockade runner, *Alabama* (known originally by its code number, "No. 290") to be built to Southern orders in a British port. Britain denied that the circumstances constituted a breach of neutrality, and the dispute was eventually submitted to international arbitration, where Britain was found responsible for all the depredations of the *Alabama*, damages of £15,500,000 in gold being awarded.

On June 23, 1862, the United States minister in London reminded the United Kingdom Government of a Confederate privateer which had earlier been built at Miller's Yard in Liverpool and allowed to leave port with a spurious clearance, actually to proceed to Nassau where her armament was completed. The minister referred also and more particularly to a more powerful vessel which was now being built at Lairds Yard at Birkenhead, within the port of Liverpool; this latter vessel also—the "290"— was in fact intended, so the minister alleged, for hostilities against the lawful Government of the United States. The vessel was being jealously guarded by its builders, and access to her could be obtained only by means of the password—"290." She was alleged to be a fighting vessel, pierced for guns, with magazine and racks for shot and canister, and the sockets for her gunbolts laid down.

In the main, the facts alleged by the United States minister were not denied by the British Government; but, although the vessel as she lay in the float at Birkenhead could easily be *converted* into a vessel of war, or could be later fitted with offensive arms, she was not, in the view of the authorities, *at that present time* either an armed vessel or a vessel equipped for war; nor did she as yet carry any stocks or cargo contrary to national law, or contrary to proper international usage.

By the time the vessel was completed in July, however, additional evidence became available. On July 28, "No. 290" left her berth, ostensibly for a trial run. She was now alleged to have six guns and a number of cutlasses concealed on board. Her tug at the "trial run" returned to Liverpool, so it was alleged, in order to ship certain beams evidently for use as gun carriages, and to embark men. The United States consul again urged that this was a flagrant violation of neutrality.

The Collector of Customs at Liverpool telegraphed the Board of Commissioners in London on July 29 that the vessel "No. 290" had left its berth the previous evening (for its trial run). On the 31st the Commissioners in London telegraphed Liverpool instructions to seize the ship. But the *Alabama* never returned from her trial run—as all the world knows. She proceeded, first to the coast of North Wales and then to the Azores, where she received her armament, and then commenced her destructive career.

The two telegrams are here reproduced, pages 96 and 97.[3]

[3]Photostats by courtesy of the Commissioners of H.M. Customs and Excise, London.

CHAPTER SIX

Manchester, Bradford, Dundee—St. Andrews

MANCHESTER AND THE LANCASHIRE COTTON FAMINE

IN 1860 Lancashire and neighbouring counties had about 2,000 cotton factories, running over 300,000 power looms and 21,000,000 spindles and employing 500,000 operatives. Over 1,000,000,000 pounds of cotton were used in England in that year. The industry was in a prosperous condition. Bumper American cotton harvests lowered the cost of the raw material, while heavy demands for cotton goods in India and the Far East provided manufacturers with a market for the goods they were producing in unusually large quantities. By May 1860, however, the demand had slackened and unsold cotton goods were accumulating. So the immediate result of the American Civil War was to benefit many manufacturers since in 1862-3 they were able to sell stocks of goods at higher prices than they had anticipated. English exports of cotton goods rose in value though they declined in quantity. Some agents flourished on "half trade at treble prices"—as did successful blockade-runners and gamblers on "futures." These financial gains explain the building of new mills at the height of the crisis. On the other hand, small inefficient mills disappeared. As the crisis continued many industrialists lost heavily and those who tried to run the blockade and to gamble on futures were not always successful. The depression in the cotton industry lasted throughout the 1860's. The financial difficulties of 1864 and the panic of 1866 delayed full recovery until about 1870.

One of the main causes of the difficulties with which the cotton industry had to contend was Lancashire's dependence upon America for about 80 per cent of her raw cotton. Owing to the blockade of the Southern ports during the Civil War Britain's cotton imports dropped from 1,261,000,000 pounds in 1861 to

533,000,000 pounds in 1862 and did not reach the 1861 figure again until 1866. Efforts were made—for example by the Cotton Supply Association—to foster cotton growing in many parts of the world, and increased supplies were obtained from India, Egypt, and elsewhere. But the quality of cotton from new districts was generally disappointing and prices were high.

The crisis led to severe unemployment and distress among the operatives. By the end of November 1862 over 400,000 operatives were out of work or on short time. The Poor Law was inadequate to deal with the situation and had to be modified. Thus an "educational test"—attendance at an adult school—was sometimes applied instead of a "labour test." The Union Relief Aid Act of 1862 helped to relieve the financial burden of those parishes and unions which had been most severely hit by the crisis. The Public Works Act of 1863 enabled local authorities to carry out necessary public works on borrowed money; £1,846,000 was borrowed and improvements were carried out in the sanitary conditions of Lancashire, but only 4,000 operatives were employed. The unemployed cotton operatives were also helped by private charity. In addition to local funds there were two big national funds—the Mansion House Fund (over £500,000) and the Bridgewater House Committee's Fund (over £800,000).

Nevertheless the workers suffered severely. It was reported in 1862 that "taking the mass of the cotton workers with their families as a whole, their average income . . . from all sources is nearly 2/- per head per week. This is exclusive of clothing, bedding and firing which are now usually supplied in addition." Illness increased during the period of the Cotton Famine: drunkenness declined. The number of illegitimate births increased somewhat. Crime, however, was not above the average and there were no serious disturbances except at Stalybridge in March 1863.

From a trade report of Messrs. Fraser, Son & Company, 1864[*]

Taking the board of trade returns of the exports of cotton goods and yarn for the last five years, and adding to them an

---

[*]Quoted by John Watts, *The Facts of the Cotton Famine* (London, 1866), pp. 370-1.

George Fraser, Son & Company was founded between 1800 and 1808; *The Times* of January 8, 1934, carries a photo of the founder's portrait in golfing estimate of the amount consumed at home, which we will take at one-third the exports, we obtain a rough approximation to the whole value of the cotton manufacturers of Great Britain. If we deduct from this the price paid by our spinners for the raw material consumed, we obtain the amount of profit which the internal industry of the country reaps from the trade. The following tables exhibit the diminution of this profit:—

	1860	1861	1862	1863	1864
			(million £)		
Export of cotton goods and yarns	52	47	37	47	56
Add one-third for home consumption	17	16	12	16	19
Total value of production	69	63	49	63	75
Estimated price paid by the trade for the raw material consumed	29	35	27	42	53
Profit to the country	40	28	22	21	22

From these figures it will be seen that, in 1860, a sum of £40,000,000 was distributed among the industrious population of Lancashire, engaged in the cotton trade or the branches dependent upon it. During the last three years this amount has declined to about one-half. Of course there are many modifying circumstances which might be mentioned, such as the profit made upon old stocks held when the war commenced. But, again, it must be remembered that the exports of 1861 and 1862 were greatly swollen by the shipments of these stocks, and represent more than the real production for these years. Taking all into account, and making allowance for 1860 being a year of remark-

costume, golf club in hands, by William Bradley (1801-57). My father, Charles Fay, commenced his five years' apprenticeship in the firm in February 1860 and after remaining at Manchester until 1883, was appointed as manager of the firm's shipping office in Liverpool where he continued till his retirement in 1921. I therefore was born in Liverpool, January 13, 1884. The firm went into voluntary liquidation in 1930. It did very well latterly in the China trade (white shirtings) till hit by Japanese competition: and in the River Plate trade (correspondents, Drabble Bros.) till disturbed by currency restrictions, and Japanese competition again. [C. R. F.]

able prosperity, it seems fair to assume that the manufacturing industry of Lancashire has suffered to the extent of £15,000,000 per annum, or more, for the last four years, in consequence of the stoppage of the cotton trade with the Southern States; and it is evident that, if this exhausting drain upon its capital continues for another year or two, serious consequences must follow, in the shape of commercial embarrassment and want of credit. The crisis hitherto has been borne wonderfully well, but the day of trial is not yet over.

From the letters of "A Lancashire Lad" *

. . . Hard times have come; and we have had them sufficiently long to know what they mean. We have fathers sitting in the house at mid-day, silent and glum, while children look wistfully about, and sometimes whimper for bread which they cannot have. We have the same fathers who, before hard times came, were proud men, who would have thought "beggar" the most opprobrious epithet you could have hit them with; but who now are made humble by the sight of wife and children almost starving, and who go before "relief committees," and submit to be questioned about their wants with a patience and humility which it is painful, almost shocking, to witness. And some others of these fathers turn out in the morning with long besoms as street sweepers, while others again go to breaking stones in the town's yard or open road-side, where they are unprotected from the keen east winds which add a little more to the burden of misery which they have to bear just now. But harder even than this, our factory women and girls have had to turn out; and plodding a weary way from door to door, beg a bit of bread or a stray copper that they may eke out the scanty supply at home. Only the other day, while taking a long stroll in the country lying about the town in which I live, I met a few of these factory girls, and was stopped by their not very beggar-like question of "Con yo help us a bit?" . . . I have heard of ladies whose lives seem to be but a changing from one kind of pleasure to another. . . . Why should they not hear our Lancashire girls' cry of "Con yo help us a bit"? Why should not they be reminded that these girls in cotton gowns and wooden

The Times, April 14, 1862.

clogs are wending their way towards the same heaven—or, alas,
towards the same hell—whither wend all the daughters of Eve,
no matter what their outer condition and dress? Why should not
they be asked to think how these striving girls have to pray daily,
"Lead us not into temptation," while temptations innumerable
stand everywhere about them? . . . Those of us who are men
would rather do much than let our sisters go begging. May not
some of us take to doing more to prevent it? I remember some
poetry about the "Sister bloodhounds, Want and Sin," and know
that they hunt oftener together than singly. We have felt the
fangs of the first: upon how many of us will the second pounce?

From Lord Derby's speech at Lancaster, 1862*

. . . There are three points on which objection has been
taken. . . . One has been that the relief we have given has not
been given with a sufficiently-liberal hand; the next—and I think
I shall show you that these two are inconsistent, the one answer-
ing the other—is that there has not been a sufficient pressure on
the local rates; and the third is, that Lancashire has not hitherto
done its duty with reference to the subscriptions from other parts
of the country. . . .

First, the amount to which we have endeavoured to raise our
subscriptions has been to the extent of from 2 shillings to two
shillings and sixpence weekly per head; in this late cold weather
an additional sixpence has been provided, mainly for coal and
clothing. Our endeavour has been to raise the total income of
each individual to at least two shillings or two shillings and sixpence a week. Now, I am told this is a very inadequate amount,
and no doubt it is an amount very far below that which many
of the recipients were in the habit of obtaining. But . . . there
is some misapprehension when we speak of the sum of 2 shillings
a week. If anybody supposes that 2 shillings a week is the *maximum* to each individual he will be greatly mistaken. Two shillings
a head per week is the sum we endeavoured to arrive at as the

*Lord Derby spoke at Lancaster (County meeting) on December 2, 1862,
appealing for funds for the distressed Lancashire operatives. The extract gives
Lord Derby's answer to criticisms that had been made concerning the conduct of
those responsible for levying rates, the raising of voluntary subscriptions, and the
distribution of relief. Quoted by John Watts, *The Facts of the Cotton Famine*
(London, 1866), pp. 188-94.

average receipt of every man, woman, and child receiving assistance; consequently a man and his wife with a family of three or four small children would receive not 2 shillings, but ten or twelve shillings from the fund—an amount not far short of that which in prosperous times an honest and industrious labourer in other parts of the country would obtain for the maintenance of his family. . . . If we had raised their income beyond that of the labouring man in ordinary times, we should have gone far to destroy the most valuable feeling of the manufacturing population—namely, that of honest self-reliance, and we should have done our best, to a great extent, to demoralise a large portion of the population, and induce them to prefer the wages of charitable relief to the return of honest industry.

But then we are told that the rates are not sufficiently high in the distressed districts, and that we ought to raise them before they come on the fund. In the first place, we have no power to compel the guardians to raise the rates beyond that which they think sufficient for the maintenance of those to be relieved, and, naturally considering themselves the trustees of the ratepayers, they are unwilling, and, indeed, ought not to raise the amount beyond that which is called for by absolute necessity. . . . I must say however . . . that . . . there are some districts which have applied to us for assistance which I think have not sufficient pressure on their rates. Where I find, for example, that the total assessment on the net ratable value does not exceed ninepence or tenpence in the pound I really think such districts ought to be called upon to increase their rates before applying for extraneous help. . . . I ask you to consider the effect of a sudden rise of rates as a charge upon the accumulated wealth of a district. It is not the actual amount of the rates, but it is the sudden and rapid increase of the usual rate of the rates that presses most heavily on the ratepayers. In the long run the rates must fall on real property, because all bargains between owner and occupier are made with reference to the amount of rates to be paid, and in all calculations between them that is an element which enters into the first agreement. But when the rate is suddenly increased from 1 shilling to 4 shillings it does not fall on the accumulated wealth or on the real property, but it falls on the occupier, the ratepayer—men the great bulk of whom are at the present moment themselves struggling upon the verge of pauperism. . . . Any attempt to increase those rates would only increase the pauperism, diminish the number of solvent ratepayers, and greatly aggravate the distress. . . . In Stockport the rate is . . . twelve shillings or more per pound and there it is calculated that at the next levy the defalcations will be at least forty per cent, according to the calculations of the poor-law commissioner himself. To talk, then, of raising rates in such districts as these would be absolute insanity; and even in districts less heavily rated any sudden attempt considerably to increase the rate would have the effect of pauperising those who are now solvent, and to augment rather than diminish the distress of the district.

The last point on which I would make an observation relates to the objection which has been taken to our proceedings, on the ground that Lancashire has not done its duty in this distress, and that consequently other parts of the country have been unduly called on to contribute to that which I don't deny properly and primarily belongs to Lancashire. Gentlemen, it is very hard to ascertain with any certainty what has been done by Lancashire, because, in the first place, the amount of local subscriptions and the amount of public contributions by themselves give no fair indication of that which really has been done by public or private charity. I don't mean to say that there are not individuals who have grossly neglected their duty in Lancashire. On the other hand, we know there are many . . . who have acted with the most princely munificence, liberality, and generous feeling, involving an amount of sacrifice of which no persons out of this country can possibly have the slightest conception. . . .

I will appeal to an authority which cannot, I think, be disputed—the authority of the commissioner, Mr Farnall himself. . . . A better authority could not be quoted on the subject of the comparative support given in aid of this distress in Lancashire and other districts. . . . I find that, including some of the subscriptions which we know are coming in this day, the total amount which has been contributed is about £540,000. Of that amount we received . . . £40,000 from the colonies; we received from the rest of the United Kingdom £100,000; and from the county of Lancaster itself . . . £400,000 out of £540,000. Now, I hope that these figures, upon the estimate and authority of the government poor-law commissioner, will be sufficient, at all events, to do away with the imputation that Lancashire, at this crisis, is not doing its duty. But if Lancashire has been doing its duty . . . there is no reason why Lancashire should relax its efforts; and of that I trust the result of this day's proceedings will afford a sufficient testimony.

We are not yet at the height of the distress. It is estimated that at the present moment there are three hundred and fifty-five thousand persons engaged in the different manufactories. Of these forty thousand only are in full work; one hundred and thirty-five thousand are at short work, and one hundred and eighty thousand are out of work altogether. In the course of the next six weeks this number is likely to be greatly increased; and the loss of wages is not less than £137,000 a week. This . . . is a state of things that calls for the most active exertions of all classes of the community, who . . . have responded to the call which has been made upon them most nobly, from the Queen down to the lowest individual in the community. . . .

From report of Mr. Somerset to the Manchester Board of Guardians, March, 1863[*]

Almost every conceivable variety of fraud, it would appear, has been practised upon the officers of the Board, as the reports of the special visitors now employed prove every week. Children recently dead have been booked as living; children that never existed have been booked; children have been borrowed to make up families; concealment or misrepresentation of wages seems almost to have been the rule in some districts of the city; men, whose regular work was at night, have obtained relief for want of work in the daytime; sick men have been found drunk in bed; men discharged by employers for drunkenness have obtained relief as decent, respectable artisans; persons have left employment avowedly because they could get a living easier by charity

[*]*Manchester Daily Guardian & Times*, March 20, 1863, quoted by W. O. Henderson, *The Lancashire Cotton Famine, 1861-1865* (Manchester, 1934), pp. 85–6, who quotes R. A. Arnold, *The History of the Cotton Famine* (London, 1864), pp. 363–4.

or parish relief than by work; men have been found who, having work at home, were attending the school or the farm; men have been found who were working, but not at their homes, and the short hours required of those sent to the school or the farm, have enabled many to secure wages of which they gave no account whatever; and, to finish this most unpleasant recital, the reports referred to have made the Guardians acquainted with the existence, in one district at least, of an amount of immorality which they had not before heard of, a large number of persons living in adultery having obtained relief as married people.

Our Factory School*

ELIJAH MOSS

You factory folk of Lancashire, a song we'll sing to you
Of a school now formed at Higher Hurst, and every word is true.
Our masters are determined to care well for their hands
If they will only come to school and there obey commands.

Chorus
Then old and young attend the school, your teachers there obey,
There's military exercise and military pay.

Our mules and looms have now ceased work, the yankees are the
  cause,
But we will let them fight it out, and stand by English laws;
No recognising shall take place, until the war is o'er;
Our wants are now attended to; we cannot ask for more.

Potatoes, ham and bacon are now to us being sold,
With comforts such as these, we have no fear of winter cold;
Every one seems hearty glad, and sings with joyous glee
For men and master now do meet in love and unity.

Amongst our scholars there are some whose age is past three score
Who have for learning, wages, which they never had before;
The pencils, slates and copybooks are free for us to use
And every morning on each desk is laid the daily news.

*Quoted in Reports of Factories for the half-year ending October 31, 1862, *Parliamentary Papers*, XVIII, 1863, pp. 479-80, and reprinted by W. O. Henderson in the *Transactions of the Historic Society of Lancashire and Cheshire*, LXXXIV, 1933.

A system of good order rules supreme from morn till night;
There's grammar and arithmetic and nearly all can write;
Reciting too with moral song, to suit the gay and grave,
And often we do close our school with singing "Sailor's Grave."

Now old and young, forget your cares, and join in singing praise,
The time is not far distant when we shall have better days;
Then comforts soon to everyone, with joy we shall abound
Contentment, peace and plenty may we have on British ground.

*Report of Robert Rawlinson, Esq., Civil Engineer, to the Right
Honourable C. P. Villiers, M.P., President of the Poor Law
Board**

Office of Public Works (Manufacturing Districts) Act, 1863,
St. Peter's Square, Manchester, 7th April 1864.

SIR,

I beg again to report as to progress made under the powers
of the Public Works (Manufacturing Districts) Act, 1863. . . .

In respect . . . to the money devoted to the purposes of this
Act, the present position is as follows:—

Amount ordered by the Poor Law Board	£1,147,865
Amount of applications at present under consideration	209,527
	1,357,392
Leaving for future applications	142,608
	£1,500,000

Of the works undertaken, the great bulk of expenditure will
be upon town sewerage and street improvements, including the
formation of roads, paving, flagging, and channelling of streets.
This class of works will improve the several districts to the greatest
extent. Of the £1,147,865 already ordered by the Board, it is
proposed that £229,558. 17s. 6d. shall be expended on main
sewers, and £555,086. 2s. 6d. on street improvement works,
amounting together to £784,641, or 68 per cent. of the total sum.

The length of main sewerage thus undertaken is 344,760 yards,

*Printed by R. A. Arnold, *The History of the Cotton Famine* (London,
1864), pp. 559-62.

or 195 miles. The area of paving and street works undertaken in respect of the above-mentioned sum of £555,082. 2*s*. 6*d*., is 3,186,768 square yards (about 3*s*. 6*d*. per square yard). This area makes 658 acres, the length of streets being 341,187 yards, or 194 miles, and costing about £2861 per mile.

The local authorities fully appreciate the advantages of the Act, as there are but few places in the cotton district that have not or will not ultimately avail themselves of its provisions.

The local authorities have, in most cases, wisely selected works which will be of enduring benefit to the population of this district, both as facilitating means of traffic and as promoting comfort and health.

In some places to which loans have been granted the local authorities have not yet commenced work, but . . . annexed to this Report, there are now forty-nine places in which works are actually progressing. With reference to employment afforded by the Act, my last monthly return, March 26th . . . shows that during the last week in March, there were 4838 men directly engaged upon works, of whom 3435 had been factory operatives, the average wages of such factory operatives amounting to about 12*s*. 6*d* per week. Two places make no return. To these 4838 men must be added, as previously intimated, the large number who are directly employed under the Public Works Act in obtaining and conveying materials furnished by contractors, which both experience and inquiry lead me now to estimate at not less than 3000 additional. This makes a total of 7838 men employed directly and indirectly, and receiving payment from funds provided by the Public Works (Manufacturing Districts) Act.

Some doubt having been thrown upon my estimate of the numbers dependent upon these men, the surveyor of one of the most important towns (Oldham) was good enough, at my request, to make special inquiry, when it was found that 141 men working in that borough represented 684 persons, or 4.85 each man. Adopting this estimate, with reference to the numbers employed under the Public Works Act (7838), the result would show that there are about 38,014 persons supported by means of the public works.

The measure of the benefits of the Act are however but very partially represented by this statement. The public works are popular with those who are employed, and the moral effect of the work, in prospect as well as in action, has been very valuable in its influences upon the unemployed population.

A number of small shopkeepers have been delivered from a condition little above the level of pauperism by the timely expenditure of large sums now paid in weekly wages through the provisions of the Public Works Act.

There are more than 1000 men (besides those I have now mentioned) engaged in out-door labour in the towns of this district, whose wages are derived from private funds or from public funds obtained before the passing of this Act; 629 men are so employed and paid at Preston.

This experiment in Lancashire ought to inculcate a lesson for future use, namely, that unskilled men may soon be taught the use of tools, where practical means are found to furnish employment.

The work must, however, be necessary and useful; the men must have reasonable treatment and equitable payment, if possible by measurement. All notion of work as a punishment must be removed, and the men must be intelligently and kindly taught. Many of the Lancashire operatives, who never worked outside the walls of a cotton-mill before this period of distress, can now execute sewer and drain trenching in a workmanlike manner, and can even lay and join sewer and drain pipes equal to any skilled labourer.

The men have, for the most part, striven to be useful, and to escape from living on the dole of charity. More men might have been earlier at work if in every town and district there had been that diligence and willingness which the crisis demanded; but I do not think any additional external interference or assistance by Government or even remonstrance, would have done so much as the quiet and silent force of local example has done.

Government provided legal powers, and money, under certain specified and favourable conditions, but did not, in any respect, meddle or dictate as to the sort of works to be executed, other than as the Act requires, namely, that works must be locally necessary;

nor has Government interfered as to the manner of executing such works. Advice has been given by myself when asked for.

The Central Relief Committee has rendered most material assistance to the successful working of the Act. This committee has provided and distributed to distressed cotton operatives going on public works, 3000 suits of warm woollen clothing for winter wear; as also 300 pairs of stout water-tight boots for men working in water; such wise expenditure of money has encouraged men to go on the works: has enabled them to bear up against the severity of this severe winter; and, in my opinion, has prevented much sickness and misery, as also saved many lives.

The works are generally progressing in a very satisfactory manner, and the operatives, in increasing numbers, are becoming skilled in the labour of carrying them out.

The returns do not give the actual state of the works in hand. The "skilled" and "unskilled" men are in many cases mixed; but there are instances of town sewers and land drains being completely executed as respects trenching, timbering, and earthenware-pipe laying, by so-termed unskilled men; that is, by men who previously earned their living within the four walls of some cotton factory. Before the coming summer is far advanced, I may strike out of my future reports the terms "unskilled labourers."

When the vast amount of work now commenced under the Public Works Act shall have been accomplished, and the one hundred and ninety-five miles of main sewers are in work, discharging sewage into the nearest watercourse or river, other equally necessary and beneficial improvements will require to be added: cesspools and cesspits, now crowded in amongst houses, must be abolished, and the refuse must be intercepted from the rivers and streams in such manner as to prevent nuisance, and, where practicable, improve agriculture. The high death-rate prevailing in Lancashire towns has its main cause in the foul cottage cesspit. An inspection of any town in the district will show this; and medical returns indicate that the prevailing diseases in Lancashire towns are those due to foul air. In the Metropolis, the number of waterclosets exceeds the number of houses; cesspools and cesspits have, within the last 30 years, been abolished by thousands, even over the flat areas of Lambeth and Bermondsey;

soil-pans and waterclosets have been substituted; the river Thames has been fouled, but sickness has been prevented; and many lives have been prolonged by the simple abolition of the putrid cess-pool, and dilution of fermenting refuse in the open river. The intercepting sewers now in course of formation in the metropolis will improve the state of the river, and the metropolis will then continue to show a comparatively low death-rate. If the population of Lancashire is placed in a sanitary state only as favourable as that of the metropolis, there will be an annual saving of some ten thousand lives, and an improved state of health throughout the entire population.

I have, etc.,

(Signed) ROBERT RAWLINSON,
Civil Engineer.

BRADFORD

In 1861, the census returns showed that during the previous decade the population of Bradford Parish[1] had increased by only some 6,500, while that of Bradford Township had fallen by nearly 4,000. Many inhabitants of Bradford, used as they were to spectacular increases in their town's population, found these statistics to be an unexpected and unpleasant surprise. The Bradford Chamber of Commerce heard its President give a long and detailed address explaining possible reasons for the sudden check. To the *Bradford Observer*, however, there was but one probable reason—the census figures were wrong![2]

[1]Population of Bradford Township and the Parish of which it was a part:

	1801	1811	1821	1831	1841	1851	1861	1871
Township	6,393	7,767	13,064	23,223	34,560	52,493	48,648	64,440
Parish	29,794	36,358	52,954	76,967	105,257	149,543	156,053	207,142

[2]The resumption of the upward trend between 1861-71, on something like the scale previous to 1851, raises the question, why the check between 1851 and 1861? The reasons given by H. W. Ripley, the President of the Bradford Chamber of Commerce, centre on the adoption of labour-saving machinery. The combing machine, coming increasingly into use after 1845, had displaced 21,900 hand wool combers and provided employment for only about 10,000 of them, leaving some 11,900 combers and their families to find other employment in the district, or migrate elsewhere, which many of them did (see *infra*). In weaving, he esti-

When one examines earlier census returns, it is understandable that this abrupt slowing down in the rate of growth of Bradford's population should excite attention. From a figure just short of 30,000 in 1801, the population of Bradford Parish had grown to 52,954 in 1821, had then more than doubled itself to 105,257 by 1841, and had further increased to 149,543 in 1851.[3] In comparison with these increases, an increase of a mere 6,000 seemed to be a paltry figure.

The rapid expansion of the population of Bradford during the first half of the century, its resumption after 1861, and the intervening check are associated with and explained by developments in the worsted industry.[4] By 1860 almost the entire worsted industry in the country was concentrated in part of the West Riding of Yorkshire[5] and, of this area, Bradford had become the undisputed industrial and commercial centre for worsted.

---

mated that the spread of the power loom and the adoption of the system of one weaver tending two looms had resulted in an increase of productivity in weaving, of 60-70 per cent, with the same number of weavers. Again, in spinning, a 25-30 per cent increase in production had been obtained, "without any increase whatever in the number of hands," but resulting wholly from the introduction of "Cap spinning" and the system of "one hand attending two sides of a frame." A 40-50 per cent saving of labour had been made in dyeing during the same period. It is interesting to note that Ripley expected a large increase in Bradford's population during the next ten years, since "machinery has now got to something like its limit in point of productive power and . . . any material improvement would probably be in quality and not in quantity." As far as population was concerned, he was correct in his anticipations. (For a report of his speech, see the *Bradford Observer*, May 16, 1861.)

The earlier increases in Bradford's population came largely from immigration into the district. Thus, A. Redgrave, the Factory Inspector for the Bradford district, reported in 1855 that "not one half of the Bradford population current were born in Bradford," and particularly noticed the greatly increased employment of Irish labour within the last ten years. It would be this inflow of labour which the labour-saving improvements mentioned by Ripley would check.

[3] It is claimed by J. James, *History of the Worsted Manufacture in England* (London, 1857), p. 611, that between 1801 and 1851 the rate of growth of Bradford's population was greater than that of any other town in the country.

[4] Bradford was overwhelmingly a one-industry town, devoted either to producing cloth and yarn, or to ancillary industries, such as textile-machine making, particularly Jacquard machines. There were two famous and important iron works at Low Moor and Bowling but, again, their activities were very much bound up with the local textile industry for which they supplied boilers, steam engines, shafting, etc. Similarly, the local stone quarrying and coal industries supplied local industrial demands.

[5] Roughly within an area bounded by Keighley in the northwest, Halifax and Huddersfield in the southwest, Wakefield in the southeast, Leeds in the east, and Otley in the northeast.

Between 1830 and 1860, the worsted industry of Bradford both expanded and changed its character. Hand weaving and hand combing were extinguished by the power loom and the combing machine, and the domestic weavers and combers were absorbed into the rapidly increasing number of factories. The efficiency of the power-driven machines was greatly increased. The predominant type of cloth made in the district changed from pure wool to a mixture of wool and cotton, or mixtures of alpaca, mohair, silk, and cotton, while, at the same time, the variety of fabrics produced was widely extended. Finally, as her industry developed, Bradford attracted merchants and became the commercial centre of the worsted industry.

1. *Spinning*

Of the three main manufacturing processes in the worsted industry, combing, spinning, and weaving, spinning was already a factory industry by 1830. Of the 33 mills which James lists as having been built in the town by this date,[6] at least 25 were occupied either by spinners or by manufacturers who combined both spinning and weaving, the latter still having their fabrics mainly woven by outworkers, to whom they supplied yarn manufactured in their own mills.

In the absence of detailed and reliable statistics for most of the period, it is difficult to give a precise account of the increase in the number of worsted spinning mills, or the number of spindles employed, between 1830 and 1860. It is not until 1850 that a distinction is drawn between mills which either spun, or wove, or did both, and the accuracy of the existing returns is doubtful.[7] Fortunately, however, as far as spinning is concerned, some anonymous enthusiast collected particulars of the worsted spin-

[6]James, *History of the Worsted Manufacture in England*, p. 606, gives a list of mills and firms for 1833, and the dates at which these mills were built. By checking this list against contemporary directories, I have obtained this figure for the number of spinning mills. Of the rest, one was a weaving mill, the others do not appear.

[7]James himself observes that the 1834 Factory Inspector's returns for the worsted industry are incomplete and that the 1837 returns confuse "mills" and "firms." Much later, in 1873, the Bradford Chamber of Commerce sent a deputation to the Home Office, complaining of the inaccuracy of the factory returns. This inaccuracy was freely admitted. The following reasons were given: many of the sub-inspectors were newly appointed and did not know the district; further, they were "not qualified to deal with statistics"; finally, the compilers of the returns had

ning mills in the Bradford area in 1839,[8] giving particulars of spinning frames, the name of each firm, and allocating an average of 96 spindles per frame.[9] Assuming this to be at least a reasonable average and, further, that the statistics given are fairly accurate,[10] one can draw the following conclusions.

In 1839, in the same townships in Bradford Parish for which returns are given in 1850, there were 98 spinning firms, with 2,196

---

assumed that firms which did not answer their questionnaire no longer existed, a poor reading of the attitude of business men towards the filling in of official forms. (For details see *Bradford Observer*, May 28, May 30, June 19, 1873.)

When one looks at James's *History*, one realizes the problems of interpreting the official returns. Quite apart from their other deficiencies, they do not, of course, include domestic outworkers, so that, particularly in the case of weaving, a comparison of the returns for, say, 1834 with those for 1850 tell one nothing about the productive capacity of the industry.

The particulars of factories which James gives for 1833 are based on personal knowledge and do not distinguish between different types of firms. The official statistics which are quoted for 1835, 1838, and 1841 again fail to distinguish different types of firms and contain no information as to the number of spindles and looms employed. Further, the geographical basis of the returns varies between Bradford Borough and Bradford Parish. It is not until 1850 that one has anything like a satisfactory situation, when a distinction is drawn between the three main types of firm and the number of spindles and looms is given for each township within Bradford Parish. (The returns for 1835, 1838, and 1841 are for Bradford Borough.)

But here, again, these returns are concerned with the number of firms, whereas the 1835 and 1841 returns gave the number of mills, a very different matter when it was common for more than one firm to occupy the same mill.

[8]Bradford Reference Library, Case 24, D.B. 17, no. 6. This important document was undated by its anonymous compiler. Someone has subsequently dated it "c. 1830," but this is too early. The inclusion in the list of firms of J. & S. C. Lister of Manningham means that it cannot be earlier than 1838, since this firm did not begin business until that year. (See *Lord Masham's Inventions Written by Himself*, Bradford, 1905, p. 7. Lord Masham=Samuel Cunliffe Lister, the great woolcombing machine inventor.) On the other hand, however, John Hanson of Keighley, who also appears, was sold up in 1839. (See J. Hodgson, *Textile Manufacture, and Other Industries, in Keighley*, Keighley, 1879, p. 161: ". . . we recollect passing the Hope Mill about forty years ago, when an auction sale was going on and on enquiring whose property they were selling we were told that it was Johnny Hanson's machinery.") It therefore seems safe to assign the year 1839 to this document.

[9]The figure of 96 spindles per frame seems reasonable enough. Although the average number of spindles per frame employed by John Foster and Son at Black Dike Mills, Queensbury, was 105, it must be noted that this firm did not start spinning until 1832. Their spinning machinery, therefore, would presumably be fairly new and larger than the many early spinning frames which would still be in use by firms which had been spinning much longer.

[10]Since the names of firms are given, it is possible to check them from the contemporary directories and to see that these returns do not exaggerate the number of firms. Given that the number of frames returned for each firm is reliable, this document therefore seems to be fairly accurate.

frames, or 210,816 spindles. By 1850 the corresponding figures were 141 firms, employing a total of 382,334 spindles,[11] an increase in spinning capacity of over 160,000 spindles in eleven years. The factory returns for six years later show a further increase in the total number of spindles to 467,416, although the number of firms had fallen to 115.[12] Thus, between 1839 and 1856, not only was there a large increase in the spinning capacity of the worsted industry, but the average number of spindles per firm also increased considerably: from 2,151 in 1839 to 2,711 in 1850 and 4,064 in 1856. It must, of course, be remembered that, while these increases were taking place, there was also an increase in the efficiency of spinning machinery, so that increasing amounts of yarn could be spun with the same number of spindles. Thus, in 1832, the application of the "dead" spindle in place of the "fly" spindle produced a finer and stronger yarn and increased the production of yarn per spindle.[13] Three years later the invention of the "screw gill" enabled the wool fibres to be kept straight in the "drawing" process and produced a more firmly twisted yarn.[14] The emphasis of these two inventions is upon increased yarn strength, an emphasis further reflected in the increasing practice at this time of mixing the long combing wool with shorter wool to give strength coupled with softness, and resulting from the concurrent displacement of the hand loom by the power loom, for which a stronger yarn was needed.

Between 1825 and 1850, the speed at which spindles were turned increased from 1,400–1,800 revolutions per minute to 2,800.[15] This increase was due not only to the fact that the frames were "now made with all the nicety of clockwork,"[16] but to improvements in steam engines, an increased willingness to work the engine up to its full capacity, better gearing, and the use of sperm

[11]1850 factory returns, quoted James, *History*, p. 609.

[12]The 1856 returns, quoted *ibid.*, p. 610, do not give returns for three townships which had previously been included, so that these returns err on the conservative side.

[13]*Ibid.*, p. 444. This was an American invention.

[14]*Ibid.*, p. 445.

[15]Henry Forbes, "The Rise, Progress, and Present State of the Worsted, Alpaca and Mohair manufactures of England," lecture to the Society for the Encouragement of Arts, Manufactures and Commerce (Royal Society of Arts), 1852.

[16]James, *History*, p. 535.

and other finer oils instead of gallipoli oil in lubricating the machinery.[17]

The expansion of the spinning branch of the worsted industry was only partly due to the local demand for worsted yarn. Bradford spinners had various other markets for their products. The hosiery trade of Nottingham and Leicester, the neighbouring worsted industry at Huddersfield, Lancashire and Scottish makers of *mousseline de laine*, all took yarn from the Bradford district. Even more important, however, was the export of worsted yarns to the Continent, particularly to Germany and France,[18] a trade which had been growing steadily since the 1820's. This partial independence of the spinners of their own local demand explains why the total number of spindles in the Bradford district continued to expand between 1850 and 1856 while the number of looms declined.

2. Weaving

Whereas spinning had been entirely a factory industry for the whole of the period 1830–60, worsted weaving was being transformed from a domestic occupation into a factory process. In addition, the nature of the woven fabric was being radically changed.

The first attempts to introduce the power loom into the Bradford area in the 1820's had provoked riots, the last of which, in 1826, apparently marks the end of the hand-loom weaver's violent opposition to the power loom. From the late 1820's onwards the hand loom was being displaced by the power loom. By 1860, there were very few hand-loom weavers left in the Bradford area. The kind of situation reported in 1834, "Harvest being

[17]Forbes's lecture. These more general considerations would also apply to the other branches of the industry. On the question of improvements in the 1850's, note Ripley's remarks quoted *supra*.

[18]John Foster and Son established their own warehouse in France in 1853, and had also, by this time, a very large trade with worsted manufacturers in Germany, Russian Poland, and elsewhere on the Continent. The importance of the French trade is reflected in the fact that Lister and Holden, in spite of the political disturbances of that year, established a machine-combing factory near Paris in 1848, and by 1853 had three large combing factories in France, catering for the French manufacturers. (For details, see the *Holden-Illingworth Letters*, privately printed, 1926.)

nearly over, the weavers are returning to their looms and the Manufacturers are consequently more inclined to purchase [more yarn from the spinners],"[19] a facet of the traditional picture of hand-loom weaving, had disappeared by 1860 from Bradford's industrial scene.

Although the power loom had been at least partly adopted by some firms in 1830, notably by Horsfall's who had provoked the 1826 riot, the total number of power looms in the whole industry in 1835 was only 3,082. Within twenty-one years the number of power looms in Bradford Parish had risen to at least 17,636. As the number of power looms rose, so the number of hand looms fell. In 1838 there were, in Bradford Parish, some 13,800 hand looms, the concentration of these diminishing as one draws nearer to Bradford itself, where only twenty were to be found. By 1851, there were only 1,117 left in the district, and six years later James wrote, "Comparatively very few pieces are now woven by hand in Bradford Parish."[20]

The report of the Hand-Loom Weavers' Commission in 1840 provides valuable evidence on the extent to which the process of displacement had gone by 1838, when evidence was taken for the Bradford district, and on the effects which this displacement had had on local hand-loom weavers. At this date, the power loom had still a long way to go before its conquest of hand labour was complete. Of the manufacturers examined, some, like George and Robert Leach of Thornton, still employed only hand-loom weavers. Others, such as T. Willett and Co., John Milner, and Willett, Oxley and Co., all of Bradford, employed partly hand-loom and partly power-loom weavers.[21] Robert Leach believed that "the power-loom manufacturers would eventually be able to drive us out of the market . . . it is certain that there are many manufacturers beginning to work figures by power."[22]

Already, in 1838, some hand weavers were turning to the last

[19]*Bradford Observer*, Sept. 4, 1834.

[20]James, *History*, p. 603.

[21]Hand-Loom Weavers' Commission, *Report*, 1840. Since the Commission investigated hand-loom weavers, no evidence seems to have been taken from manufacturers who employed only power looms.

[22]This statement does not appear in Leach's evidence as reported in the official version of the Commission, but was given in the *Bradford Observer* (Oct. 4, 1838), whose reporter was present at the inquiry in Bradford.

stronghold of domestic labour in the worsted industry, hand combing, or to other occupations, such as stone quarrying.[23] Their already depressed rates of pay were bad enough, but they suffered further in that a depression saw the manufacturers first turn off their hand weavers, and lastly their power-loom weavers, since they wished "of course, to work . . . fixed capital as long as possible."[24] Faced by circumstances such as these, and by the rapidly increasing efficiency of the power loom, in which, between 1839 and 1850, the speed of the shuttle movements more than doubled on a 6/4 loom,[25] the hand-loom weaver was squeezed out of his cottage, either into the factory or to find a new job elsewhere.[26]

The progress of the power loom at the expense of the hand-loom weaver is only one aspect of change in worsted weaving in Bradford between 1830 and 1860. During the same period, the introduction of the cotton warp had revolutionized the nature of the woven product and given a powerful impulse to the further expansion of the worsted industry.

Changes in fashion, favouring "light, elegant and cheap articles of dress which, lacking the wearing qualities of former stuffs, were yet more showy and attractive,"[27] threatened the Bradford trade unless it could be adapted to meet these new demands.

In addition to changes in fashion, however, there were two other factors which favoured the introduction of cotton warps. First, their substitution for wool warps meant cheaper cloth. This was important, since the ladies' light dress goods which were mainly produced in Bradford competed with cotton fabrics, a fact which had to be taken into account by the trade expert of the *Bradford Observer* when assessing the future prospects of the worsted trade. In 1835, and again in 1836, the *Observer* warned

[23]See evidence of Julius Ackroyd and John Robinson, as reported in the *Bradford Observer*, Oct. 4, 1838. Once again there appear here statements which do not appear in the published official report. John Robinson had himself turned from hand weaving to hand combing. Ackroyd stated: "Many weavers are leaving to comb. . . . All the stout young men are going to the quarries to work."

[24]Hand-Loom Weavers' Commission, *Report*, p. 564.

[25]See Forbes's lecture.

[26]Males predominated in hand-loom weaving, but women and girls in power-loom weaving, so that many of the men who were displaced from hand-loom weaving must have had to seek jobs in other trades.

[27]James, *History*, p. 471.

Bradford that high wool prices were dangerous. Farmers must be content with "a good remunerating price" for their wools, otherwise "other articles of cotton manufacture may be substituted."[28] Again, "If a check is not speedily put to advancing prices other manufactures, such as Cottons, will supersede our fabrics."[29]

The second factor lay in the foreign trade policy of the Zollverein. When, in 1842, a high German tariff on worsted goods was threatened, a deputation was sent from the West Riding to Sir Robert Peel, protesting and asking for help. Prominent in this deputation was Edward Akroyd of Halifax, one of the largest worsted manufacturers in the country. He "proceeded to account [to Sir Robert] for the large and increasing demand for worsted goods in the countries of the German League. High rates of duty had been imposed on cotton and silk goods, amounting on many qualities to more than one hundred per cent of their value, whereas the duty upon worsted goods had hitherto been comparatively trifling. This article therefore being placed in a more favourable position, was forced into unnatural popularity and it was owing to this increasing demand for worsted and cotton and worsted fabrics that the towns where they were principally made . . . although now suffering, had not been placed in the same state of extreme destitution as the districts of the cotton manufacture."[30] In view of this, it is not surprising that from the late 1830's onwards Bradford became the home of a rapidly increasing number of German merchants.

Although the cotton warp was not successfully introduced into the Bradford trade until 1837–9, experiments with it had been proceeding since 1825. The main difficulty was in dyeing and finishing the mixed wool and cotton fabrics, since the two fibres, one animal and one vegetable, reacted in different ways to the same dyes. This problem was overcome in 1839, but at first there was some difficulty in inducing Lancashire cotton manufacturers to supply warps for a trade which they thought would be ephemeral and for which they needed special machinery.

However, the cotton warp, once introduced, stayed and helped

[28]*Bradford Observer*, June 4, 1835.
[29]*Ibid.*, Aug. 11, 1836.
[30]Reported *ibid.*, July 7, 1842. It was reported in the *Leeds Mercury* (July 7, 1842) that the demand for this tariff came from the German cotton manufacturers, who had only succeeded in bringing competition from Bradford to replace that of Lancashire.

Bradford to overcome what would otherwise have been a difficult period. As Akroyd said in the same interview with Peel: "Articles made entirely of worsted, which formerly constituted the staple trade, such as merinos and lastings, were difficult of sale. . . . The only trade left which was possessed of life and vitality was that consisting of mixed goods of cotton and worsted."[31] Thus from 1839 onwards the cotton warp transformed the Bradford trade. By 1857 the use of the cotton warp was so general in the Bradford district that James could write: ". . . now most of the warps used in the worsted manufacture consist of cotton."[32] Bradford was now, more than ever, connected both directly and indirectly with the cotton industry: indirectly in that her products were now, more than before, competing with Lancashire cottons; directly in that an important part of her raw material now came from Lancashire.[33]

The increasing variety of the cloth produced in Bradford as a result of the introduction of the cotton warp was further augmented by the introduction in the late 1830's of two new fibres, alpaca and mohair, both of which had to be woven with a cotton warp and which henceforward became an important part of the Bradford trade.[34] As far as the increasing variety of cloth is concerned, the number of different types of cloth made by one of the leading firms in the Bradford trade increased from 14 to 70 between 1841 and 1860.[35]

3. *Combing*

This expansion of the spinning and weaving sections of the Bradford worsted industry carried with it two further important consequences which must finally be noticed, the necessary mechanization of wool combing, and the corresponding development of Bradford as the industry's commercial centre.

[31]*Bradford Observer*, Aug. 4, 1842.

[32]James, *History*, p. 579.

[33]By 1863 there were 18 cotton spinners, doublers, and twisters and 5 cotton-warp sizers in Bradford.

[34]It is almost true to say that an entire town was built on alpaca. Sir Titus Salt, who introduced this manufacture and built up a vast business in manufacturing it, moved his entire works and working staff from Bradford in 1853, and built a model town, Saltaire, near Shipley in the Aire valley.

[35]Messrs. John Foster and Son Ltd., Stock Books, 1838-90, deposited by the firm in the Brotherton Library, Leeds University.

The hand comber performed the main process preparatory to spinning, i.e. combing the long wool fibres so that they lay parallel to each other and, at the same time, removing the short fibres, or "noil," from the locks of wool, these then being sold to the woollen industry. Until the successful advent of the combing machine, this operation was done entirely by hand with two steel-toothed combs, the teeth of which were heated in a pot. Working in a hot and smoky atmosphere, the hand comber's was an unhealthy job. Some of the large spinning firms had a combing shop attached to their works, but generally the combers were scattered over the countryside, working in small establishments for a small master comber, to whom the spinner sent his wool to be combed on commission.

Since the invention of Cartwright's "Big Ben" in the early 1790's, the threat of machine competition had been hanging over the hand comber's head, but "Big Ben" was a cumbersome and inefficient combing machine and it was not until the late 1840's that the threat of successful machine combing became a reality. Traditionally a truculent and turbulent class of workers, pioneers in the trade union movement in the eighteenth century, the combers were shorn of their earlier power by the 1840's. Not only the threat of the machine, but the failure of their great strike in 1825, had reduced them to pleading for, rather than demanding, improvements in their wages and conditions, and their poverty was a byword. In 1845 a committee was appointed in Bradford to examine their condition. Its report "is one of the most distressing documents that can be perused."[36] In the town and neighbourhood of Bradford there were upwards of 10,000 hand combers, "the major part of whom were compelled to make workshops of their sleeping apartments. . . . Unable to pay the rent for a comfortable dwelling, a large number huddled together in one apartment. . . . That their physical well-being was neglected, the emaciated appearance of most plainly betokened."[37] Their sufferings, however, were not as prolonged as those of the hand-loom weavers. By 1851 the number of hand combers in the Bradford district had been reduced to 5,600[38] and six years later they were almost extinct.

[36]James, *History*, p. 548.
[37]*Ibid.*
[38]Bradford Reference Library, MS giving total numbers of hand weavers and hand combers for Bradford area, June 23, 1851.

The history of the successful introduction of the combing machine is complicated and the sources for its study would seem to consist chiefly of innumerable legal cases and patent records.[39] Heilmann, Preller, Collier, Donnisthorpe, Lister, Holden, and Noble all had a hand in the process, and all at about the same time, so that there was enormous scope for confusion and infringement. There were many other inventors, whose names are less well known.[40] The evolution of the combing machine proceeded by a complex cross-fertilization of ideas and this is not the place to unravel their respective merits.

The delay in the successful adoption of the combing machine until the late 1840's was caused by the technical difficulties involved. As Lister, one of the most successful of the inventors and business men connected with combing, wrote: "There is nothing like it recorded in the history of any invention. Indeed, I doubt if the steam engine, the locomotive, the spinning frame and the power loom, all put together, have occupied so many minds and taken as much effort, time and expenditure as the wool combing problem; and yet, at the end of more than fifty years after Cartwright's great invention no one had succeeded and it appeared almost hopeless to think that anyone would."[41]

Nevertheless, by 1845, after three or four years of intensive effort, the main problems of combing had been solved and machine combing had become a practical proposition.[42] Un-

[39]James Burnley, *History of Wool and Wool-Combing* (London, 1889). Burnley did an enormous amount of work on the question, and his book is still the authority on the subject. But his apparent mistake in attributing the idea for the "square motion" comb to Holden in 1848, whereas Lister had already brought out a patent for the same invention two years before, of which Burnley had no knowledge, brought Lister's wrath upon his head. Burnley was sued, the publication of his book was stopped, and Lister wrote the story of his inventions by himself, *Lord Masham's Inventions, Written by Himself*, 1905, showing that there was little doubt in his mind, at least, as to who was responsible for the introduction of successful machine combing. From another angle, the *Holden-Illingworth Letters* throw light upon much of the "inside story" of combing, with correspondence between Holden and Lister, and letters by Holden to others.

The litigation in which the combing-machine inventors were involved, particularly Lister and Holden, almost made the legal profession an ancillary trade to wool combing! At one point Holden had eight cases running at once, for all of which he prepared his own briefs.

[40]Burnley, in his Appendix, *History of Wool and Wool-Combing*, lists 156 principal inventions in combing between 1790 and 1860.

[41]*Lord Masham's Inventions*, p. 9.

[42]*Ibid.*, p. 14. "It had taken me just three years ['43, '44, and '45] to do what the whole trade and a host of inventors had failed to do in fifty and what looked to be at the time almost impossible."

doubtedly, the central figure in the whole process was Lister
(Samuel Cunliffe Lister, 1st Baron Masham, 1815–1906), who by
1853 had Donnisthorpe under close contract and Isaac Holden as
partner; had bought the patent rights of Heilmann's and Noble's
machines for Britain and owned or controlled the patent rights of
the Lister-Cartwright machine, the "square motion" and "nip"
machines;[43] had commission combing factories at Addingham,
Halifax, Bradford, and Leeds; and in addition had the controlling
interest, in partnership with Holden, in three combing factories
in France.

Apart from Lister's own immense combing business, his control of all the important patent rights for the machines in England
put him in a monopolistic position as far as the sale of combing
machines was concerned. Having decided to produce only the
"nip" machine, he sold it to worsted spinners for the "sum of
TWELVE HUNDRED POUNDS A MACHINE OR A THOUSAND POUNDS
PATENT RIGHT, the machine costing about two hundred. But even
at that price it was highly profitable and for years I sold a large
number."[44]

The "nip" machine cut the number of workers needed from
one to three per machine in comparison with earlier models.[45]
Not only was a higher standard of work produced by it, but in
comparison with hand combing, the cost of combing per pound
of wool was reduced by 1s. 6d.[46] It is hardly to be wondered,
therefore, that the early 1850's saw the rapid extinction of the
hand comber.

This extinction created a serious social problem. According
to H. W. Ripley, 11,900 combers were entirely displaced.[47]
Worsted spinning was done by women and children, weaving
mainly by women and girls and, in any case, did not call for an
expanded labour force in the 1850's.[48] There was therefore little
scope for the hand comber to find alternative employment within
the worsted industry. Except in so far as he could find local employment outside the industry, and this in an area overwhelmingly

---

[43]*Ibid.*, p. 45. For details of his factories in England and France, see *Holden-
Illingworth Letters*, p. 783.

[44]*Lord Masham's Inventions*, p. 46. The capitals are Lord Masham's own.
See also p. 43: "It was the largest patent right that was ever paid for a machine."

[45]*Ibid.*, p. 46.   [46]*Ibid.*, p. 53.

[47]H. W. Ripley, 1861, see *supra*, note 2.

[48]*Ibid.*

devoted to worsted production, his only salvation lay in emigration from Bradford.

The surviving correspondence of the Woolcombers' Aid Society,[49] a charitable body formed to deal with the situation, reveals the actual fate of many of these displaced combers. The Society acted as an employment agency for the combers and attempts were made to place them in other employment. Firms

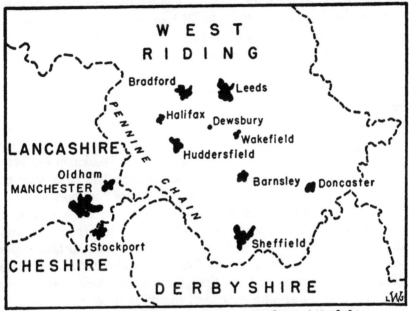

Manchester, Sheffield, and the West Riding of Yorkshire

in other parts of the country were canvassed.[50] Advertisements were inserted in the newspapers: "Situations as passenger or Goods Porters for 100 Strong, Active, Honest and Industrious Woolcombers, from 22 to 40 years of age, varying in height from five foot, six inches to six feet. . . ." When all else failed, the

[49]Bradford Reference Library, Empsall Collection. The Society was a committee of the Christian Mutual Provident Society. The letters are only a fragment of the original correspondence and fall mainly between May and July, 1854.

[50]Amongst the firms which were canvassed were the following: Messrs. Balcoes, Middlesborough; Leeds and Bradford Railway (for jobs as porters); Liverpool Constabulary Force; East Lancashire Railway, at Bury; Manchester Constabulary Force; Leeds, Halifax and Bradford Junction Railway; Eston, Middlesborough and Witton Park Iron Works; Tees Iron Works; Alfred Jobson, "mines and coke mills"; a wool textile mill at Garstang; Ormesby Iron Works, Middlesborough; South Durham Iron Works, Darlington; Midland Railway, Derby; King's Cross Station, London (porters).

Society gave the comber a testimonial in order to induce the public to help him to emigrate: "The Bearer of this, Thomas Cavanagh, belongs to that unfortunate class of Operatives, the Woolcombers. . . . He has been out of work since the 11th. of March last, and has in vain sought employment since that date. He has tried to acquire the trade of a Painter but has failed through the slackness which pervades that branch of business. His only resource is Emigration. . . . A small donation from twenty or thirty persons would thus, in all human probability, rescue a young man from the jaws of Pauperism." Bradford combers were dispersed all over the country, to the rising iron industry at Middlesborough, to work as dock labourers at Liverpool, to jobs as farm labourers, railway porters, and servants. Their letters back to the Society, often barely legible, show their varying fates. Some, who went as labourers to Middlesborough, were fortunate. In spite of the heavy work in a hot temperature, "both Marsters bear a Very Good Name and all the Workmen are very civel to us." At Middlesborough, however, one had to beware of the Irish: ". . . if you send men hear in Large Numbers and the Marsters begin to turn the irish of[f] it will very likely lead to a disturbance." At Liverpool, the combers were less fortunate, and the work was dangerous and heavy: ". . . We have to load ropes varying in weight from one to five tons without the assistance of a Crane to be rolled up the plank in the best manner we can . . ." and the employer treated them "as if we were not men but something lower and had no feelings." Elsewhere, there were complaints of the "robbery committed by thoas who kep lodgines . . . at sume lodgines hear thay will not heaven mend yor stockin for you and thay Charge half a Crowne a week."

These dislocations and sufferings of domestic workers were part of the price paid for the continued rapidity of the expansion of the Bradford worsted industry.

IV

There was, however, another part of the price, which was paid by other towns which had earlier been important centres of worsted manufacture and merchanting. Norwich, by 1850, had almost lost its worsted industry to Bradford, "probably the classical case of industrial migration in English history."[51] Wakefield at the beginning of the century had been not only a centre of worsted production, but also a very important wool and goods market for the industry. Very early, in 1817, her Piece Hall had been closed, and by 1857 Wakefield had "ceased to be a stuff producing district, its mills being employed in spinning hosiery yarn for the Nottingham and Leicester trade."[52] Halifax had succeeded in retaining an important worsted producing industry amongst its mixed activities, but had not advanced with anything like the same rapidity as Bradford. Its great Piece Hall, once one of the chief piece goods markets for the worsted industry, was almost deserted by 1857, for "Most of the Halifax manufacturers now carry their goods to the great Mart of the worsted industry,— Bradford market."[53] This process was already started in 1836, when it was reported: ". . . the manufacturers are removing to Bradford as fast as they can get accommodated with rooms and so long as the merchants can get what they want at the latter place, it is not likely they will attend Halifax."[54]

The same trend of decline in worsted manufacturing and marketing is also observable in Leeds between 1830 and 1860. In 1830 the bulk of worsted merchanting was done at Leeds, where 53 per cent of the worsted merchants of Leeds, Bradford, Halifax, and Wakefield combined had their warehouses.[55] By 1853 Leeds could claim only 16 per cent of West Riding worsted merchants, while Bradford had increased its proportion from 30 per cent in 1830 to 75 per cent in 1853.[56] The situation whereby in 1834-5 Messrs. John Foster and Son, with their mill on the far side of Bradford from Leeds, had sent over £32,000 worth of their goods to Leeds, and only £3,710 worth to Bradford merchants,[57] had been reversed by 1860.

[51]J. H. Clapham, "The Transference of the Worsted Industry from Norfolk to the West Riding," *Economic Journal*, XX, 1910, pp. 195-210.

[52]James, *History*, p. 630.

[53]*Ibid.*, p. 616. This desertion of the Piece Hall would be due not only to the migration of merchants to Bradford, but to the transition from the "domestic" to the "factory" system in the worsted industry, the Piece and Cloth Halls of the West Riding being the mercantile concomitant of small-scale manufacture.

[54]*Bradford Observer*, Sept. 5, 1836.

[55]Cf. table *infra*.

[56]*Ibid.*

[57]Messrs. John Foster and Son Ltd., Ledgers, 1834-5. The figures are for the period June 1834–July 1835.

Not only was there a migration of merchants to Bradford from Leeds, but also from Manchester where, before 1830, there was already a colony of German merchants trading in both cottons

NUMBERS OF WORSTED MERCHANTS, 1822-1861*

	Leeds	*Bradford*	*Halifax*	*Wakefield*
1822	24	5	6	2
1830	42	24	12	1
1834	44			
1837	52	25	12	0
1842	51	54	21	0
1847	42	71	14	0
1851		98		
1853	28	128	14	0
1861	17	157		

*Sources, contemporary directories.

NUMBERS OF FOREIGN WORSTED MERCHANTS*

	Leeds	*Bradford*
1822	0	0
1830	2	3
1834	4	
1837	7	8
1842	10	25
1847	7	34
1851		38
1853	5	55
1861	3	65

*I.e. with recognizably foreign names (included in the above totals).

and worsteds. The extent to which foreign merchants participated in this movement is reflected in the increasing extent to which such distinctive names as Behrens, Schlesinger, Schuster, Schunk, Albrecht, Wurtzburg, Gustavus Gumpel, Zigomala, Zossenheim, and d'Hauregard appear in the contemporary Bradford directories. By 1861 there were sixty-five merchants bearing foreign names, the great majority of whom were Germans.[58] As a distinct colony, the German merchants became one of the features of Bradford, holding regular meetings of their Schiller Verein, sending a contingent of sons to fight for the Fatherland in the Franco-Prussian War, and making an important contribution to the cultural life of the town.

An outstanding personal example both of migration from Leeds and of immigration from the Continent was Jacob Behrens.[59] A Hamburg wool textile merchant, he first visited Leeds in 1832 and 1833, settling there in 1834, one of the first foreign merchants to take this step. He realized that "the commission merchant on the spot in England, buying for foreign customers with expert knowledge and at market prices, had obvious advantages over the stock-holding merchant on the Continent who,—far from knowledge or control of his source of supply—bought from one or two manufacturers at whatever rates they chose to fix."[60] These advantages were at the root of the immigration of the German merchants into the West Riding and of their settling in Bradford. To be "on the spot" in worsted dealing soon meant to be in Bradford. Jacob Behrens transferred his business to Bradford in 1838. Other merchants, foreign and English, soon followed his example. Rapidly, others came direct to Bradford. By 1861, over 45 per cent of Bradford worsted merchants bore distinctively foreign names.

By 1860, therefore, Bradford was the commercial and industrial hub of the British worsted industry. The period 1830-60 saw the foundations of this supremacy laid and realized, a supremacy which still remains.[61]

[58]The German merchants settled close to each other. One of the Bradford police beats is still officially known as "Germany."

[59]Knighted 1882.

[60]*Sir Jacob Behrens, 1806-1889*, a privately printed memoir published in 1925. I am indebted to Mr. Edgar Behrens, O.B.E., for permission to quote from this book.

[61]Bradford was not content to allow unaided economic forces to contribute toward her expansion. The linking of Bradford with other northern towns by railway was to be a stroke of policy deliberately designed to foster her mercantile supremacy. The Editor of the *Bradford Observer* pointed out that Leeds and Manchester were already linked by railway. Bradford ought therefore to build a railway line which would enable her to intercept Manchester merchants on their way to Leeds: ". . . as long as there is no railway communication between this town and Manchester, so long will the Leeds stuff merchants have the advantage over those of Bradford." *Bradford Observer*, Dec. 14, 1843.

DUNDEE–ST. ANDREWS*

Dundee, honoured with the appellation of the second Geneva at the time of the Reformation,[1] came to worship Mammon, almost without reservation, at the beginning of the nineteenth century. So spectacular was the development of this thriving industrial and commercial centre that its population practically doubled in thirty years and by 1831 reached 45,355 inhabitants, excluding some 2,500 seafarers. Formerly lumped together with St. Andrews, Cupar, Perth, and Forfar for the purposes of parliamentary representation, Dundee in 1832 gained an M.P. of its own and elected, first, George Kinloch of Kinloch who died in London during his initial session, and then Sir Henry Parnell "whose character was well known among political economists by his treatise on Finance."[2]

By that time the hodden grey and broad bonnets, for the manufacture of which Dundee was once famous, had practically disappeared. No longer was any importance attached to the making of plaiding and glass, or of thread and cotton. Flax in large quantities was obtained from various parts of Europe, especially Prussia and Russia; and, to meet the large demand at home and abroad, it was converted into such linen fabrics as sacking and sail-cloth, sheetings, and Osnaburghs by upwards of 30 spinning mills, which employed some 3,000 adults and children for twelve and a half hours a day, used machinery valued at roughly £500,000, and turned out almost 7,500,000 spindles of yarn per annum.[3] Business throve; wealthy families appeared; and, if wages were low, the workers were reasonably content and comfortable. During the winter curling, the "roaring play" imported from Dumfriesshire, was enjoyed by many; and, to while away the summer hours of leisure, cricket, the favourite game of merry England, was introduced.

From south of the Scottish border, too, came the idea that flax might be replaced by jute; for at Abingdon in 1815 experiments were made to produce a new fabric from a raw material, sent home by the East India Company from the Ganges valley where Hindus of all ages and both sexes had spun and woven

*The reader is referred to the map on page 5.
[1] By the Rev. Robert Edward in 1678. Quoted in *New Statistical Account of Scotland* (1834-45), vol. XI, p. 6.
[2] *Ibid.*, p. 12.   [3] *Ibid.*, p. 26.

coarse jute cloth and twine for several centuries. But the initial venture was no more successful in England than it was in Dundee in 1822; for the jute was too intractable for the existing machinery and was lacking in tensile strength. Soon, however, dry goods, packed in jute gunny bags, came from India to this country where the vast expansion of industrial output emphasized the urgent need of a packing material more suitable and less expensive than cotton. So in 1832 a Dundee linen manufacturer named Watt resumed the experimentation with jute; and, in order to make more pliable the hard and rough fibres, he resorted to whale-oil of which there was almost a local glut in consequence of good catches and a growing tendency to replace oil by coal gas for domestic and street lighting. By this bright idea Watt rescued the whalers and started a boom in jute manufacture. A further fillip came in 1838 when a Dundee firm received a large order from the Dutch government for jute bags to carry coffee beans from the colonies; in 1846 when the repeal of the Corn Laws encouraged increased trade in grain; and in 1854 when the outbreak of the Crimean War stopped the supply of flax from Russia, handicapped the linen manufacturers, and encouraged more and more of Dundee's spinners and weavers to switch over to jute. If the Indian Mutiny caused some growing pains to the lusty infant industry, the American Civil War, which came in 1861, brought it to manhood by diverting much of the home demand from the scarce and expensive cotton to a more plentiful and cheaper fabric.

If, to the extent indicated, some English pioneers helped to place "Jutopolis" on the industrial and commercial map, an Englishman too was destined to pave the way towards the eventual eclipse of Dundee. In 1853 George Ackland after a chequered career settled in Calcutta. Learning that jute bags were being transported all the way from the east of Scotland to the west of India, he decided, with much enterprise, to get a Dundee firm to send appropriate machinery to Bengal. When the plant arrived in 1855 it was accompanied by a Dundee technical expert, the first of many who left Angus to industrialize Calcutta. But in the early stages factory work had little appeal for the natives. To ease the transition from the traditional habits of the Hindus spinning alone was attempted. However, as the new industry gathered momentum, power looms were sent from Scotland. By 1859 there were 192 of them in the mills of Calcutta; and within a few years Dundee had to face serious competition in its home markets for manufactured jute.

Across the Tay and some ten miles south of Dundee stood St. Andrews which Daniel Defoe had described as "an ancient and once flourishing City, the Metropolis of all *Scotland*, . . . a most august Monument of the Splendour of the *Scots* Episcopal Church in former times; . . . remarkable for a fine Situation, surrounded by extensive Corn-fields, . . . and the pleasant downs, called the *Links*, lying on the Sea-side towards the North."[4] Although the first ill-fated Tay bridge, spanning commerce and culture, as it were, was not constructed until 1878, communication between Angus and Fife was much improved in 1852 when the railway penetrated to St. Andrews. Yet "this asylum of repose, the best Pompeii in Scotland," as Lord Cockburn had called it in 1844, no less than Dundee had long had a close connection with India. Part of the evidence lay in the existence of Madras College, founded in 1832 on the site of a Dominican or Black Friars' monastery. This famous co-educational school, which in its heyday had 800 pupils, was the result of a munificent bequest by the Rev. Dr. Andrew Bell who, a native of St. Andrews and a graduate of its venerable University, had gone to Madras in 1787 under the auspices of the East India Company, become the superintendent of its Orphan Asylum and, having invented the monitorial system of tuition, decided to make provision for its application primarily in St. Andrews and also in some other Scottish towns.[5] Bell's own moral education, however, probably owed most to a regular round of golf, a wonderful training for mind and body and medically eulogized in the *New Statistical Account* in 1838 as "the best prophylactic in preventing dyspepsia and hypochondriasis."[6] Possibly he contributed his quota to the development of the game in Madras. Certainly in his time Madras and Calcutta too were getting their share of an annual output of upwards of 10,000 rather short-lived feather

[4]*A Tour through the Whole Island of Great Britain* (7th ed., 1769,), vol. IV, p. 185.
[5]C. J. Lyon, *History of St. Andrews* (Edinburgh, 1843), vol. II, pp. 213-20.
[6]Vol. IX, p. 453.

golf balls,[7] retailed at 1*s.* 8*d.* each and produced for the most part by such celebrated St. Andreans as Allan Robertson, "the cunningest bit body that ever handled a club" who eventually in 1858 established a record of 79 strokes for the Links;[8] Tom Morris who in partnership with Robertson was never defeated, but stole his thunder through his son, "Young Tom," who not only broke Robertson's record, with a 77, but won four open championships before he died at the age of 24—probably as a result of making golf balls with feathers;[9] and a famous caddie and character called "Long Willie." But for the St. Andrews Roland there came in 1848 an Indian Oliver in the form of gutta percha which was moulded into gutta balls—missiles which flew all the better when painted, cut, and dented, and soon displaced the "featheries" from circulation. Meanwhile, in 1845 the Golfing Society of Bombay, in token of gratitude, presented a silver medal to the St. Andrews Club for competition among its members at the Spring Meeting. Thirty-seven years were to elapse before Calcutta came into line by sending to the Royal and Ancient "a handsome silver Cashmere Cup, value sixty guineas," partly met by petty fines in the Calcutta Club, and beautifully fashioned by Indian craftsmen out of silver rupees.[10]

Probably Hugh Lyon Playfair (1786-1861)[11] did more than most men to undermine Kipling's dichotomy between East and West. Before his long and distinguished Indian military service during which incidentally he helped to pioneer the game of golf out there, he had received his early education in Dundee High School. Thence he proceeded to St. Andrews—most fittingly, because while one relative issued a scholarly edition of Adam Smith's *Wealth of Nations* in 1806 and published, in nine volumes, *British Family Antiquities* in 1809-11, another was Principal of the United College of St. Salvator and St. Leonard during the first two

---

[7]*Ibid.*, p. 476.

[8]J. S. F. Morrison, *Around Golf* (London, 1939), p. 54.

[9]Feathers were stuffed into the leather cover by a blunt pointed iron instrument called a stuffing iron with a sort of crutch which the maker fixed to his shoulder or chest. Ball makers frequently died of consumption resulting from the continuous pressure of the stuffing iron or from swallowing minute particles of feather.

[10]H. S. C. Everard, *History of the Royal and Ancient Golf Club of St. Andrews 1754–1900* (London, 1907), p. 214.

[11]The son of James Playfair, Principal of St. Andrews, and Margaret Lyon of Ogil. He was the uncle of Lyon, first Lord Playfair (1818–98).

decades of the nineteenth century; and also because the young man desired to frequent the Links and study the lore of golf. Soon he learned how in 1457 James II of Scotland, in defence of archery, had given the lead to his immediate successors by decreeing that "golfe be utterly cryit downe and nocht usit"; how in 1552 John Hamilton, Archbishop of St. Andrews, in return for permission to plant and plenish "cunninggis" (rabbits) within the north part of the Links next adjacent to the Water of Eden, grudgingly acknowledged the community's right "inter alia, to play at golf, futball, schuting, at all gamis, with all utter maner of pastime, as ever thai pleis"; how in 1627-9 James Graham, Marquis of Montrose, like most of his student contemporaries, devoted the bulk of his time to golf and archery;[12] and how in 1754 twenty-two "Noblemen and Gentlemen, being admirers of the ancient and healthfull exercise of the Golf" had met at St. Andrews and formulated the embryonic "Rules of Golf," subsequently revised in 1812 and 1828 to cope with the (ungentlemanly) development of the game.[13]

On his retirement from the Indian Army, Playfair inevitably settled in St. Andrews; and in 1835, acting on behalf of fifty-eight golfers and archers for whom the "19th hole" had previously been Bailie Glass's, the Black Bull, or some other convenient tavern in the town, founded the Union Parlour Club with premises suitably near the 1st tee and 18th green and with all the necessary amenities. Two years later he rejoiced when the royal patronage was obtained and His Majesty King William IV presented, for competition, a gold medal, inscribed "To the Royal and Ancient GOLPH CLUB of St. Andrews." Presumably he was elated still more when in 1840 he won that coveted trophy, with a score of 105 strokes for a round of the Links. But his greatest triumphs were yet to come. In 1842 he was elected Provost of St. Andrews. In that role he proved to be a very energetic reformer, with modern ideas of sanitation and a propensity for removing slums, middens, forestairs, and other relics of antiquity. However, his thoughts, always on the Links, were translated by G. F. Carnegie into the poetic "Golfiana":[14]

[12]Everard, *History of the Royal & Ancient, St. Andrews,* chap. II.
[13]*Ibid.,* chap. III.
[14]*Address to St. Andrews* (1842).

St. Andrews! they say that thy glories are gone,
Thy streets are deserted, thy castles o'erthrown:
If thy glories be gone, they are only methinks,
As it were by enchantment, transferr'd to thy Links.
Though thy streets be not now, as of yore, full of prelates,
Of abbots and monks, and of hot-headed zealots,
Let none judge us rashly, or blame us as scoffers
When we say that instead there are Links full of golfers,
With more of good heart and good feeling among them
Than the abbots, the monks, and the zealots who sung them:
We have red coats and bonnets, we've putters and clubs;
The green has its bunkers, its hazards and rubs:[15]
At the long hole across we have biscuits and beer,
And the Hebes who sell it give zest to the cheer:
If this make not up for the pomp and the splendour
Of mitres and murders and mass—we'll surrender;
If golfers and caddies be not better neighbours
Than abbots and soldiers with crosses and sabres,
Let such fancies remain with the fool who so thinks,
While we toast old St. Andrews, its Golfers and Links.

In 1854 Playfair was a prime mover in establishing the Royal and Ancient Club in what was destined to be its world-famous home; and in 1856 he, now a belted knight, attained the acme of bliss by becoming its Captain and *ipso facto* winner of the Queen Adelaide Medal, presented in 1838 by the spouse of King William IV "for the purpose of distinguishing the Captain in Office from the other Captains present, their uniforms being all alike."[16] Nominated by these predecessors in the spring, he had an ordeal to undergo before an assembled host at eight o'clock on the morning of the Autumn Medal. At that fateful hour and to the accompaniment of a loud report from an ancient piece of ordnance sited in the immediate vicinity, he drove a ceremonial ball from the first tee down the fairway in the general direction of a swarm of caddies, one of whom, more agile or luckier than his fellows, retrieved it and, returning it to the Captain, received a warm handshake and the traditional golden sovereign. Nor was Playfair's reward limited to the Queen Adelaide Medal. It also embraced the celebrated Silver Club, originally presented by

[15]Lucky breaks.
[16]Everard, *History of the Royal & Ancient, St. Andrews,* p. 143.

twelve members in 1754. But at that time competition for it was "open to all and sundry," with the proviso that "every victor was to append a silver ball to the club for the year he won."[17] In 1773, however, the competition for the Silver Club was restricted to St. Andrews golfers and the Honourable Company then at Leith. In 1819 the old Club could not hold any more balls and a new one had to be provided. After 1824 it automatically and without competition became the perquisite of the Captain who accordingly appended a silver ball (or a gold one if he happened to be a member of the royal house), of the correct golfing dimensions, and inscribed with his name, his arms, and the date of his Pyrrhic victory. Such was the crowning glory of Sir Hugh Lyon Playfair, still also Provost of the city. He had no more worlds to conquer; and in 1861, when he had run his course, he had the honour of the company not only of the baillies and magistrates of the Royal Burgh but also of the draped regalia and leading members of the Royal and Ancient Golf Club as he went to join the immortals in the hallowed burial ground of the Cathedral and Abbey of St. Andrews.

> The wind blaws keen at Aberdeen
>   Sae does it at Dundee
> O'er mony a stately town it blaws
>   In Scotland's cauld countrie.
> But of a' the towns the wind blaws o'er,
>   There's nane sae dear to me
> As the grey towers o' St. Andrews town
>   St. Andrews-on-the-Sea.
>
> For there I ween dwell Golfers keen,
>   A jolly companie;
> And mony a leal and trusty friend,
>   And mony a fair ladye;
> And there "the major" keeps his state,
>   And rules the auld citye;
> A mighty man of heart and hand,
>   And the pink of courtesye
> The Major of St. Andrews Town—
>   St. Andrews-on-the-Sea.

[17]*Ibid.*, p. 57.

CHAPTER SEVEN

The Clyde

[*This is the famous river whose economic history, strange to relate, has not yet been given to the world. But its shipbuilding has been written, and I have the honour of presenting in lecture form a survey of that part of the story which falls within our period. I desire to repeat my obligation to Dr. W. S. Cormack. C. R. F.*]

IN THE *Port of Glasgow*, a sumptuous volume issued by the Clyde Navigation Trust, January 1, 1947, and rich in maps, photos, statistics, and historical advertisements, there is under "Clydeside War Effort" the following notice, page 101:

JOHN BROWN & CO., LTD.

Vessels completed at Clydebank

58 ships of approximately one third of a million tons displacement, and filled with machinery of approximately two million horse power. The liner "Queen Elizabeth", the battleship "Duke of York", the aircraft carrier "Indefatigable" and the battleship "Vanguard" are included in the foregoing totals.

For close on a century Glasgow has been known the world over as the centre of the shipbuilding and engineering industries of the west of Scotland. Over the same period the Clyde has held first place among the rivers of the United Kingdom for output of ships and engines, the quality of which is acknowledged in the significance attached to the phrase "Clyde built." The thirty-year period covered by this survey is an important one in the economic history of the area. The direct-acting steam-engine with separate condenser, invented by James Watt of Greenock some sixty years earlier, had already been applied to sea, rail, and road transport. By 1825 over three hundred steam-engines averaging 20 h.p. were working in the city and suburbs of Glasgow.[1] Half of these were supplying power for textile and other manufacturers, 58 were winding and pumping at pits, 7 were working in stone quarries, and 68—aggregating 1,926 h.p.—in steam-boats. By 1830 iron was being smelted at a rate of 30,000 tons per annum—more than half the Scottish total—in four ironworks in the immediate vicinity of Glasgow. Cort's discovery (in 1783) of the technique of rolling plates had been applied to building the hulls of vessels, and a small iron passenger boat, the *Vulcan*—motive power one horse!— had been plying between Glasgow and Coatbridge on the Monkland Canal since its launch there is 1819.[2] For three years before our survey commences, the first Clyde-built iron steamboat—the *Aglaia*—had been sailing Loch Eck, facilitating the overland journey from Glasgow (via Dunoon by steamer) to Inverary.

Yet by 1860, when our study of the Clyde ends, iron had only just established its superiority to timber as a material for the hulls of vessels, and the issue of steam or sail was still undecided. Throughout these three decades the foundations of the ship-building and marine engineering industries were being laid but it was only after 1860 that they became the principal industries of the district. Before that time they did not appear to contemporary writers to be of sufficient importance to justify the collection and publication of statistics of yearly output; consequently figures for the period under review are fragmentary.

To present a clear picture, the historic material available has been grouped in three parts each dealing with an aspect of the subject. Also, since the opening date has been chosen somewhat arbitrarily, a few paragraphs at the beginning of each chapter sketch the background existing in 1830.

I. The River and Its Workshops

The geographical position of Glasgow conforms to an ancient pattern: the town at the ford on the river, catching the coastal road trade and controlling the market for goods going to and coming from the hinterland. As a future port it was severely handicapped, being twenty-two miles from the open firth at Greenock. The river between was a wide but shallow winding

[1] James Cleland, *Historical Account of the Steam Engine* (Glasgow, 1825).
[2] The boat—not the horse!—was still at work in 1875.

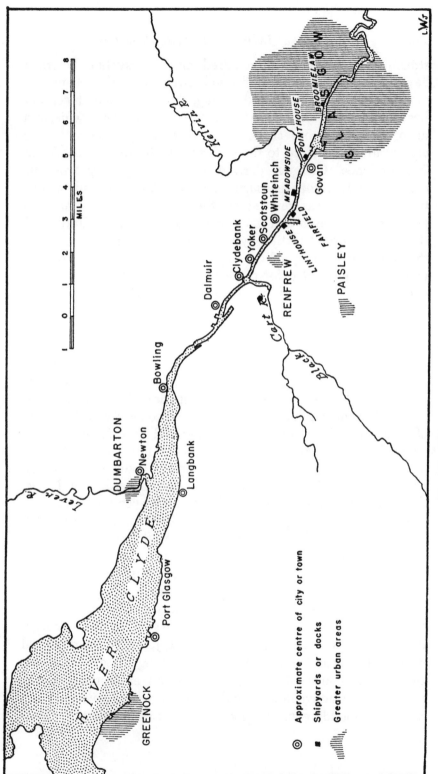

The Clyde from Greenock to Glasgow

stream the bed of which required much excavation before a navigable channel could be formed. Even today this channel is maintained only by constant dredging. Till the nineteenth century boatbuilding was confined to the estuary, which is long, wide, and deep, with numerous sheltered lochs along its shores. In the eighteenth century, up to the outbreak of the American War of Independence, Glasgow derived its wealth mainly from its *entrepôt* trade in tobacco, sugar, and rum. After a decade of disturbance trade was revived by the export of home-produced goods, chiefly cotton and linen fabrics and ironware. Until 1840 the manufacture of textiles by steam-driven machinery remained the principal industry of the city; indeed, the engineering skill and technique needed for the construction of ships and marine engines was developed by the requirements of textile manufacture. It was during the period with which this review is concerned that Lancashire took the lead in the making of cotton goods. As a consequence much of the capital, labour, and plant employed locally in these manufactures was transferred to the newer industry of shipbuilding in which, to achieve its pre-eminence, the Clyde had to meet severe competition from the Thames.

By 1825 the depth of the river at the Broomielaw in the centre of Glasgow was 7 to 8 feet at low water and 12 to 15 feet at high water. Records show that vessels up to 300 tons actually tied up in the harbour, which extended to 7 acres of water with quayage of 1,100 yards. Thirty-two years later the Cunard liner *Persia*, 3,600 tons, was able to dock at Glasgow, but even then large vessels in their journey up the river from Greenock often grounded in the shallows and were compelled to await the next tide. The primary reason for deepening the river was to permit the loading and discharge of ships in the harbour, but improvements in the channel rendered possible also the construction and launch of equally large vessels in, and in the vicinity of, the city. Prior to this, the important shipbuilding yards were situated on the margin of deep water at Greenock, where, in 1711, John Scott had opened a yard for the construction of the local herring "busses." For over two centuries successive generations of this enterprising family maintained an active interest in the business which developed into Scotts' Shipbuilding and Engineering Co., Ltd. Before the advent of the nineteenth century the grandson of the founder of the firm had opened the first dry-dock on the Clyde. In 1790 a local foundry was taken over, and in 1825, under the name of Scott, Sinclair & Co., the manufacture of steam-engines was begun. Three years later the firm was employing 220 men at a weekly wage bill of £180 and engines up to 200 n.h.p.[3] were being made. Quite early Scotts specialized in steamships and in 1838 received their first Admiralty order for H.M.S.S. *Hecla* and *Hecate*. To them fell also the honour of building H.M.S. *Greenock*, the first steam frigate launched on the Clyde, representing one of the earliest attempts at geared screw propulsion. Other early ship-builders of Greenock and Port Glasgow were: R. & A. Carswell, Robert Duncan & Co., John Hunter, James McMillan, Joshua Muiress, James Munn, Robert Steel & Co., and John Wood. The last named built the *Comet* and many other early passenger steam-boats at his Port Glasgow yard. Caird & Co. opened a foundry in Greenock in 1809 and fifteen years later were manu-facturing marine engines. Later still they extended their activities to shipbuilding and throughout the nineteenth century this firm was one of the most important on the Clyde. Wm. Simons & Co.[4] commenced business in Greenock in 1817.

On the upper reaches of the river, within a few miles of the city, Barclay, Curle & Co. (of Whiteinch) and Alexander Stephen & Sons (of Linthouse) opened up in the 1820's. But priority of commencement had little influence on the extent of later develop-ment. In general the firms which prospered were those that antici-pated and prepared for the triumph of steam and iron at a time when sail and timber were still favoured by most ship-owners. As the river was alternately widened and deepened, shipbuilding yards tended more and more to approach the city, whence by road and rail came supplies of raw materials, engines, and fittings.

---

[3]Nominal horse power, derived from the formula:

$$\text{n.h.p.} = \frac{\text{area of piston (sq. in.) x effective pressure x piston speed}}{33000}$$

Effective pressure was assumed to be 7, sometimes 7½, lb. per sq. in. and piston speed was estimated by an arbitrary rule issued by the Admiralty. After 1820 the modern measure, indicated horse power (i.h.p.), was introduced but n.h.p. con-tinued in use for many years, though as effective pressures and piston speeds in-creased n.h.p. ceased to represent even approximately actual values.

[4]Now situated in Renfrew, they specialize in dredgers.

Later, when the harbour at Glasgow was repeatedly extended, many of the yards moved west again.

The foundations of some of the engineering enterprises that later achieved distinction were laid before 1830. Already the Napier family—John and his son David—had constructed in Camlachie Foundry the boiler for the *Comet*. Robert Napier (1791–1876), a cousin of David, who had been apprenticed to his father in Dumbarton, opened an engineering business in Glasgow in 1815 and early in the 1820's leased Camlachie Foundry from David, who had moved his workshop to Lancefield Street nearer the river. Robert's first marine job for the *Leven*, built by Lang of Dumbarton in 1823, outlasted three hulls and was finally put permanently on view on a pedestal at Dumbarton pier. In a race with other Clyde steam-boats in 1827 the *Clarence* was adjudged the fastest vessel on the river and the *Helensburgh* second. Both had been engined by Robert Napier who consequently achieved an enviable and deserved reputation as an engineer. Although Camlachie Foundry was equipped with only a few 10″ and 12″ lathes (having wooden shears!), a rude horizontal boring mill, a vertical drill, hand tools and casting appliances, it turned out first-class reliable workmanship. Business extended and Napier was fortunate in choosing David Elder[5] as his manager. In 1828 he took over the Vulcan Foundry and eight years later his cousin's Lancefield Street works also. In 1838 he made his first successful tender for a government contract comprising two sets of 280 n.h.p. side-lever engines for H.M.S.S. *Vesuvius* and *Stromboli*, the price being £13,480 per set. He started several steam-boat companies, including the City of Glasgow Steam Packet Co., forerunner of the Cunard Company. In 1839, Samuel Cunard, the East India Company's agent in Halifax, Nova Scotia, having received the Atlantic mail contract, came to Britain to arrange for the construction of suitable steam-ships. As Robert Napier had engined several boats for the East India Company, Cunard sought his aid both technically and financially. The outcome of these negotiations was the formation of the Cunard Company, the principals of which were Cunard himself, George Burns,[6] David and Charles

---

[5]Father of the patentee (in 1853) of the compound marine engine.
[6]Also of the Glasgow firm Messrs. G. & J. Burns, now the Burns and Laird Lines, Ltd., running the Glasgow-to-Ireland service from the Broomielaw.

McIver (who from 1830 to 1840 had organized the Liverpool-to-Ireland service), and Robert Napier. Four steam-ships—the *Britannia, Acadia, Caledonia,* and *Columbia*—were built by Robert Duncan, John Wood (of Greenock and Port Glasgow), Charles Wood, and Robert Steel respectively, and all were engined by Robert Napier. They were of approximately the same dimensions and power—206 ft. x 44 ft., 1,150 tons, 440 n.h.p. The *Britannia* was the first to make the crossing and accomplished it in the record time of 14 days 8 hours, arriving at Boston on July 4, 1840. A month later the *Acadia* reduced the passage time to 12 days 18 hours. The aim of the Company being to give a regular and reliable Atlantic service, all their vessels prior to 1855 were wooden paddle steamers.[7]

Meanwhile, in view of the difficulties being experienced with ocean liners with timber hulls, the energetic Robert determined to add iron shipbuilding to his other business interests. He acquired land for this purpose at Dumbarton, but then changed his mind and sold it to Messrs. Denny. In partnership with his two sons he opened at Govan in 1841. His brother James also joined the firm and they acquired the services of William Denny[8] as designer. Their first iron vessel, the *Vanguard,* was launched in June 1843. In the two following years the first iron steamships for the British Navy—H.M.S.S. *Jackal, Bloodhound,* and *Lizard*—were built there, followed by the first iron frigate—H.M.S. *Simoon* of over 2,000 tons. In the early fifties the firm transferred to what was known as the Govan yard. One of the first vessels launched there was the *Persia,* the first of the Cunard Company's iron ships —350 ft. x 45 ft., 3,300 tons, 3,600 i.h.p. Still paddle driven, she was the largest vessel afloat at that time and made the passage from New York to Liverpool in 9½ days. Even after this the Company continued till 1864 to order both wooden and iron paddle steamers. Subsequently they built up a fleet of iron screw-propelled ships. From 1840 to 1865 the engines for the entire Cunard fleet were constructed in Napier's workshops. The firm

[7]Up to the middle of the 1880's, when twin screws came into general use, steam vessels of all types—even the large Atlantic liners—carried sails for use in the event of engine breakdown and to help to manage the ship when sailing "light" or in heavy seas.

[8]This was the William Denny who later resuscitated and made famous the old Dumbarton firm, dating from the early years of the nineteenth century.

were also responsible for the engines of many ships of the P. & O., Pacific, Royal Mail, Castle, and other leading shipping companies as well as for warships for various European powers. In 1856 Napier's yard launched the *Erebus*, the first British armoured vessel. The armour plate was four inches thick and Napier, under a penalty of £1,000 a day for late delivery, was allowed six months for the whole job. Actually it was completed in the incredibly short time of three and a half months, having been launched complete with machinery installed. Five years later the *Black Prince* (10,000 tons), second in point of time of all British ironclads and the first of its kind to be built on the Clyde, was launched from the Govan yard. When such warships were contemplated, Napier took over Parkhead forge, the management of which he entrusted to his son-in-law, Mr. Rigby, and the firm operated under the title Rigby and Beardmore. Rigby died in 1872 and the forge was carried on by Beardmore alone. On the death of Robert Napier in 1876 the shipyard and engine works were sold to John and James Hamilton and A. C. Kirk for a sum of £270,000 but the old title of the firm was retained for many years. Later still it passed into the ownership of Wm. Beardmore & Co. and the yard was moved to Dalmuir, six miles down and on the other side of the river.[9]

Though probably the most famous Clyde shipbuilder and engineer of the period and the man to whom, more than any other, the industry in the west of Scotland owes its distinction, Robert Napier held no monopoly. The oldest established building yard on the upper reaches of the river was that founded by Robert Barclay at Finnieston in 1818. Later the firm became Barclay, Curle & Co. Till 1857 this firm confined itself to shipbuilding; after that engineering and boiler-making were added. Wingate & Co. began shipbuilding in 1823, followed a year later by James Stephen. Two of David Napier's shop foremen, David Tod and John Macgregor, entered into partnership as marine engineers and iron shipbuilders in 1834. A year later[10] they built the first iron vessel actually constructed on the banks of the Clyde and

[9]Beardmore's yard was closed on grounds of redundancy after the end of the First World War. The site is now occupied by the Royal Ordnance Factory.
[10]See also p. 154 below.

launched into the river. In 1846, owing to harbour extensions, the yard was moved to Meadowside. All except two of the Inman Line vessels—the *City of Berlin* and the *City of Chester* which Caird of Greenock built—were constructed in this yard. Their *City of Glasgow*[11] was the first twin-screw vessel to ply regularly between Glasgow and New York. About 1874 David Tod, Jr., sold out to David and William Henderson and under that title the shipyard still operates, but for repairs only, at Meadowside, Partick. Another partnership which later developed into a top-ranking firm was formed in 1834 by Charles Randolph and R. S. Cunliffe, with a small millwright's shop in Tradeston district. Three years after this John Elliot joined the partnership and the title of the firm was altered to Randolph, Elliot & Co. In 1852, John Elder, Jr., who was Robert Napier's chief draughtsman, joined the firm and the name became Randolph, Elder & Co. In 1854 they added boiler-making and in the same year, from the original shop in Centre Street, Tradeston, came the first successful compound marine engine. Next they branched into shipbuilding in 1860 in a small yard within the city boundaries but four years later removed to Fairfield, just beyond Govan. The first four vessels they built were blockade runners for the American Civil War. Ample room for expansion existed here and large vessels could be launched without difficulty. Randolph and Cunliffe both retired in 1868 and a year later Elder died. The firm was reconstituted and continued its successful career as the Fairfield Shipbuilding and Engineering Co.

In 1847 two brothers, James and George Thomson, who had been foremen in Robert Napier's shop, opened engineering premises in Finnieston Street, Glasgow. Four years later they added shipbuilding, beginning in a yard at Govan and confining their attention to iron vessels. When harbour extensions later necessitated a removal they went to the new suburb of Clydebank and adopted the title the Clydebank Co., which is now John Brown & Co. The actual site of this yard was chosen with amazing foresight opposite the spot where the last tributary—the River Cart—enters the Clyde, which today is 800 feet wide at that point.

[11]Built in 1859 for other owners but purchased later by the Inman Line.

It is this circumstance which makes safe the launching of very large vessels (e.g., *Lusitania, Aquitania,* H.M.S. *Hood,* and the two *Queens*); no other shipyard on the Clyde can do it.[12]

In the same year (1847) Anthony and John Inglis commenced business as engineers and millwrights with premises in Warroch Street, and twenty years later opened up as iron shipbuilders at Pointhouse, Glasgow, on the north bank of the river. Another firm with very early origins is Denny Brothers of Dumbarton. At the beginning of the century William Denny's father, in partnership with James Maclachlan, had begun boatbuilding in a small way at the Woodyard on the west bank of the River Leven at Dumbarton. In 1814 William Denny built the paddle steamer *Marjory,* the first of its kind to ply for hire on the Thames, and several other early steam-boats. On his death in 1833 his son John, one of a family of eleven, succeeded to the business but a few years later he too died. Thereafter the firm disappeared to be revived in 1844 by three brothers of the deceased owner, William, Peter, and Alexander, who had recently established in Glasgow a partnership as marine architects. The Woodyard was equipped for iron shipbuilding and in the following decade produced forty-five vessels some of which were as large as 1,500 tons and 300 n.h.p. Among these was the *Water Witch*—240 tons, 35 h.p.—the first merchant screw vessel from any Clyde yard. The firm of Denny Brothers progressed rapidly, being ready at all times to adopt the latest inventions; it staked its fortunes on steam propulsion. In 1850 engineering and boiler-making were commenced by an associated firm, Tulloch and Denny, which in 1862 became Denny & Co. Important contracts for G. & J. Burns, the shipowners, were executed in 1851-2. As business extended new sites were occupied and today the shipyard and engine shops are among the most important on the Clyde. Peter Denny survived till 1895 and the firm's success must be attributed in very large measure to his energy, foresight, and skill.

[12]The *Queen Mary* was launched by John Brown, September 1934, the *Queen Elizabeth,* September 1938. When siting the yard and shipways used by John Brown, the firm had in mind the possibility of requiring the mouth of the Cart for launching very large vessels. But it has not been called upon even for the *Queens,* because the tugs were able to manoeuvre them in the River Clyde. However the mouth of the Cart is dredged and kept clear in case the ship at launching should not be brought under control in time.

By 1853 there were eight or nine shipbuilding concerns in the immediate vicinity of the city and this number doubled in the next ten years. Mention may be made of Smith and Rodger—which became the London & Glasgow Engineering and Iron Shipbuilding Co.—Charles Connell & Co., and Hedderwick & Co. Many new engineering firms sprang up. Harbour extensions forced many of the older firms to move to new premises down the river. Wingate & Co. went to Whiteinch; Barclay, Curle & Co. likewise to Whiteinch at Clydeholm yard; Stephen to Linthouse, Connell to Scotstoun and, as already mentioned, J. & G. Thomson to Clydebank. Napier, Hedderwick, and the London & Glasgow Co. alone remained on their original sites on the south bank, and Stephen & Sons[13] on the north bank of the river. Most of the firms were founded or managed by men who had served their apprenticeship or worked with Robert Napier. Among them were William Denny, James and George Thomson, John Elder, William Beardmore, Smith and Rodger, David Tod and John Macgregor, Aitken and Mansel, Shanks and Bell, Miller, Scott, Dunsmuir and Jackson—truly a famous roll.[14]

Meantime the city was increasing in size and beginning to acquire the elements of modern municipal organization. The Scottish Muncipal Reform Act of 1833 gave the ratepayers the right to elect their own town council. A regular police force had been authorized by an act of 1800 and other acts concerned with this followed in 1821, 1837, 1843, 1846, and 1866. Gas lighting was inaugurated by a private company in 1818 and a second gas company started up in 1843. The adjacent district of Blythswood was annexed in 1830. The Burghs of Calton and Anderston and the Barony of Gorbals, each of which up to this time had its own magistracy and police force, were annexed by the city in 1846, thereby increasing the population to over a quarter of a million.

But our chief concern is with the river and its development; these other matters are mentioned only to indicate that progress and expansion were taking place in all directions. Until 1834 river and harbour dues were disposed by public sale; after that date they were collected by the Trustees. In 1840 the fifth act relating

[13]Afterwards Aitken and Mansel, and not to be confused with Stephen of Linthouse.
[14]Changes in the names of firms are summarized in Appendix A.

to Clyde navigation was put on the statute book. The river was now 15 feet deep, the quayage extended to over a mile, and the harbour had an area of 23 acres. Annual revenue from dues was approaching £50,000. The new act authorized a depth of 17 feet for the river and altered the constitution of the Trust to include nominees from the Chamber of Commerce, the Merchants' House, and the Trades' House. Of the total membership of 33, the Town Council had 23 seats. As yet there was no dock in the city and the 1840 act authorized the provision of that convenience, but no immediate attempt was made to fulfil this part of the act. Six years later another act repeated the provision but the project was not undertaken. In the same year (1846) a basin 3½ acres in extent was opened by the Forth & Clyde Canal Co. at Bowling, some ten miles down the river from Glasgow.

The seventh Clyde Navigation Act was passed by Parliament in 1854. Its provisions were purely financial, extending the borrowing powers of the Trustees, making regulations for the establishment of a sinking fund, etc. Two miles of quayage were now available but still no dock or tidal basin, simply 51 acres of open harbour. In 1856 the Clyde Trust opened a basin 8½ acres in extent at Bowling. The eighth act a year later continued, renewed, and extended the powers already granted and in 1858 another legislative measure consolidated and, in minor points, amended those already in operation. The constitution of the board was again altered, the number of members being fixed at 25, to be elected as specified in the act. A new title was conferred on the board, "The Trustees of the Clyde Navigation"—hence the abbreviated name by which the body is currently known, Clyde Navigation Trust. At the harbour some 19 cranes, of which 4 were operated by steam, dealt with the loading and discharge of cargo, the largest being capable of lifting 60 tons. As yet there was no public graving or dry dock though a private one (450 ft. x 55 ft.) belonging to Tod & Macgregor was completed in 1858.

Between 1770 and 1857 no less than £2,676,505 was expended on river and harbour improvements. Of this sum £574,708 went in purchase of land, £658,473 on the construction of works, £253,963 on dredging and deepening the channel, and the remainder—£1,189,361—on management, maintenance, interest on money borrowed, etc. The irony of the situation was that much of the land which had to be bought at a high price was land actually created during the early operations—when the channel was being narrowed to promote scouring—by the material excavated from the river bed and thrown on the banks behind the jetties and dykes. The expense incurred in the improvement of the river was borne by local effort and finance, no government assistance being received at any time. Shipping dues were by 1860 bringing an income of over £80,000 per annum. Improvements in the facilities offered were constantly under review and dredging of the channel went on all the time. In 1852 and again in 1861 diving bells were called into service to remove large boulders from the bed of the river. The first wet dock—Kingston Dock—was opened in 1867 and the first public graving dock—at Plantation—in 1875.

The consequence of thus making Glasgow accessible by water is obvious in the extensive trade which the city has conducted for so many years. Prior to the river improvements the revenue collected by the Crown from Glasgow's trade was negligible; by 1856 it was nearly £2,800,000. Population too was steadily increasing; and, whereas in the middle of the eighteenth century the total rental of the city amounted to only a few thousand pounds sterling, a hundred years later it was over £1,300,000.

II. Technical Advances: Iron versus Timber and Steam versus Sail

Since the pre-eminence of the Clyde in shipbuilding is related to the use of iron for hulls, a few facts concerning iron smelting in and around Glasgow will serve to introduce this section. Carron Works, erected near Falkirk in 1760, were the first large ironworks in Scotland. In 1786 Clyde Iron Works at Tollcross, near Glasgow, were opened by Edington & Co.[15] Ten years later there were eight blast furnaces in the Clyde area, three of which had forced blast supplied by steam-engines. Early in the nineteenth century David Mushet, an employee of Clyde Iron Works, discovered large deposits of blackband ironstone about five miles from the works.

---

[15]These are still the largest and most important ironworks in Glasgow and district; they are now owned by Colvilles' Ltd.

This provided the necessary raw material for many years. In 1828 James B. Neilson, a Glasgow engineer, devised and initiated the hot blast, thereby reducing from 8 to 2½ tons the coal required to smelt one ton of ore. In his *Enumeration of the Inhabitants of the City of Glasgow and County of Lanark* (Glasgow, 1832), Dr. James Cleland pointed out that the city is equidistant—twenty-six miles—from the Atlantic Ocean on the west and the North Sea on the east. Communication with the latter was by the Monkland and Forth and Clyde Canals. "With these advantages," he wrote, "for obtaining the materials, and sending the manufactured article to market Glasgow must become the seat of a great iron manufacture. She has already large establishments for the manufacture of steam engines and machinery, and for making the machines employed in the processes of cotton spinning, flax spinning, and wool spinning. In these works everything belonging to, or connected with, the millwright or engineer departments of the manufacture is also fabricated. Having these important and valuable portions of the manufacture already established, and with the advantages which the district possesses for carrying on the trade, there is every reason to expect its rapid growth, and its extension to every article of the iron manufacture." The omission of any reference to the building either of sailing ships or of steamboats or to the manufacture of marine engines as local industries is significant of the meagre contribution made by these activities to the commercial position of Glasgow, of which Dr. Cleland in his census report (1832) was making a detailed examination. However the foundations were being laid in the general engineering trades, and the production of iron for local consumption and for export extended rapidly in central and western Scotland. Ten ironworks were operating in Scotland in 1832, four of them being in the immediate vicinity of Glasgow, and the others, though more distant, were all within forty miles of the city. These four had a combined output of 31,000 tons per annum out of a Scottish total of 55,000 tons. The output per furnace increased steadily as a result of improvements in the technique of working and the adoption of larger units. By 1836 another establishment had been opened at Coatbridge and Scottish production had increased to 110,000 tons per annum, of which about one quarter was exported.

Three years earlier it had been only 44,000 tons and the increase may be attributed principally to the extension of the hot blast technique. After 1836 the iron industry made rapid strides and by 1860 Scottish output was in the region of a million tons per annum.

The first sea-going vessel of iron had been built on the Mersey in 1815 and the first on the Clyde[16] in 1827. Despite this iron vessels were rare until after 1840 and even then the output can be described as moderate only. For the six years 1846-51 the average launching of iron ships on the Clyde amounted to 13,000 tons per annum. All were steam-ships. From about 1850 onwards—until displaced by mild steel some thirty years later—iron hulls became the established practice for steam-ships. They were still considered unsuitable for sailing ships and it may be pointed out that in 1860 the sail tonnage launched was twice that of steam.[17] For the decade 1852-61 output of iron ships on the Clyde averaged 57,000 tons per annum, almost all being steam-ships. The long delay in the general adoption of iron was due in part to deep-seated prejudices[18] from which neither the Admiralty nor maritime underwriters[19] were immune. There was certainly no shortage of iron.[20] The only substantial objection was the compass deflection caused by the large mass of metal in the hull. It was found, however, that the placing of two iron balls, one on either side of the compass—a noticeable feature of the binnacle—gave reasonable protection. True, for many years the initial cost of an iron ship exceeded that of a timber one of the same size,[21] but the price of iron fell as output increased whereas the cost of English oak rose as the forests were decimated; consequently many wooden

[16]The thirty-ton *Aglaia* by David Napier; see p. 140 above.

[17]Not till 1870 did steam tonnage launched exceed sail and again in 1875 and 1876 sail substantially exceeded steam. The last recovery of sail was in 1885-6 when its tonnage was 45 per cent of the total launched in these two years. Of course, owing to the difference in average speeds of the two types, a "steam" ton even at that date represented a carrying capacity twice to three times that of a "sail" ton.

[18]*Milestones*, a play by Arnold Bennett, has as its central theme this prejudice against iron and the similar prejudice later against mild steel when it replaced iron.

[19]They charged higher insurance premiums for iron than for timber vessels. Lloyds did not issue rules for iron vessels till 1855.

[20]See Appendix D for statistics.

[21]About 1846 an iron ship cost £25 and a timber one £20 per registered ton.

vessels were built in India instead of in Britain. Canada and the United States had unlimited quantities of pine and, though the soft nature of this wood caused it to deteriorate rapidly, it was sufficiently cheap to warrant its use even if frequent replacement were required.

The decisive factors which made the ultimate triumph of iron inevitable were: (i) the ever increasing size of ships, the limit of length for a wooden hull being about 300 feet; (ii) the replacement of paddles by the screw propeller, timber not being able to stand up to the vibration, whereas iron could be given local strength at the required points. Composite ships in which the beams and framing were of iron while the planking was of wood were tried,[22] but, except in the period when clippers flourished, this device did not gain the favour of shipowners. The last wooden vessel of any considerable size built on the Clyde was the *Canadian* by Scott of Greenock in 1859, but not until mild steel was beginning to displace iron in the 1880's had iron entirely displaced timber.

Returning to the history of early iron vessels built in the vicinity of Glasgow, we may note that John Neilson of Oakbank in 1831 constructed the first iron steam-boat to ply on the Clyde. As the building yard was situated at the Old Basin, Hamilton Hill, near Port Dundas[23] on the Forth and Clyde Canal, some two miles from the Clyde, the boat had to be conveyed on lorries to be put in the water at the Broomielaw. She was named the *Fairie Queen* and carried passengers on the Largs route. In 1832 Messrs. Wingate & Co. launched their first iron vessel, a lighter for the Glasgow and Paisley Canal. Three years later the recently founded firm of Tod and Macgregor launched their first, the *Vale of Leven.*[24] The first sea-going iron steamship from the Clyde was the *Iron Duke* (393 tons) in 1840.

The Clyde and the Mersey were the rivers upon which the pioneer work in iron shipbuilding was done. "To the Clyde builders," writes William Fairbairn, F.R.S., "may be referred some of our most important constructions, and there is probably no part of the United Kingdom where greater energy and enterprise in

[22]Lloyds in 1867 issued special rules for this type.
[23]Named after Lord Dundas, Governor of the Forth and Clyde Canal Co.
[24]See also pp. 146–7 above.

this branch of industry is displayed."[25] By 1850 Glasgow and Dumbarton were specializing in iron steam-ships, while Port Glasgow and Greenock remained "thirled" to timber for many years after.[26]

The rivalry of steam and sail started with the *Comet*, which was the first commercially successful (wooden) steam-boat in Britain. It may be said to have inaugurated in 1812 the era of the steam-ship. The story need not be repeated here. Its promoter and owner, Henry Bell, died in 1830. The boat itself had been wrecked ten years before off Craignish Point, Argyllshire. Following on its success a number of similar steam-boats, all built locally, were soon plying on the river. As Bell took out no patents, others were free to apply his ideas and indeed to improve on them. Thus began the tourist industry in the west of Scotland and, with the availability of a steam-boat service, the population of coast resorts increased. In all, from 1812 to 1901, no fewer than 309 passenger vessels were built and engined on and for the river.[27] Of these 73 were in service before 1830, and 139 were built and put into commission between 1830 and 1860. After service on the river for a longer or shorter period many were transferred to the West Highland service; others were sold to English or foreign owners.

In 1818 the first steam-boat to navigate the open sea, the Irish Channel, had been launched by Denny at Dumbarton and engined by David Napier, who became the pioneer of hull design for deep-sea steam navigation. He conducted experiments with models on the Molendinar Burn[28] and discovered that a wedge-shaped bow gave much better results than any of a rounder type.

[25]*Treatise on Iron Shipbuilding* (London, 1865).

[26]Stakes marking the site of the enclosures into which the logs were floated are still to be seen on the south bank of the river between Langbank and Port Glasgow.

[27]James Williamson, *The Clyde Passenger Steamer: Its Rise and Progress during the Nineteenth Century, from the "Comet" of 1812 to the "King Edward" of 1901* (Glasgow, 1904). The year 1904 saw the first merchant vessel with steam turbines—*King Edward*, 250 ft. x 30 ft., 562 tons, 400 shaft h.p.—launched by Denny Brothers. It was the forerunner of a number of similar pleasure steamers, fast and luxuriously furnished.

[28]A stream which has its source in Hogganfield Loch to the northeast of the city. It is now covered in for the greater part of its course and serves as a common sewer. At that time it was a very pretty burn, flowing behind the old College garden and uniting with the Camlachie Burn near Jail Square just before it entered the Clyde at the west end of the Glasgow Green.

In the fifteen years following the launch of the *Comet* no significant improvements had been made in marine machinery[29] and, until these did materialize, extended voyages over open sea could not be undertaken on account of the quantity of coal consumed, which, on the average, amounted to 25 lb. per h.p. per hr. Consequently the cargo-carrying capacity of a vessel of, say, 100 tons, driven by a 50 h.p. engine, would have been reduced by 50 per cent on a four-day voyage since no less than 50 tons of coal would be consumed in that period. Excessive coal consumption was due partly to the inefficiency of the boilers, which were able to sustain only a low pressure—5 lb. per sq. in. above atmospheric was common—and partly to the engines, which used an inordinate amount of steam. Gradually both defects were eliminated, and many of the inventions to that end were made by Clyde engineers.

In 1830 James Napier, a cousin of David, patented the haystack boiler which achieved a 25 to 30 per cent saving of coal. In company with his cousin William Napier, James was at this time carrying on business at the Swallow Foundry, Washington Street, Glasgow. In the same year they furnished several steam-boats incorporating the new type of boiler and these gave every satisfaction. Haystack boilers, with pressures of 60 to 70 lb. per sq. in., were still being used for river steamers under construction in the 1890's. A departure from the side-lever engine was made by the London engineer, Joseph Maudslay, when in 1827 he invented the oscillating cylinder, a type so well suited to river paddle steamers that it held its place for over half a century.[30] John Neilson of Oakbank fitted one in the *Fairie Queen*.[31] In 1832 David Napier invented the steeple engine, so called because the connecting rod,

[29]Verification of this is to be found in a testimonial to Bell. Dated April 2, 1825, it runs: "We the undersigned, engineers in Glasgow, having been employed for some time past in making machinery for steam vessels on the Clyde, do certify, that the principle of the machinery and paddles, used by Mr. Henry Bell in his steamboat the 'Comet', in 1812, has undergone little or no alteration, notwithstanding several attempts, by ingenious persons, to improve it. Signed: Hugh and Robert Baird, John Neilson, David Napier, Duncan McArthur, Claud Girdwood & Co., Murdoch and Cross, Wm. McAndrew, William Watson, Robert Napier." The order of signing is by commencement of business. James Cook comes second, between Baird and Neilson.

[30]William Murdock had used the same idea experimentally for his road carriage more than forty years before.

[31]See also p. 154 above.

crack, and framework projected well above the deck of the vessel. For the next forty years it proved to be by far the most popular type for river work.[32] The first steam-boat equipped with it was the *Clyde* (342 tons, 160 n.h.p.) launched in 1836. The double steeple soon followed. Many other inventions stand to the credit of David Napier; some achieved practical success whilst others remained merely designs. Among the successful we may note the feathering paddle in 1841 and, ten years later, an arrangement for forced draught to marine boilers. Of his unsuccessful designs the most interesting from our point of view was his rotary engine. In 1852 he had a vessel, the *Rotary*, built to his specification by Henderson of Renfrew and engined by Wingate & Co. After a few trial trips, regarding which great secrecy was maintained, the vessel was converted to ordinary paddles. Under a different name it sailed the Clyde for many years. As a solution to the problem of sewage disposal, he suggested that barges should carry the waste material to the Firth and there dump it in deep water. Rejected at the time, his idea was later adopted by the Clyde Navigation Trust. Though he possessed a fertile inventive brain from which issued many brilliant designs and ideas, the machines produced in his workshops were rather poor in quality and workmanship. In consequence he was involved in much trouble and litigation of which one instance may here be cited. In 1835 the boilers of one of his vessels, the *Earl Grey*, burst as she lay at Greenock. Many persons were killed and injured. After this David Napier removed to London where he built steamers for the Margate trip. Subsequently his London shipyard was taken over by Scott Russell in connection with the construction of the *Great Eastern*.

The successful application of the screw propeller in 1836 by John Ericsson, a Swede engaged in civil engineering practice in London, must be noted. It had revolutionary consequences in the

[32]Of the 119 river steam-boats built between 1835 and 1860, records of the type of engine with which they were equipped are extant for 70 of them, and of these 70, 50 were steeple type and only 10 oscillating cylinder. When the present writer was on his way to Skye for summer holidays in 1929, he boarded the steamer *Glencoe* at Kyle of Lochalsh for Portree. As he stepped on deck he was amazed to observe that its motive power was a steeple engine. Inquiry showed that the vessel was the renamed *Mary Jane* (165 ft. x 20 ft., 223 tons, 120 n.h.p.), Clyde built and engined by Tod & Macgregor in 1846!

development of the steam-ship.[33] The next step was to drive the
propeller through gearing to give it a higher rate of revolution
than the engine had, i.e. the engine was "geared up." Built by
Scott & Sons in 1849, H.M.S. *Greenock* was the first steam frigate
constructed on the Clyde and was the largest iron warship of that
time. She was one of the earliest to be equipped with geared
screw.

From the workshops of Randolph, Elder & Co., founded in
1852 to take over the business of Randolph, Elliot & Co., came a
number of important improvements in marine machinery. Between 1853 and 1867 this firm registered no fewer than fourteen
patents. The most important, and one which foreshadowed the
ultimate disappearance of sail, was that dated January 24, 1853,
defining the principles of construction of the compound marine
engine.[34] It was tried out successfully in the *Brandon* in 1854.
Coal consumption, already reduced by boiler and engine improvements to 4 lb. i.h.p. per hr., dropped to 3¼ lb. Another patent
revived the discarded steam jacketing of cylinders, designed to
prevent heat losses to the air and to reduce initial condensation—
the source of the mysterious "missing quantity"—in the cylinder.
The second and third ships to be fitted with the new compound
engine were the *Inca* and the *Valparaiso*. Steam pressure in these
was 30 lb. per sq. in. above atmospheric and the cylinders were
partly jacketed; fuel consumption as low as 2½ lb. per i.h.p. per
hr. was reached. Such a degree of economy, never before realized,
rendered practicable what had hitherto been impossible: trade
by steam-ship across the Pacific Ocean. Further improvements in
a short time reduced the figure to 2¼ lb. The development by John

[33] For ocean voyages paddles had serious defects. Owing to the weight of fuel
required the ship started off low in the water. As the coal was consumed the vessel
floated higher and higher; consequently from a somewhat low figure at the commencement of the voyage, the efficiency of the paddles increased for the first two
thirds of the trip and decreased again during the remainder. Paddles have obvious
disadvantages for fighting ships; hence, partly at any rate, justification for the
Admiralty's reluctance to go in for steam-driven ships in a large way. On the other
hand the screw propeller is equally effective at varying draughts provided it is
submerged. It is indifferent to rolling though adversely affected by heaving. It
can be used for large or small powers. With the development in later years of
higher engine speeds it was possible to dispense with gearing.

[34] Hornblower in 1781 had patented a single-acting compound engine and in
1804 Woolf patented a double-acting compound engine. Neither proved suitable
for marine work.

Elder of a three-cylinder compound engine solved the problem of unbalanced forces almost completely. Rowan and Horton in 1860-1 also took out patents for boiler improvements and for a type of three-crank compound engine. The first ship to be fitted with a surface condenser, auxiliary to its compound engine, was the *Thetis*, built by Scott of Greenock and engined by Rowan of Glasgow, in 1858. It had water tube boilers working at 115 lb. per sq. in. On trial, as certified by Professor Rankine, F.R.S., the coal consumption was only 1.018 lb. per i.h.p. per hr. The twin screw, an advance towards which David Napier contributed, came into use in a few vessels shortly after 1860.

The size of ships also increased. In the early days of steam-boats a length equal to four times the breadth was considered suitable. By 1860 lengths of seven or even eight times the breadth were not uncommon. Hull design improved greatly as a result of the competition between steam and sail. In the latter class the fast clipper was evolved and many of these were built in Clyde yards. Efficiently manned and with some luck when crossing the doldrums, they achieved phenomenally fast passages, rivalling at times those of the most up-to-date steam-ships of their day. As an example the Clyde-built iron clipper, *Lord of the Isles*, launched in 1856, may be cited. This vessel on one occasion made the passage from Shanghai to London with 1,030 tons of tea in 87 days. On another trip she averaged 320 miles per day (i.e. 13.3 m.p.h.) for five consecutive days. A very good steam-ship average on the Atlantic in the 1860's was 320 miles in the twenty-four hours. The Clyde shipyards had a full share in the building of these "China clippers," being responsible for 37 (totalling 28,637 tons) out of the 85 (totalling 64,658 tons) constructed in Britain between 1852 and 1869. One of the last and most famous of them, the *Cutty Sark*, was built by Scott & Linton—a firm now long defunct—at Dumbarton. The opening of the Suez Canal in 1869 killed the clipper ship; it shortened the route from Britain to the East by 3,000 to 5,000 miles for steam-ships, sailing ships being unable to negotiate the Canal. Foremost among the Clyde builders of sailing ships were Russell & Co. of Port Glasgow and Connell & Co. Not till 1894 did they too turn over to steam. In contrast it may be mentioned that Caird & Co. of Greenock in 1853 launched the

P. & O. Line steamer the *Atrato*, the largest ship in the world. She was 354 ft. long and 3466 tons burthen.[35]

It is clear that the period with which we have dealt was important in laying the foundations of a great industry in which the Clyde engineers and shipbuilders played a leading part. Alike in design and in workmanship the ships and engines produced in the west of Scotland were unsurpassed by those from any other area of the United Kingdom. Here lived and worked many of the pioneers of iron ships; from here came the first steam-boats in Europe. But even the most visionary of these men could scarcely have conceived the extent and importance of the later developments for which they supplied the impetus.

III. Output and Wages

In response to a request of His Majesty's Government for a summary of trade prospects in the west of Scotland, the Lord Provost of Glasgow in February 1823 rendered a statement in the course of which the following passage occurred:

Periods of great prosperity are naturally followed by others of an opposite description. And as the extent of business has, during the last year, been unusually great in this department, it is not difficult to foresee a change, the more especially as the increased production of the present time will require more extensive markets; that a pressure causing great stagnation, and consequently lower wages, and distress among the operatives must take place at some time, probably not far distant, seems to be beyond all question. And much will depend on the political circumstances of the country, as to the period when such a pressure may be expected to occur. It may be added, that the recent practice of our manufacturers exporting their goods to foreign markets on their own account, and of obtaining advances on their goods from commission merchants, to whom they consign them, seems likely to lead to over production, to occasion more frequent gluts in distant markets, and consequently to give rise to greater vicissitudes in trade, than the system which formerly prevailed.

It is evident that even at this comparatively early date the outstanding features of the trade cycle had been recognized—this

---

[35]The following year saw the laying of the keel of the ill-fated *Great Eastern*, nearly twice the length and more than three times the tonnage, at Millwall in London. She was launched in 1858.

at a time when the imminent depression could not be ascribed to any war, famine, or other exceptional occurrence.

The year 1831 marked the bottom of the trade depression which, in accordance with prophecy, had affected the whole of Britain since 1825. The depression in steam-boat building arrived a year later, probably on account of the time such vessels took to build. Tonnage of steam-boats built on the Clyde fell from the 1826 peak of 1,332 tons to 194 tons in 1831. None at all were launched in 1827. A period of expansion now set in and continued till 1841 with a temporary check around 1835. Clyde output of steam-ships was approximately 6,500 tons in 1841. Then followed a period of unparalleled distress, the hungry forties. In 1845 tonnage built was only one-thirteenth of that for 1841. However, the decade 1846-55 was one of prosperity. Railway construction boomed and gold was discovered in California and in Australia. The discovery of gold had a long-term effect in raising prices but it had an immediate consequence too: emigration increased and this required shipping space. The Crimean War of 1854-56 added considerably to the calls made on shipping and, of course, stimulated orders for men-of-war. In output for the whole of Britain sail still predominated, net tonnage built in 1854 being twice and in 1855 three times that of steam. Nevertheless the majority of Clyde firms continued to specialize in steam-ship building, a choice which proved of great importance in the later development of the area.

Two methods of propulsion were now available, paddles and screw. Denny Brothers were producing little else but screw vessels, while paddles still predominated in the output of the towns on the left bank. The yards in Glasgow were executing 50 per cent of the total steam-ship construction and workshops 75 per cent of the marine engine work of the west of Scotland. Of the engines for ships built elsewhere than on the Clyde, Glasgow firms accounted for one-half. Apart from new construction, ship and engine repairs, for which no figure can be computed, also added considerably to the industrial activity. Launches touched a maximum of 84,750 tons in 1855. Thereafter another downward loop of the trade cycle began and, at the close of the period which is our special concern, tickets for soup, coal, blankets, etc., were still being distributed to the unemployed of Glasgow.

The year 1860 marks also the date after which the Clyde became the leading river in the United Kingdom for shipbuilding and engineering.[36] For the decade 1853-62, Clyde output of iron vessels aggregated 586,824 tons and to convey some idea of what this represented in money values we may cite the details for 1861:

81 iron steam-ships (60,185 tons), hulls and fittings	£1,252,300
Engines for above (12,493 n.h.p.)	456,800
5 iron sailing ships (3,060 tons), hulls and fittings	50,560
	1,759,660

This statement gives average costs:

Steam vessels without engines	£21 per ton
Steam vessels with engines	28 per ton
Sailing vessels	16-10 per ton
Engines	36 per n.h.p.

If allowance be made for wooden vessels, repairs, and engines for ships built elsewhere, the sum accruing annually to the west of Scotland from these industries probably exceeded £2,000,000 for an average year. Taking a backward glance, this figure may be compared with the period 1813-19 when the value of steam-boats built on the Clyde averaged £20,000 per annum. A typical vessel was the *Albion* of 20 h.p., launched by John Wood of Port Glasgow and engined by James Cook of Glasgow in 1816:

Hull	£1,000
Upholstery and equipment	850
Engine, boiler, and paddle mechanism	1,600
	3,450

In that seven-year period 42 steam-boats aggregating 3,200 tons constituted the Clyde ouptut of steam-driven vessels.

Of the period 1849-60 the historian MacGregor wrote: "Shipbuilding was becoming a most important industry of Glasgow and its neighbourhood."[37] Looking back from our present vantage

[36]For the past seventy years output from the Clyde averages one-third of that for the United Kingdom and this proportion is still being maintained; see Appendix for further statistics of output.

[37]George MacGregor, *The History of Glasgow* (Glasgow, 1881).

point we could well add that after 1860 it became *the* most important industry of the district.

At various places in this survey sums of money have been stated. As we are all too painfully aware from the record of the twentieth century, money values change. Prices rise and fall so that a given amount of money buys less or more at different times. No attempt has been made to assess the changes in purchasing power in the period with which we have been dealing. Moreover such changes are nation-wide, often world-wide, so that a detailed treatment would be out of place in the study of a locality. But changes in purchasing power are closely bound up with changes in wages and conditions of labour, to which in conclusion we advert. For purchasing power the following table must suffice:[38]

Period	Nominal wages	Prices	Real wages
1810-30	Falling	Falling fast	Rising slowly
1830-52	Nearly stationary	Falling slowly	Rising slowly
1852-70	Rising fast	Rising	Rising considerably

As for wages, complete records of wages in shipbuilding and engineering are not available but a few selected figures, referring to Glasgow and the Clyde, are given; they show the normal rates in shillings and pence per week:[39]

Year	Shipwrights	Ship joiners	Mechanics, turners, fitters	Pattern-makers	Smiths
1830	21/0		23/6	21/6	18/0
1835	21/0		23/6	21/6	18/0
1840	21/0		20/0 to 30/0		
1845	21/0		20/0 to 28/0		
1850	25/6	24/0	20/6		
1855	35/0	27/0	24/0		
1860		26/0			

[38]Abstracted from W. T. Layton, *An Introduction to the Study of Prices* (London, 1920).

[39]Abstracted from paper to the Royal Statistical Society by Professor Bowley and George H. Wood, March, 1905.

Of the several shipbuilding districts in Britain the Thames paid the highest rates. This was in part at least the result of a strike in 1825 by which the London engineers obtained a "price book." When the character of the work changed, this "book" was maintained and consequently London shipbuilding costs were higher than in the north. Clydeside wages were about 25 per cent lower than Thameside, while the Tyne and Wear in general came between these extremes. There can be no doubt that many orders came to the Clyde as a result of the lower contract prices which west of Scotland shipbuilders and engineers were able to quote. Normal hours in these industries were 60 per week. As now, in bad times unemployment hit the heavy industries a particularly hard blow.

IV. CONCLUSION

We have come to the end of our thirty years' survey. Generalizations are always dangerous but it will not be misleading to say that the shipbuilding industry on the Clyde was made possible by the huge expenditure on river development incurred primarily to maintain the status of Glasgow as a port. If we compare the river today with the river as it was a century or more ago we shall appreciate the terse description with which an economic historian concludes his survey of the changes: "Glasgow," he wrote, "has created a river out of a ditch."[40] In the second place there was the fact that the textile industries had already established an engineering industry in the city. A decisive factor was the proximity of the Lanarkshire coalfield and the contiguous iron deposits. Finally there were the men: the inventors, the organizers, the business men prepared to risk investment in industries that had not yet proved themselves, and—not least—the skilled artisan class taking a pride in the job of work to be done. Of course it is not quite so simple as this; a full-length study would draw attention to the part played by many other factors. But perhaps enough has been said to show that the west of Scotland attained the industrial position it holds today neither by deliberate planning nor yet by chance occurrence.

[40]Adam Kirkaldy in his book *British Shipping* (London, 1914).

APPENDIX A

CHANGES OF NAME AND OWNERSHIP OF CLYDE FIRMS

The following list gives, in order of their output for the year 1949, the principal firms on the Clyde (firms producing only yachts, motor boats, and small craft have been omitted):

Shipbuilders and engineers

John Brown & Co., Clydebank
Harland & Wolff, Govan and Greenock
Fairfield S. & E. Co., Govan
Alex. Stephen & Sons, Linthouse
Barclay, Curle & Co., Whiteinch and Scotstoun
Wm. Denny & Bros., Dumbarton
Scotts' S. & E. Co., Greenock
Wm. Simons & Co., Renfrew
Ailsa S. & E. Co., Troon and Ayr
Yarrow & Co., Scotstoun
Lobnitz & Co., Renfrew
Ferguson Bros., Port Glasgow
Fleming and Ferguson, Paisley

Shipbuilders (only)

Lithgow's Ltd., Port Glasgow
Wm. Hamilton & Co., Port Glasgow
Blythswood Shipbuilding Co., Scotstoun
Chas. Connell & Co., Scotstoun
Greenock Dockyard Co., Greenock
James Lamont & Co., Port Glasgow
A. & J. Inglis, Pointhouse
George Brown & Co., Greenock
Ardrossan Dockyard Co., Ardrossan
Scott & Sons, Bowling
Millen Bros., Paisley
D. & W. Henderson, Partick (ship and engine repairs only)

Engineers (only)

John G. Kincaid & Co., Greenock
David Rowan & Co., Glasgow
British Polar Engines, Glasgow
Bergius Co., Glasgow
Rankin & Blackmore, Greenock
Aitchison, Blair, Clydebank
McKie & Baxter, Govan

In addition to the absorptions indicated below, Lithgow's own the firm, Wm. Hamilton & Co., Port Glasgow, and have a controlling interest in David Rowan & Co. (founded 1865) and the coal business of James Dunlop & Co.

Barclay, Curle & Co. in 1925 acquired the business of the North British Diesel Engine Co. (previously Burmeister & Wain) of White-inch, Glasgow; but it is now itself controlled by Swan, Hunter and Wigham Richardson, the Tyneside firm of shipbuilders.

Harland & Wolff, who began business at Queen's Island, Belfast, in 1858, have a controlling interest in D. & W. Henderson, A. & J. Inglis (both of Glasgow), and Archibald McMillan & Son (of Dumbarton). Together with John Brown & Co. this Belfast combine acquired a large interest in David Colville & Co. (now Colvilles' Ltd.), steelmasters.

Several shipping companies have a direct interest in shipbuilding yards, and some shipbuilding firms, no doubt to assure preferential supplies of plates and forgings, have interests in steel manufacture.

The following shows the fate of many of the early firms mentioned in the text. (Changes prior to 1860 appear in the text.)

Aitken & Mansel, Govan—defunct

Blackwood & Gordon, Port Glasgow, later the Clyde Shipbuilding Co.—now James Lamont & Co., still extant

Caird & Co., Greenock—taken over in 1916 by Harland & Wolff

Dobie & Co., Govan—defunct; yard taken over by Harland & Wolff

D. J. Dunlop & Co., Port Glasgow (later Dunlop, Bremner & Co.)—now Lithgow's

Dunsmuir & Jackson, Engineers, Yoker—defunct

Mackie & Thomson, Govan, occupied Robert Napier's yard—now occupied by Harland & Wolff

Muir & Houston, Engineers, Govan—now McKie & Baxter

Robert Napier & Sons, Govan, became Wm. Beardmore & Co.—yard transferred to Dalmuir; now defunct

A. Rodger & Co., Port Glasgow, taken over in 1912 by Russell & Co.—now Lithgow's

Ross & Duncan—defunct

Russell & Co., Port Glasgow—now Lithgow's

Shanks & Bell, Old Kilpatrick, later became Napier, Shanks & Bell, later still Napier & Miller—defunct

Smith & Rodger, Govan, became the London & Glasgow Engineering
and Iron Shipbuilding Co.—taken over in 1911 by Harland & Wolff
Robert Steel & Co., Greenock—defunct; yard taken over by Scotts'
S. & E. Co.
J. & G. Thomson, Finnieston, later became the Clydebank Co.—now
John Brown & Co.
Wingate & Co., Whiteinch—defunct

APPENDIX B

OUTPUT OF STEAM AND IRON VESSELS ON THE CLYDE

Number and tonnage of steam vessels built on the Clyde, from
John Strang, *Social and Economic Statistics of Glasgow* (1855):

Year	No.	Tonnage	Year	No.	Tonnage	Year	No.	Tonnage
1812	2	55	1826	11	1,332	1840	11	3,074
1813	2	118	1827			1841	9	7,786
1814	9	550	1828	3	124	1842	7	1,973
1815	6	529	1829	4	595	1843	5	1,157
1816	7	509	1830	4	540	1844	12	3,038
1817	2	105	1831	2	194	1845	2	576
1818	4	286	1832	6	728	1846	17	7,125
1819	7	892	1833	3	306	1847	26	16,999
1820	3	187	1834	10	1,837	1848	34	12,409
1821	6	792	1835	20	3,528	1849	23	11,798
1822	4	337	1836	13	2,078	1850	32	18,604
1823			1837	8	2,023	1851	42	27,724
1824	3	175	1838	11	2,010	1852	78	52,945
1825	3	305	1839	10	1,845	1853	86	61,044

Number and tonnage of all iron vessels built on the Clyde (figures
for 1846-52 from paper by John Strang, read to Statistical Section of
British Association meeting at Belfast, Sept. 7, 1852; for 1853-62, evidence given by John Scott of Greenock before the Royal Commission
on the Depression of Trade and Industry in 1886):

Year	No.	Tonnage	Year	No.	Tonnage	Year	No.	Tonnage
1846	17	7,125	1852	69	49,716	1858	60	40,522
1847	23	11,514	1853	79	54,750	1859	78	35,705
1848	32	10,292	1854	129	70,530	1860	88	47,833
1849	22	11,513	1855	107	84,750	1861	88	66,801
1850	29	13,791	1856	102	58,530	1862		69,987
1851	41	25,322	1857	98	57,416			

APPENDIX C

Number and tonnage of steam vessels launched and engines constructed at Clyde ports will be found in table below (from paper by John Strang, read to Statistical Section of British Association meeting at Belfast, Sept. 7, 1852).

Year	Wood No.	Wood Tonnage	Iron No.	Iron Tonnage	Total No.	Total Tonnage	Paddles	Screw	Total	HP Wood hull	HP Iron hull	HP Total	For ships not built on Clyde	Avg tonnage Wood	Avg tonnage Iron
Glasgow															
1846			11	5,717	11	5,717	11		11		2,490	2,490	300		519
1847			11	6,152	11	6,152	11		11		2,650	2,650			560
1848			13	4,464	13	4,464	10	3	13	2,810	2,081	4,891	580		344
1849			16	9,799	16	9,799	13	3	16		2,756	2,756	120		606
1850			16	7,255	16	7,255	9	7	16	1,660	2,237	3,897	180		453
1851			20	14,321	20	14,321	11	9	20		4,299	4,299	140		716
1852	1	200	35	22,733	36	22,933	15	21	36	2,140	6,026	8,166	3,400	200	649
Totals	1	200	122	70,441	123	70,641	80	43	123	6,610	22,539	29,149	4,720	200	576
Dumbarton															
1846			5	1,080	5	1,080	2	3	5						216
1847			7	1,439	7	1,439	2	5	7						206
1848			5	650	5	650	2	3	5						130
1849			4	1,264	4	1,264	2	2	4						316
1850			8	3,136	8	3,136	2	6	8		400	400			392
1851			9	3,908	9	3,908	5	4	9		610	610			434
1852			20	18,284	20	18,284	5	15	20		2,605	2,605	200		914
Totals			58	29,761	58	29,761	20	38	58		3,615	3,615	200		512

APPENDIX C—Continued

Year	Wood		Iron		Total		Paddles	Screw	Total	Horse power of engines				Average tonnage	
	No.	Tonnage	No.	Tonnage	No.	Tonnage				Wood hull	Iron hull	Total	For ships not built on Clyde	Wood	Iron
Greenock and Port Glasgow															
1846			1	328	1	328	1		1						328
1847	3	5,485	5	3,923	8	9,408	8		8		1,120	1,120	410	1,828	785
1848	2	2,117	14	5,178	16	7,295	11	5	16		640	640	354	1,059	370
1849	1	285	2	450	3	735	2	1	3		150	150	260	285	225
1850	3	4,813	5	3,400	8	8,213	3	5	8	65	845	910	440	1,604	680
1851	1	2,402	12	7,093	13	9,495	6	7	13		1,260	1,260	800	2,402	591
1852	3	3,029	14	8,699	17	11,728	10	7	17	64	1,424	1,488	2,250	1,010	621
Totals	13	18,131	53	29,071	66	47,202	41	25	66	129	5,439	5,568	4,514	1,393	548
All Ports on Clyde															
1846			17	7,125	17	7,125	14	3	17		2,490	2,490	300		418
1847	3	5,485	23	11,514	26	16,999	21	5	26		3,770	3,770	410	1,828	500
1848	2	2,117	32	10,292	34	12,409	23	11	34	2,810	2,721	5,531	934	1,059	327
1849	1	285	22	11,513	23	11,798	17	6	23		2,906	2,906	380	285	524
1850	3	4,813	29	13,791	32	18,604	14	18	32	1,725	3,482	5,207	620	1,604	475
1851	1	2,402	41	25,322	42	27,724	22	20	42		6,169	6,169	940	2,402	618
1852	4	3,229	69	49,716	73	52,945	30	43	73	2,204	10,055	12,259	5,850	807	720
Totals	14	18,331	233	129,273	247	147,604	141	106	247	6,739	31,593	38,332	9,434	1,309	555

APPENDIX D

STATISTICS OF IRON PRODUCTION

British production prior to application of hot blast:

Year	England and Wales (tons)	Scotland (tons)
1740	17,350	
1788	61,300	7,000
1796	108,973	16,086
1806	243,966	23,240
1823	417,566	24,500

After introduction of hot blast:

Year	England and Wales (tons)	Scotland (tons)
1830	615,917	37,500
1833		44,000
1836		110,240
1839	1,051,021	196,960
1842		276,250
1852	1,926,000	775,000
1861		1,040,000

CHAPTER EIGHT

Ireland—American Finance

The Irish Scene

[*As a contribution to Anglo-Irish understanding, nothing can be more helpful than an objective survey of the Irish scene, assembled by an Irish scholar and embracing the years of social stress which were the prelude to Home Rule and the recognition of Eire. C.R.F.*]

Disraeli, 1844. "I want to see a public man come forward and say what the Irish question is. One says it is a physical question; another a spiritual. Now it is the absence of the aristocracy; now the absence of railways. It is the Pope one day and potatoes the next. . . .

"A dense population in extreme distress inhabit an island where there is an Established Church which is not their Church; and a territorial aristocracy, the richest of whom live in a distant capital. Thus they have a starving population, an absentee aristocracy, an alien Church, and in addition the weakest Executive in the world. Well, what then would honourable gentlemen say if they read of a country in that position? They would say at once "the remedy is revolution." But the Irish could not have a revolution, and why? Because Ireland is connected with another and a more powerful country. Then what is the consequence? The connection with England became the cause of the present state of Ireland. If the connection with England prevented a revolution, and a revolution was the only remedy, England logically is in the odious position of being the cause of all the misery of Ireland. What, then, is the duty of an English Minister? To effect by his policy all those changes which a revolution would do by force. That is the Irish question in its integrity."

Before the Famine, 1830–1845

The problems that faced a dissolving society are stated and illustrated in the following extracts. It was easier to diagnose the disease than to prescribe a remedy. Population had increased from about five millions in 1801 to over eight millions in 1841. In a period of industrial decline, these growing numbers pressed ever more heavily on the land. The results were shown in a progressive shrinking in the size of holding and in a dependence on the potato that became still greater in the years preceding the Famine. At this time, when the long leases that were freely granted in the past were falling in, many landlords resumed direct control of their properties. They found middlemen subletting at profit-rents and occupiers subdividing. The first task of an improving landlord was often to remove as many occupiers as possible. In a country where land afforded practically the only means of obtaining a livelihood, this was not easy; nor could it be accomplished without a struggle. There were remedial measures that could have been taken: cultivation of waste lands, drainage, and above all, instruction in the arts of agriculture. Such measures were recommended by the commission that sat to examine the need for a poor law in 1833–6 and by the Devon Commission that examined land tenure in 1843–5. Even if their recommendations had been accepted, which they were not, such measures were long-term remedies and involved a degree of state intervention that was repugnant to contemporary thought. Inevitably, attention was focused on the immediate over-population instead of on the means by which it might be eased.

"The war with France raised considerably the profits of the occupier, who was thus enabled to pay a large rent to the mesne lessee. These causes produced throughout the country a class of intermediate proprietors, known by the name of middlemen, whose decline after the cessation of the war, and the fall of prices in 1815, brought with it much of the evils we have witnessed of late years. Many who, during the long war, had amassed much wealth, had become proprietors in fee; others, who had not been so successful, struggled in after years to maintain a position in society which their failing resources could not support. Their sub-tenants were unable to pay 'war-rents.' The middleman himself, who had come under rent during the same period, became equally unable to meet his engagements. All became impoverished; the middleman parted with his interest, or underlet the little land he had hitherto retained in his own hands; himself and his family were involved rapidly in ruin. The landlord in many cases was obliged to look to the occupiers for his rent, or, at the expiration of the lease, found the farms covered with a pauper, and, it may be, a superbundant population."*

"A remarkable instance of the various interests possessed in the same estate was detailed respecting a large piece of land in the barony of Kilconnell, county Galway. The proprietor in fee is Mr. Alderman Harty, who purchased from an individual in whose favour it had been confiscated after the battle of Aughrim, in the revolution of 1688. Alderman Harty receives 9d. per acre from Major Warburton, the first lessee; Mr. Handy pays under an old lease, 2/6d. an acre to Major Warburton; John North holds under Mr. Handy, and pays 6/– an acre; John North has sublet to several small tenants, and receives from them on an average of £1.7.0 an acre."†

"The high prices of agricultural produce during the late continental war, and the consequently increased value of land, appear to have much increased subletting, by enabling the large farmers, without personal trouble, to derive from their leaseholds considerable incomes in the form of profit rents.

"The attention of the proprietors has been latterly more called to the ruinous consequences of this practice; and their exertions, aided by the operation of the Subletting Acts, have considerably diminished the frequency of its occurrence. . . .

"Though from the above-mentioned causes, the practice of subletting is now much less prevalent than it formerly was, it appears that the practice of subdividing farms as a provision for the children of tenants still continues to a very great extent, notwithstanding the most active exertions of proprietors and agents.

"This evil is one difficult, or almost impossible to prevent. The parent possessed of a farm looks upon it as a means of providing for his family after his decease, and, consequently, rarely induces them to adopt any other than agricultural pursuits, or makes any

*Her Majesty's Commissioners of Inquiry into the State of the Law and Practice in Respect to the Occupation of Land in Ireland (Devon Commission), *Report* (1845).
†Poor Law Commission, *Third Report* (1836), Appendix F, p. 142.

other provision for them than the miserable segment of a farm, which he can carve for each out of his holding, itself perhaps below the smallest size which can give profitable occupation to a family. Each son, as he is married, is installed in his portion of the ground, and in some cases, even the sons-in-law receive as the dowries of their brides some share of the farm. In vain does the landlord or agent threaten the tenant; in vain is the erection of new houses prohibited, or the supply of turf limited. The tenant relies on the sympathy of his class to prevent ejectment, and on his own ingenuity to defeat the other impediments to his favourite mode of providing for his family.

"The fear of this subdivision, and its ruinous consequences, appear, from the testimony of many, to be the principal causes preventing the grant of leases, as the power of the landlord to resist them, though always insufficient, is considered to be much diminished where the tenant holds by lease, no matter how stringent the convenants against subdivision may be, it being stated that the difficulty of enforcing the covenants in leases is in general very great."[*]

"The general tenor of the evidence given before the commissioners proves that, with the exception of some districts in the north, and some particular localities and estates, or individual farms in other parts of the country, the usual agricultural practice throughout Ireland is defective in the highest degree, whether as regards the permanent preparation and improvement of the land essential to successful tillage, the limited selection of the crops cultivated, or the relative succession and tillage of those crops. . . . It has been stated almost universally throughout the evidence, that the lands in nearly every district of Ireland require drainage; that the drainage and deep moving of the lands or subsoiling have proved most remunerative operations wherever they have been applied; that these operations have as yet been introduced to a very limited extent. . . . Some [witnesses attribute] the apathy that exists to want of capital. . . . Others, and by far the most extensive class of witnesses, attribute the inertia to the fact of the occupiers not

[*]Her Majesty's Commissioners of Inquiry into the State of the Law and Practice in Respect to the Occupation of Land in Ireland, *Digest of Evidence* (Dublin, 1847), pp. 417–19.

having any certainty of receiving compensation, if removed immediately after having effected valuable improvements; and to their not generally having leases, or that security of tenure of their farms which would justify them in expending labour or money in their improvement, as, if they did so, the proprietor would then have the power of immediately increasing the rent."*

"It appears that in Great Britain the agricultural families constitute little more than one-fourth, while in Ireland they constitute two-thirds of the whole population; that there were in Great Britain in 1831, 1,055,982 agricultural labourers; in Ireland, 1,131,715—although the cultivated land of Great Britain amounts to about 34,250,000 acres, and that of Ireland only to about 14,000,000. We thus find that there are in Ireland about five agricultural labourers for every two that there are for the same quantity of land in Great Britain. It further appears that the agricultural produce of Great Britain is more than four times that of Ireland; that agricultural wages of Ireland vary from sixpence to one shilling a day; that the average of the country in general is about eightpence halfpenny; and that the earnings of the labourers come on an average of the whole class to from two shillings to two shillings and sixpence a week or thereabouts for the year round. . . . A great portion of them [the labourers] are insufficiently provided at any time with the commonest necessaries of life. Their habitations are wretched hovels; several of the family sleep together on straw, or on the bare ground, sometimes with a blanket, sometimes not even so much to cover them. Their food commonly consists of dry potatoes; and with these they are at times so scantily supplied as to be obliged to stint themselves to one spare meal in the day. . . . They sometimes get a herring or a little milk, but they never get meat except at Christmas, Easter, and Shrovetide."†

"We perceive then that no general area can be given as to the quantity of land that would support a family; that, in the particular case examined, the ordinary defective method of cultiva-

---

*Her Majesty's Commissioners of Inquiry into the State of the Law and Practice in Respect to the Occupation of Land in Ireland, *Digest of Evidence* (Dublin, 1847), pp. 13-15.
†Poor Law Commission, *Third Report* (1836).

tion requires above one-half more land to support the family as compared with what would be necessary if the occupier knew his trade well, and if the land were in an improved state. But in *ordinary land,* the above mode of calculation would lead us to say, that about eight acres, well improved and well managed, would be as safe a minimum average as could be fixed; and would agree with the opinions of a larger number of the witnesses than any other extent that could be suggested.

"Taking this basis for our calculation . . . we find that there are at present 326,084 occupiers of land (more than one-third of the total number returned in Ireland) whose holdings vary from seven acres to less than one acre; and are, therefore, inadequate to support the families residing upon them.

". . . the consolidation of these small farms, up to eight acres, would require the removal of about 192,368 families, and . . . the first class of improvable waste land in Ireland would furnish to those removed families locations of about eight acres each; or the first and second qualities of improvable waste land, taken together, would furnish them with locations of about twenty acres each.

"[These estimates] do not contemplate the modification that this calculation might admit of, as considering the occupiers of those small holdings partly in the capacity of farmers on their own account, and partly as labourers, deriving a portion of their support from extraneous employment by others. Unfortunately the data do not exist to lead to such an analysis, although they might be easily collected through the poor law department. At the same time, when it is considered that the professed day labouring class is not included in the tables referred to; that the demand for their services is generally stated in the evidence as being quite inadequate to give them employment, even at the low rate of wages prevalent in most districts; that there are only 141,819 farms returned between twenty and fifty acres, 45,394 between fifty and 100 acres, and 25,037 above 100 acres, there can be very little doubt that the full amount of relief suggested by the above calculation would be required to place the supply and demand of the labour market upon any thing approaching to a healthy state."*

*Her Majesty's Commissioners of Inquiry into the State of the Law and Practice in Respect to the Occupation of Land in Ireland, *Digest of Evidence* (Dublin, 1847), pp. 398–400.

"The cause which most frequently, at the present day, leads to the eviction of a number of tenants on a particular estate, is the wish of the proprietor to increase the size of the holdings, with a view to the better cultivation of the land; and when it is seen in the evidence, and in the returns on the size of farms, how minute those holdings are frequently found to be, previous to the change, it cannot be denied that such a step is, in many cases, absolutely necessary, and called for by a due regard to the interest of both landlord and tenant....

"It now frequently happens, that upon the expiration of a long lease, a landlord finds his property occupied by a multitude of paupers, who had obtained an occupation of a few roods or acres, either through the want of a clause against subletting in the former demise, or the failure of the landlord through some legal defect, or his own neglect to enforce that covenant, if existing. Many of these poor people are found living in a most miserable way, and quite incapable of managing their land properly, or so as to derive from their small holdings a sufficient supply even of food for their subsistence.

"It becomes absolutely necessary, with a view even to the condition of the people themselves, as well as towards any general improvement in the country, to make some change.

"A humane landlord, finding himself thus circumstanced, if he is resident, or if he has an intelligent and active agent, will have much communication with the individual occupiers. He will inform himself of their respective position and character. He will select a sufficient number of those best qualified to occupy a farm, and will establish them in holdings of such size as will enable them, with industry, to live comfortably, and to pay a reasonable rent. He will encourage and assist some who may be willing to emigrate. He will aid others in settling themselves on waste land belonging to himself, or will assist them in procuring it from others, and for some of the poorest he will find employment as labourers.

"In this way he will be enabled at the same time to improve the condition of his property, and to benefit the population with which he has had to deal....

"On the other hand, if a landlord, finding a portion of his estate thus overrun with pauper tenants, looks only at the benefit to be derived from a new arrangement of it, without a sufficiently close attention to the effects of this upon individuals, a great extent of misery will often be produced.

"Arrangements hastily adopted—rules arbitrarily laid down and enforced, for the remodelling of estates, grounded perhaps on some preconceived theory in regard to the size of farms—will often be found to disappoint the expectations of the proprietor, and to produce much individual misery, however lavish the expenditure. ... Perhaps the agent after selecting a sufficient number to remain on the farm, advises the giving of a sum of money to the rest. But it is difficult to say what compensation, apart from land, will be adequate in a country where land alone affords a permanent security for food.

"The money is soon spent in the temporary maintenance of the family. They may be willing to labour, but can find no employment.

"Some of them may be ready to emigrate, but require the advice and assistance of a kind friend to put them in the way of taking this step with advantage.

"Others may be desirous of exerting their industry in the reclamation of some waste land, but know not where to apply, or by what means to encounter the first difficulties of such an undertaking.

"Thus it is, that a proceeding which under the existing circumstances of Ireland is often indispensable, may become a source of comfort or of misery, according to the spirit in which it is carried out."*

Tenant Right, 1845–1860

The potato crop failed in the autumn of 1845 and again in 1846. A failure had not been unknown before then but its prolongation over two successive seasons gave the year 1846–7 a gloomy pre-eminence in Irish history. Grain and cattle were produced and exported during those years; but the dependence of the great mass of the population on the potato was so complete that starvation was general. Pestilence succeeded famine; and these years saw also the beginning of the great emigration to the

*Her Majesty's Commissioners of Inquiry into the State of the Law and Practice in Respect to the Occupation of Land in Ireland, *Report* (1845).

United States that lasted into our own times. The census of 1851 showed a population of six and a half millions. The population of Connacht had fallen by 29 per cent compared with 1841, that of Munster by 22 per cent, and those of Leinster and Ulster by 15 per cent.

By its very magnitude so great a catastrophe provided an opportunity that unhappily[1] was not taken. Thousands of small occupiers had been swept away; many landlords, whose finances had never been secure since Waterloo, had been ruined. The Encumbered Estates Acts of 1848 and 1849 were passed to allow the sale of insolvent estates. It was hoped that by this means a new class of more intelligent and more enterprising landlords would be introduced and that the standard of Irish farming would be raised nearer to the level of England or Scotland. These hopes were largely disappointed. Few buyers came from Great Britain; and the bulk of the new proprietors regarded their purchases as a business investment to be dealt with on a business basis.

The continued movement towards consolidation of holdings exacerbated the struggle between landlord and tenant. The findings of the Devon Commission, which suggested the provision of compensation for improvements and favoured short leases, were not implemented. The position of the tenant therefore was as bad after the Famine as it had been before it; and the new type of landlord was less likely to be conscious of his responsibilities than the old. Thus began the struggle that was to last for decades. The rights of property were invoked on one side; the rights of possession on the other. Attention was thus distracted from the task of improving agricultural practice which was delayed until the Land Act of 1881, followed by the Land Purchase Acts, gave legislative recognition to the arguments of J. S. Mill and ushered in a more prosperous and peaceful period.

"A class of men, not very numerous, but sufficiently so to do much mischief, have, through the Landed Estates Court, got into possession of land in Ireland, who, of all classes, are least likely to recognize the duties of a landlord's position. These are small traders in towns, who by dint of sheer parsimony, frequently

[1][But understandably, in view of the fact that English landholding on its improving side was based on regional custom and not on general law. C.R.F.]

combined with money-lending at usurious rates, have succeeded, in the course of a long life, in scraping together as much money as will enable them to buy fifty or a hundred acres of land. These people never think of turning farmers, but, proud of their position as landlords, proceed to turn it to the utmost account. An instance of this kind came under my notice lately. The tenants on the property were, at the time of the purchase, some twelve years ago, in a tolerably comfortable state. Within that period their rent has been raised . . . several times; and it is now, as I am informed by the priest of the district, nearly double its amount at the commencement of the present proprietor's reign. The result is that the people, who were formerly in tolerable comfort, are now reduced to poverty: two of them have left the property and squatted near an adjacent turf bog, where they exist trusting for support to occasional jobs. If this man is not shot, he will injure himself through the deterioration of his property, but meantime he has been getting eight or ten per cent on his purchase-money. This is by no means a rare case. The scandal which such occurrences cause, casts its reflection on transactions of a wholly different and perfectly legitimate kind, where the removal of the tenants is simply an act of mercy for all parties."*

"That duty—the duty for the performance of which I believe that Providence created landlords—is *the keeping down population*. If there were no one whose interest it was to limit the number of the occupants of land, it would be tenanted by all whom it could maintain, just as a warren is tenanted by all the rabbits that it can feed. Competition would force them to use the food that was most abundant—every failure of a crop would produce a famine; they would have no surplus produce, and therefore no division of labour; no manufactures, except the coarse clothing and furniture which every family must produce for itself; no separation of ranks, no literature—in short, no civilization. This is a mere picture of a neglected estate held in rundale in Ireland. . . . To prevent all this, Providence created landlords— a class of persons whose interest it is that the land should produce

*Letter from J. E. Cairnes (1823–75; Whately Professor of Political Economy, Trinity College, Dublin), quoted by J. S. Mill in *Principles of Political Economy* (London, 1909 ed.), p. 338.

as large as possible an amount of surplus produce, and for that purpose should be occupied by only the number of persons necessary to enable it to produce the largest possible amount beyond their own subsistence."*

"Ireland is still governed by two codes: one deriving its validity from Acts of Parliament, and maintained by the magistrate: the other laid down by the tenants and enforced by assassination."†

"Famine supervened, and wholesale emigration; the pressure was lightened in some places, while in others the return of prosperity sustained it. But the Irish farmer remained, as before, faithful to the soil of his holding, and persistent in the vindication of his right to hold it. In the result there has in general survived to him, through all vicissitudes, in despite of the seeming or real veto of the law, in apparent defiance of political economy, a living tradition of possessory right, such as belonged, in the more primitive ages of society, to the status of the man who tilled the soil."‡

"What the case requires is simply this. What is wanted in Ireland is a commission . . . to examine every farm which is let to a tenant, and commute the present variable for a fixed rent. . . . The time is passed for a mere amicable mediation of the State between the landlord and the tenant. There must be compulsory powers, and a strictly judicial enquiry. It must be ascertained in each case . . . what annual payment would be an equivalent to the landlord for the rent he now receives (provided that rent be not excessive) and for the present value of whatever prospect there may be of an increase, from any other source than the peasant's own exertions. This annual sum should be secured to the landlord, under the guarantee of the State. He should have the option of receiving it directly from the national treasury, by being inscribed as the owner of Consols sufficient to yield the amount. Those landlords who are the least useful in Ireland, and on the worst

*Nassau Senior, *Journals, Conversations and Essays Relating to Ireland* (2nd ed., London: Longmans Green), vol. I, p. 276.
†*Ibid.*
‡Commission on the Working of the Landlord and Tenant (Ireland) Act, 1870 (Bessborough Commission), *Report* (1881), p. 4.

terms with their tenantry, would probably accept this opportunity of severing altogether their connection with the Irish soil. Whether this was the case or not, every farm not farmed by the proprietor would become the permanent holding of the existing tenant, who would pay either to the landlord or to the State the fixed rent which had been decided on; or less, if the income which it was thought just that the landlord should receive were more than the tenant could reasonably be required to pay. . . .

"We are told by many . . . that in a generation after such a change, the land of Ireland would be overcrowded by the growth of population, would be sublet and subdivided, and that things would be as bad as before the Famine. . . . Those who still believe that small peasant proprietors are either detrimental to agriculture or conducive to over-population, are discreditably behind the state of knowledge on the point. . . . All prognostics of failure drawn from the state of things preceding the famine are simply futile. The farmer, previous to the famine, was not proprietor of his bit of land; he was a cottier, at a nominal rent, puffed up by competition to a height far above what could even in the most favourable circumstances be paid, and the effect of which was that whether he gained much or little, beyond the daily potatoes of which his family could not be deprived, all was swept off for arrears of rent. Alone of all working people, the Irish cottier neither gained anything by industry and frugality, nor lost anything by idleness and reckless multiplication. That because he was not industrious and frugal without a motive, he will not be industrious and frugal when he has the strongest motive, is not a very plausible excuse for refusing him the chance. There is also another great change in his circumstances since the famine: the bridge to America. If a population should grow up on the small estates more numerous than their production can comfortably support, what is to prevent that surplus population from going the way of the millions who have already found in another continent the field for their labour which was not open to them at home? And the new emigration, there would then be reason to hope, would not, as now, depart in bitterness, nor return in enmity."*

*J. S. Mill, *England and Ireland* (London, 1868), pp. 36–40.

Industry, 1830–1860

Industries, protected and subsidized by the Irish Parliament before the Union of 1801, failed to readjust themselves to the loss of these encouragements or to the impact of the Industrial Revolution. They suffered especially from the lack of capital, a result of conditions in agriculture, and from a lack of skill. The early decades of the century formed a period of decline, offset by the growth of the linen industry around Belfast and of brewing and distilling in the south. On the even of the Famine, Sir Robert Kane aroused considerable interest by his book on the industrial resources of Ireland; its effect died away in the apathy and pessimism that was created by that disaster. The post-Famine years saw the end of the declining manufactures, which could not indeed survive British competition in a contracting market. They saw also, however, the addition of one major industry, Belfast shipbuilding, which dated from the 1850's. By the end of the period these four industries, linen, brewing, distilling, and ship-building, had established themselves in the export market.

"Besides these [the linen and woollen industries] it can scarcely be said that there is any other manufacture in Ireland conducted on so great a scale as to be of so much national importance. Under the now exploded system of bounties and protecting duties, several manufactories sprang up; but not being the natural growth of circumstances favourable to their establishment, most of them gradually disappeared as soon as the undue encouragement, which had created and stimulated them, was withdrawn. Still there are to be found, in every district, establishments of various kinds conducted in the most creditable manner; but they do not exist to such an extent as to claim especial notice in a general view of the employment of the people. . . . But while the manufactures which were formed under the system of bounties have been sinking into decay, the various processes to which agricultural produce is subjected have been gradually extended and improved. Grinding, malting, brewing and distilling have made great progress within these few years. Until lately, the mills of Bristol and Liverpool enjoyed almost the exclusive advantage of converting the Irish wheat into flour. That process is now performed in Ireland. The construction of water-wheels and other machinery has been much improved, and the use of them under favourable circumstances has greatly increased; but there are few large mills in which steam is not united with water power, in order that the supply may be constant and regular during the summer as well as the winter months—a proof of a better system of trading and of more enlarged means. The malting was one of the first in which improvement became manifest; and this has gradually led to greater perfection in the quality of the beer produced. Great breweries have been established in Dublin and Cork. Irish porter is now largely exported to England; and the Dublin bottled porter successfully rivals the London porter, even in London itself. The quality of Irish produce has also considerably improved. Irish butter, Irish pork, and Irish beef bring greater prices in the English market than they did some few years ago; while the quantity produced and exported has much increased. The districts in which these improvements are most manifest are those of Cork, Waterford, Limerick, and Belfast. From north to south, indications of progressive improvement are everywhere visible, and most so in places which are accessible to the immediate influence of steam navigation; but these signs of growing prosperity are unhappily not so discernible in the condition of the labouring people as in the amount of the produce of their labour."*

"In all operations, therefore, where brute force is required, there is no question but that we possess in Ireland, in the actual population, a vast amount of power. . . . But the labouring force of man must be considered as lying truly dormant, so far as its true uses are concerned, until it be quickened by the energetic fire of industrial education. It is in this respect that Ireland is actually weakest, and that most difficulty may be expected in any future development of our industry. No matter to what side we turn, or what problem of manufacturing or agricultural improvement we proceed to, we find the difficulty of procuring skilled workmen or superintendents, and hence all such positions are occupied by natives of the sister island, to the exclusion, as it would appear unfair, of the natives of this country. Such an idea

*Commissioners Appointed to Consider and Recommend a General System of Railways for Ireland, *Second Report* (1838).

is, however, quite unjust. Irishmen are not appointed to those situations because they are not educated for them. Scotchmen and Englishmen obtain them because they learn what is necessary for such duties. The remedy for this is not to declaim against intruding foreigners, but to learn these trades so well as to make it the direct interest of the employer to give his country-men the preference. Every intelligent Englishman or Scotchman who comes to Ireland should not be looked upon as an intruder but as a schoolmaster. . . .

"No person really conversant with the progress of industry in the two countries would assert that there is more combination here than in Great Britain. . . . [But] besides the fact of the importance of such strikes [in Ireland] being magnified by the unwholesome appetite for political excitement which pervades this country, there is another, perhaps still more influential in its operation upon trade. Employers are in Ireland much less able to stand out against strikes than in the sister kingdom. They possess less capital; its rapid circulation is a matter of more pressing necessity, and hence any temporary interruption is more felt. But still more important is the circumstance, that in Ireland, employers are more dependent on their men, than those of the same class in England. They do not in general know their own trade as well. . . .

"There is another circumstance, so popularly counted on as a most material obstacle to the development of industry in Ireland, that I cannot leave the subject without briefly adverting to it, that is, the want of capital. This has been the bugbear of Irish enterprize for many years. . . . We leave our fields in barrenness, our mines unsought, our powers of motion unapplied, waiting for English capital. . . . If some money be made in trade in Ireland . . . it is withdrawn from trade, and stock is bought, or land is bought, yielding only a small return, but one with the advantage of not requiring intense exertion or intelligence, and free from serious risk. Capital cannot, therefore, increase with a rapidity at all commensurate with English progress; but that capital of great amount does truly exist in Ireland available for industrial uses, is certain. . . .

"The fault is not in the country, but in ourselves; the absence of successful enterprize is owing to the fact, that we do not know how to succeed; we do not want activity, we are not deficient in mental power, but we want special industrial knowledge."[*]

AMERICAN FINANCE, 1842–1843[†]

J. Horsley Palmer[1] *to William Cotton, Governor of the Bank of England*

(By courtesy of the Bank of England)

Letter I

"NEW YORK
30 June 1842.

"Matters are singularly interesting at the present time in this country, but I have thought that you might not object to be troubled with a line from myself in addition to the business matter of Sampson's letters; which I take for granted will merely relate to the effects of the Bankrupt law and other causes annihilating debts owing to those accounts he came here to examine, while the securities taken for debts settled will require no end of time to realise. To attempt that course at present is perfectly useless as a general measure. I have had some trouble and no little annoyance in looking after these concerns that were the immediate object of my visit here, and though the security may eventually be ample to cover the advance, yet it has been not a little mortifying to find that a desire to serve particular parties should by their want of common sense have been totally defeated. I shall probably be detained here until the end of Sept[r], hoping by that time to have put all matters straight. Pray look to my waitings[2] till the middle of October, and I will readily repay any

[*]Sir Robert Kane, *The Industrial Resources of Ireland* (2nd ed., Dublin, 1846), pp. 401 ff.
[†]Extracts by courtesy of the Governor and Company of the Bank of England.
[1]John Horsley Palmer (1779–1850), Director of the Bank, 1811–1857, Deputy Governor, 1828–1830, Governor, 1830–1833; Director of London Assurance Company, 1808–1811; author of *Causes and Consequences of the Pressure upon the Money Market* (London, 1837).
[2]The reference is to attendance at the Committee of "Daily Waiting," which was obligatory on all members of the Court and necessitated their attendance at the Bank in rotation for a week at a time to hold certain keys and to resolve points

kindness I may receive from other friends prior to that time.

"Now for a little dose of politics, currency etc. Nothing can exceed the attention and civilities that I have received from all parties both here and at Washington. Until I had visited the latter city, and seen the principal people there, I was not prepared to offer any opinion either as to the past, present or future prospects bearing upon the singular position of public credit in this country filled as it is to brim with all the elements of property and industry and productions of every kind with which the earth is blessed.

"The reckless proceedings of Jackson and Biddle have ended in that most wild and unmanageable joint stock banking system, which portends every species of speculation by the loan of their subscribed capital, deposits and circulation to a very great extent upon lands and other inconvertible securities, and brought to the ground first the private credit of individuals and subsequently themselves with all the ephemeral institutions they had tended to promote thro'out the country. This destruction of credit, both public and private, naturally brings in its train the whole credit currency of the Union, and tho' the banking interest of the Eastern States has maintained its ground, yet it is found in the unnatural state of being under the necessity of retaining, I believe, near double the amount of specie against their circulation in order to preserve their credit at the expense of the mercantile and other classes of the country. As for the Banks of the South and West, the major part are said to be so locked up in advances upon dead and inconvertible *stuff* that most, if not the whole of them, must be wound up. Those who maintain their ground most naturally keep pressing upon their debtors for payment, while the same necessity as exists with the Banks in the South will prevent their affording that usual accommodation essential in a healthy state of the circulation. This pressure upon the industrious classes for payment of debts, created during the excess of former years, is stated to be severe, but which time will to a certainty remove, for the

---

in the banking and general business which would be referred to them. Obviously Horsley Palmer's absence in New York obliged him to find a substitute in this Committee, which presumably meant that he would have to make up the time when he returned. The Committee is now obsolete, the work which it did being a part of the duties of the Executive Directors of the present day.

industry and productions are both progressing—cotton and tobacco with rice in the South and agricultural produce in the Western States, for which an improved market is expected in Canada under the new English tariff. Whether meant as a joke or otherwise I know not—but it was seriously stated the other day that the people of Ohio were seriously contemplating competing with the whale fishery in the production of spermaceti from their innumerable herds of swine. Putting aside however all such stories, there can be no doubt but that a moderate time will force the country into power by its own internal strength, assisted as it is by an immigration constantly and daily taking place by hundreds— indeed almost by thousands. Still, while the restoration is gradually taking place, we must in the meantive look at the state of public credit which is so depressed that the Gov^t, without any debt worth mentioning, and after honorably discharging all former debts, finds itself unable to borrow either at home or abroad a million Sterling. Bad as is the present state of private credit and defective as is the condition of the general currency, this strange want of power to move on the part of the Federal Gov^t seems to me to be mainly attributable to the state of political parties. The first measure indispensable for the restoration of credit is an adequate revenue to meet all the liabilities of the State: and tho' all parties, Whigs, Democrats and Locofocos,[3] admit this truism, yet they each have their own separate objects to promote—some for revenue alone—others for a tariff giving protection to home industry—some for applying the Public Lands in aid of Revenue, others adhering to their distribution among the several States, or making them available for the discharge of their respective debts.

"While all these measures are bandied about, the Treasury becomes empty—a loan is authorised by Congress, but no promise being made to meet even the interest, all parties have stood aloof. While at Washington, I enquired why the Minister did not insist upon the main question of revenue being put forward by their friends and persisted in until a decision had been obtained one way or another, the answer I got from those in authority was simply that

---

[3] A self-lighting cigar from *loco*-motive and its *fuoco* fire; applied to the anti-monopoly party of New York Democrats because at a meeting in 1835 the Tammany Democrats put out the lights, and the meeting lit candles and locofocos.

the President was in a minority in both Houses—a pretty and hopeful state this for the greatest nation upon Earth (in Yankee opinion) for freedom and liberty. Coupled with this most vital matter—revenue—arose a discussion upon the State of the Currency, and the objections raised to the formation of a National Bank. Seeing what an exposé the last has made, I confess that I should think it a false step to attempt the establishment of a new one based upon the same principles for issue and banking agency. My own opinion is in favour of the Exchequer Plan, as set forth by the Secretary of the Treasury, divested of all banking privileges and confined to issue alone and regulation of the internal exchange by transfer from one part of the Union to the other—the limitation of issue being in the first instance fixed at 15 million with a reserve of 5—all further issues being made on specie alone, convertible at the Head Office of Issue *alone,* but receivable anywhere for Gov^t dues.

"This approval of the Gov^t plan gave great satisfaction to the President, and I was subsequently asked whether it would be agreeable to offer that opinion in writing—which I as courteously declined, having no desire to mix myself up in party strife, and to be run down, as I most certainly should be by one party or another for my presumption—whereas I now stand well with all, even the Press, which is rather a singular fact—notwithstanding my intention to be a mere byestander; yet I think the principle of one Issue separate from Banking is gaining ground, and will be likely to be adopted a few years hence when a little more light has shone upon that subject in England. As to the repudiation of State debts, I have not met with a single person who advocated such a doctrine from the President downwards, all maintain that every shilling, principal and interest, will eventually be paid, but until the credit of the General Government be restored, and the currency be placed upon some more sufficient basis through the working of a sound banking system, it is impossible to move. Looking to the revenue of the several states there are various ways short of general assumption by the Federal Gov^t by which they can be aided in the general restoration of credit. Some field I have no doubt will eventually be acted upon. In the meantime some of the leading works are slowly carrying on, which when complete will give considerable aid by the revenues they will afford. The *main* railroad lines are essential in a National point of view and for their use the Gov^t appears willing (*where able*) to offer liberal terms.

"As a summary of all I have to say—let the Gov^t establish a full revenue to meet all their expenditure—then let the Public upon that security offer such loan as they may require. Lay the foundations of a sound Gov^t issue, *limited in amount,* unconnected with any banking power—and then perhaps 2 or 3 years hence opportunity may come for carrying thro' their difficulties all the now non-paying States by the aid of public lands and various other measures then at their disposal.

"Excuse this long scrawl and believe me
very truly yours
J. HORSLEY PALMER"

[Between Letters I and II the following quotation from Lord Lytton's *Alice* seems in place: ". . . money so scarce—speculation so sure in America—great people the Americans—rising people—gi-gi-giants—giants!"]

Letter II

"NEW YORK
15 Sept. 1843

"What a strange alteration I am witnessing in the internal state of this country compared with that which existed when I was here only 12 months since. All the change seems to have been effected by the bullion imports of the last year, which, cheapening money in a degree never before seen in the States, has set everything in motion—not only stocks of all kinds, but produce of every description, foreign and domestic, is passing from one end of the Union to the other. One of the chief woollen dealers told me a few days since he had never experienced so active a demand since the autumn of 1835, and coming upon very small stocks in hand had occasioned orders to some considerable amount being transmitted by the Steamers of the last two months to the old country; I trust therefore that our manufacturing districts are beginning to feel the benefit of the change on this side of the Atlantic. The Exchange you will see is high which is to be accounted for—when there are no produce bills on the market of any moment—by the large remittances on demand for payment of imports, of which I calculate a portion may consist in the non-paying stocks which our own countrymen and the Dutch are throwing back upon the market with a grievous loss to the holders. At the present prices of those securities I fancy the American stock market will take off as much as may be offered under the conviction universally prevalent here that at no distant day they will all be paid, tho' no one is able to tell you how or when. I confess myself to be of that opinion, and acting upon it decline selling a dollar of the amount in which I am now interested— Under that feeling, I thought you a little quick in making some sales of Alabama through Prime & Co. (I think a little above 50) now worth 67. That State, I am told, tho' the last to resume specie payment, will punctually meet all her engagements. The worst case, and which has done more mischief to the credit of the Union than any other, is that of Pennsylvania for which no excuse can be offered. It is now said that her interest will be paid in August 1844, presuming that they must then fund the arrears, for without a large taxation which I have no idea of the legislature imposing they cannot find the means to meet that amount.

"I have had some conversation with Blatchford relating to the assets still outstanding and belonging to the suspended Houses and confess that were the property my own, I would not only withhold forcing the sale for a 12 months, but where there are 1st mortgages on the property carrying 7% p.a. interest actually receivable from the Estates, I would authorise the redemption and thereby be enabled to take advantage of such private offers of sale as may hereafter be presented, which cannot be so easily done when the 1st mortgages are held by other parties. I allude to such properties as those in the City of Buffalo, and the warehouses belonging to the Estate of Wiggins. In the first there is a prior charge of 10,000 which (though the quantity of land is only ½ of what Sampson imagined) being discharged will, so far as I am informed, place the property under the controul of the agency here, and become valuable building ground, for the extension of that City is as certain as that of New York. I don't pretend to know the location, but Sampson does. I am merely repeating what I hear from Blatchford, with the evidence before me of a manifest advancing value on all property without any symptom at present of going ahead [*sc.* without restraint] so frequently seen on this side of the water.

"As regards my own movement I can say nothing at present. The lawyers make great professions of amity and goodwill, but whether I shall be able to make them act in that spirit is perhaps a little uncertain. I shall however complete everything that I came here to do with the litigation and must leave the decision to the Chancellor of the State.

"In the meantime the property is in safe keeping and daily improving in value. I do not therefore imagine that much will be lost by the delay beyond interest of money and that only in parts, pray then do what you can for me in my waitings. It shall if possible be the last time of my undertaking such distant trips.

"My best regards to your Deputy and all other friends.

P.S.

"I found that the Shipping lines are really taking advantage of our Tariff of last year in sending rather large quantities of provisions (beef, cheese, etc.) by almost every packet now sailing for Liverpool.

"I have not seen any late returns of the Bank, but understand those of N/Y to hold upwards of 13 million of specie (dollars) against little more than 3 million of circulation.

"Charleston not very different from former times, and below that City the circulation consists almost entirely of specie, with the exception of Alabama, which however is said to be on the eve of returning to a specie basis."

[Thus Horsley Palmer kept his Governor posted on the American financial scene, 1842–3; but by 1845 the dispute over the Oregon boundary, which threatened to end in war and was the occasion of a famous memorandum by the Duke of Wellington on Canada and its defences, February 1846, made finance of secondary importance for the time being.]

William Cotton to the Chancellor of the Exchequer

March 20 1845

". . . I hope the Americans will not give you any additional trouble or disturb the peace we heard so much of on Monday. The consols fell 5/8%."

CHAPTER NINE

With Faraday in London

I TAKE you finally to the London of a century ago, a metropolis of government, culture, and trade: as large then, relatively to the rest of England, as is the Greater London of today, and yet not so large that it cannot be epitomized in the person of a man who influenced more profoundly than any other one person its intellectual and industrial development both during his lifetime and after his death.

He was born in a London suburb (Newington); reared as a child in Jacob's Wells Mews; apprenticed to a bookbinder, M. Riebau at 2 Blandford Street; spent most of his working life in the Royal Institution, Albemarle Street, Piccadilly, W.; lived in retirement at Hampton Court; and was buried at Highgate in the same cemetery as Karl Marx. The gravestone reads:

Michael Faraday
Born 22 September
1791
Died 25 August
1867
Sarah His Wife
Born 7 January
1800
Died 6 January
1879

Thus he was a Londoner through and through, though his father was of Yorkshire stock. London made him: and he, following Davy, made London a focal point of high scientific research. Before he died he was London's universal consultant, as sought after and as admired as the greatest specialist in Harley Street. Punch hon-

oured him with a cartoon of praise, thus raising him to its immortals. We may place him among his contemporaries thus:

1791-1867   Michael Faraday of the Royal Institution
1785-1864   Leonard Horner of the Factory Inspectorate

preceding whom were

1778-1829   Humphrey Davy (1815, the miner's safety lamp)
1771-1858   Robert Owen (1816, the *New View of Society*)

And one year must be imprinted on our minds, 1831. For in that
year, when London was distracted by reform bills and cholera,
Faraday discovered the laws of electro-magnetism, to which
James Clerk Maxwell, born in this same year, subsequently gave
mathematical form, the combination of the two being of epochal
importance to physical science and the electrical trades.

How the Almighty managed it one can but guess—Watt, Ohm,
Ampère: Galvani, Volta, Oersted: mixed together in a Leyden
jar and the result a "stream of force" in the philosophic brain of
a blacksmith's son, reared in a London mews; with no "birth," no
property, and only the education which he gave himself; yet
giving to educationists in famous final evidence a guide to science
teaching in schools and college which is valid for all time.

He was, however, a poor economist, being quite immune to
the profit bug: "My desire to escape from Trade, which I thought
vicious and selfish, and enter into the service of Science which I
imagined made its pursuers amiable and liberal, induced me at
last to take the bold and simple step of writing to Sir H. Davy,
expressing my wishes and a hope that if an opportunity arose he
would favour my views; at the same time, I sent the notes I had
taken of his lectures." The notes (preserved) are in a clear and
orderly hand, put together with the neatness of an industrious
apprentice, and they appealed to the dashing flamboyancy of
Davy. And so Faraday became in 1813 Davy's assistant, or "lab.
boy" as we should say. He had only been able to attend the lectures because a certain Mr. Dance had given him a ticket for
them.

A trinity of circumstances made London an ideal workplace
for a Faraday.

1. The London of 1820-50 was renowned for its engineering and engineers. The canal boom of the previous generation had left several debouching on the Thames, in particular the Regent's Canal, which traversed the northern part of the metropolis. And London, lit hitherto by candles (incidentally the subject of Faraday's most famous Christmas lecture), was now being supplied with coal gas on the commercial scale by the Gas Light and Coke Company (1820). Gas came under the purview of Faraday thus: the Portable Gas Company—so called because it prepared, by heating animal oil, an oil gas which was compressed into metal cylinders and carried round to the homes in which it was used—provided him with an oil liquor, which by research in 1815 he had shown to be a bicarburet of hydrogen, our benzene. "It has been said that three quarters of organic chemistry is concerned with benzene and its derivatives. In particular from the series of hydrocarbons, of which benzene is the first, has come the coal-tar industry."

More important to London than canals were docks, bridges, and waterways. In our key year, 1831, Rennie's new London Bridge was opened. In 1843, after a standstill of fifteen years, the Thames (foot) Tunnel was engineered by Sir Marc Isambard Brunel. Faraday and the two Brunels, M. I. the father and I. K. the son, were friends; and there is a letter to one of them from him, arranging for a river trip and enclosing a a map for guidance to the embarkation point. There is another from Brunel *père* to Faraday of February 1836: "Could one use every kind of coal gas without confining ourselves to that made by the Metropolitan Gas Company? This Company uses Canel coals. A word or line from you will carry much greater weight among all our interested friends, and most particularly with those who lent us the money to go on with the work."

The railways followed the canals. The first main line to reach London was the London and Birmingham, 1838. The ambitious project of I. K. Brunel to connect London with New York by a broad gauge line to Bristol and thence by fast steamer service to America did not work out altogether as he hoped, but it was the prelude to the Atlantic greyhound, which in conjunction with the new river and channel steam-boat services made the Thames

Estuary for a time a centre of iron shipbuilding, as it had long been of wooden shipbuilding. It added to Faraday's work, as adviser to Trinity House, and to the importance of applying electricity to beacon lights. It added also to the dirt of Father Thames. The steam-engines of Watt, developed for the drainage of Cornish mines, were bettered by the Cornish engines of Richard Trevithick, which were installed first in 1848 by Thomas Wicksteed in the East London Water Works at Old Ford, thereby inaugurating a new era in water supply. The Thames, with its growing volume of traffic and population, was now a cesspool of sewage, and so dangerous to public health that in 1852 the intake for water supply was removed to above Teddington.

Faraday took his part in the public health campaign, writing a strong letter to *The Times*, which was the occasion of Punch's cartoon. I give the letter from *The Times* (July 9, 1855), the Punch cartoon—see page 199—and Mr. Punch's commentary (July 21, 1855).

THE STATE OF THE THAMES.

TO THE EDITOR OF THE TIMES.

Sir,—I traversed this day by steamboat the space between London and Hungerford bridges between half-past 1 and 2 o'clock; it was low water, and I think the tide must have been near the turn. The appearance and the smell of the water forced themselves at once on my attention. The whole of the river was an opaque pale brown fluid. In order to test the degree of opacity, I tore up some white cards into pieces, moistened them so as to make them sink easily below the surface, and then dropped some of these pieces into the water at every pier the boat came to; before they had sunk an inch below the surface they were indistinguishable, though the sun shone brightly at the time; and when the pieces fell edgeways the lower part was hidden from sight before the upper part was under water. This happened at St. Paul's-wharf, Blackfriars-bridge, Temple-wharf, Southwark-bridge, and Hungerford; and I have no doubt would have occurred further up and down the river. Near the bridges the feculence rolled up in clouds so dense that they were visible at the surface, even in water of this kind.

The smell was very bad and common to the whole of the water; it was the same as that which now comes up from the gullyholes in the streets; the whole river was for the time a real sewer. Having just returned from out of the country air, I was, perhaps, more affected by it than others; but I do not think I could have gone on to Lambeth or Chelsea, and I was glad to enter the streets for an atmosphere which, except near the sinkholes, I found much sweeter than that on the river.

I have thought it a duty to record these facts that they may be brought to the attention of those who exercise power or have responsibility in relation to the condition of our river; there is nothing figurative in the words I have employed, or any approach to exaggeration; they are the simple truth. If there be sufficient authority to remove a putrescent pond from the neighbourhood of a few simple dwellings, surely the river which flows for so many miles through London ought not to be allowed to become a fermenting sewer. The condition in which I saw the Thames may perhaps be considered as exceptional, but it ought to be an impossible state, instead of which I fear it is rapidly becoming the general condition. If we neglect this subject, we cannot expect to do so with impunity; nor ought we to be surprised if, ere many years are over, a hot season give us sad proof of the folly of our carelessness.

I am, Sir, your obedient servant,

M. FARADAY.

Royal Institution, July 7.

Mr. Punch's commentary takes the form of gentle irony, and runs:

A PHILOSOPHER AFLOAT

A CHEMICAL work of small size and great importance has been lately published. The production alluded to is FARADAY ON THE THAMES; a title which means even more than it appears to mean; for it not only expresses PROFESSOR FARADAY's views of the composition of the river, but also describes the sensations experienced by him during a period of brief transit upon its surface. A piece of white card, according to the professor, becomes invisible at a very small degree of submersion in the Thames water; which is of a peculiar colour—"opaque pale brown"—drab—quakerish—and a not very peculiar smell, because it partakes of that of the sinkholes; and may be described as odoriferous but not fragrant. We have often had great pleasure in hearing FARADAY explain the composition of water, pure and simple; but we rejoice much more that he has enabled the public to form a correct idea of the constituents of that of the Thames; which consists of something more than Oxygen and Hydrogen. Because we are losing brave men by war, it is rather the more desirable than otherwise that we should not also lose useful citizens by pestilence, as we certainly shall if the Thames continues much longer to be an open sewer. We hope that PROFESSOR FARADAY's publication, which takes the shape of a concise letter to the 'Times' will effect a saving of human life still greater than that which has resulted from his predecessor's safety-lamp. DAVY's invention prevents carburetted hydrogen from blowing up miners; may FARADAY's epistle avert cholera and typhus, by stirring up senatorial and municipal persons to prevent sulphuretted hydrogen from being disengaged.

In the cartoon Faraday is giving his card to the Thames—see letter. Note the bedraggled grime of Father Thames, and the monster rats, carriers of disease, floating belly up. Edwin Charwick and his Board of Health had been fighting cholera since 1848.

But Punch must have his joke at the Professor's specialty, as in this of January 17, 1865: "Just look at the facilities afforded to us by electricity. It is now 6 o'c and we are in Fleet Street, and this message was only sent from Oxford Street yesterday afternoon at 3."

2. Faraday's London was the London of the new medicine. It is fitting that in the Exhibition of Medicine in 1850, showing, 1950, at 28 Portman Square, W. 1, the visitor should find on the ground floor two cabinets of illustrations: the Florence Nightingale cabinet and the Faraday cabinet. In the former is the "command" portrait of Miss Nightingale with all the great hospitals around her, and, below, the hospital scenes in the Crimea depicting the Lady of the Lamp on her famous rounds. The metropolis housed the very rich and the many poor, and on this duality medicine was built up. The only lack was "subjects," which, however, the Jerry Crunchers[1] and Irish steam-boats supplied. The frontispiece of the catalogue is rightly Justus von Liebig by Trautschold (1845), which places it within the ambit of economic history; for his *Chemistry in Its Application to Agriculture and Physiology*, translated in 1840 by his pupil Lyon Playfair, marked the transformation of agriculture, already an art, into a science. Science was coming into its own. The Prince Consort surrounded himself with men of science—English and German in particular; and he made the Exhibition of 1851 an

[1]Not Geriatrists—they are persons who find out why you grow old. The badge of the one is an ageratum; of the other a sprig of London Pride, resting on pickaxes proper.

FARADAY GIVING HIS CARD TO FATHER THAMES;

And we hope the Dirty Fellow will consult the learned Professor.

Cartoon from Punch

International Science Exchange. From Farmer George to Poly-technic Albert!

The doctors were attracted to Faraday both by the quality of his research and by its practical application to their own pro-fession. In *Chambers's Technical Dictionary* after "farad," "Fara-day cage,—effect,—tube,—disc,—ice,—pail,—law of induction," comes

faradaic currents (Med.) currents obtained from an induction coil and used for curative purposes
faradism (Med.) The treatment of disease by the use of an interrupted current obtained from an induction coil, the wave-form being very peaky.

3. Faraday's London was the capital not only of a country but of an empire; and the Royal Institution with its great classical columns and its beautiful eighteenth-century interior was worthy of its metropolitan role. Every library in the English-speaking world should possess the portrait and life of its founder, Sir Ben-jamin Thompson, Count Rumford of the Holy Roman Empire (1753-1814). A British Sir, a continental Count, taking his title from the Massachusetts township of his wife, he was by birth an American. He lived now in America, now in Paris under the protection of the First Consul, now in Germany in the service of the Bavarian army; and his mind travelled as much as his body. He proposed at first an institution which would make science useful to the poorer classes by introducing model kitchens and improved heating—hence the Count Rumford stove, a specimen of which adorns the library of the Royal Institution, having above it the round stereoscopic mirror into which Faraday loved to peer—and as adjuncts thereto lectures, laboratory, and library. But the success of the means quickly changed the end. "We have found," writes Rumford in 1801, "a nice able man as lecturer Humphrey Davy. Bernard [Sir Thomas Bernard, philanthropist] says they are crazy about it."

Davy saved the Institution from early death; in the "they" were the nobility and intelligentsia of London, statesmen, savants, and City magnates (it was the City then of J. J. Anger-stein and the Barings and other patrons of art). Science at Davy's hand became vastly popular, but not *mirabile dictu* as popular science. It was fundamental experiment, done in the laboratory in the basement of the Institution and illustrated in the lecture hall above. Davy, indeed, was not more eloquent than the Rev. Sydney Smith, whose lectures on moral philosophy filled the hall for three years, but he had more to offer; and in unimagined novelty his results excelled even those of Faraday later. He began, on request, with practical science, the chemistry of tanning, the chemistry of agriculture—his book on this held the field until Liebig—but his pleasure and his fame came from electro-chemistry. "The discovery of potassium and sodium and their preparation by an electrolytic method [Oct. 1811] so delighted him that he danced about the room in an ecstasy." Utterly fearless, he more than once risked the life of himself and his assistant.

Such was Faraday's London.

Faraday, like his chief Davy, approached electricity through chemistry and, as he approached it, took metallurgy in his stride. This is the theme of Sir Robert Hadfield's centenary appreciation, *Faraday and His Metallurgical Researches* (1931). The frontispiece of the book is a photo of a plaque cast in steel. On the right is the box labelled by him, in which the seventy-nine specimens of steel, now in a show-case, were discovered, and on the left the blast furnace in which the work was done. "From early manhood until his closing years, he made one discovery after another, some being of such importance that vast industrial enterprises have since arisen from them. Almost the entire electrical industry of to-day is founded on his discovery of the phenomenon of electromagnetic induction."

Every writer on Faraday—Bence Jones, T. Martin, E. W. Ashcroft—endeavours to leave two impressions: the practical importance of his discoveries, and the artistry of his technique in experiment and exposition. Sir Robert concludes:

. . . in the field of alloys of steel, Faraday's work [1819–1824] stands out brightly on the dark background of an almost complete absence of any previous knowledge concerning this subject. His alloys may appear humble and imperfect beside the efforts and productions of to-day, and he would undoubtedly marvel at all that has been accomplished since he worked with his little "blast furnace," but let us not forget that in this field, too, his fame stands out in high relief between the background of the eighteenth century and the foreground of the twentieth.

Long acknowledged as a leading chemist and as the founder of the electricity industry, Faraday is now seen to have been a metallurgical investigator of great ability and brilliant inspiration.

Chemist, metallurgist, physicist, is there anything else that he was: anything that he was not? The answer, in both cases, is "Yes."

He was a universal consultant. His contribution to the sanitation of the Thames we have noticed. He was consulted by Barry on the acoustics of the new Houses of Parliament; by Sir Antony Panizzi on the substratum on which to lay the gold for the ribs of the cupola of the new Reading Room in the British Museum (1856) and on the treatment of the surfaces of the Museum sculptures (1857). This was public service of the same order as his contacts with professional friends—with J. P. Joule, who writes to him (1845): "I now feel quite certain that the heat which can increase the temperature of a pound of water by a degree is equal to about 800 pounds raised a foot high," and with James Nasmyth and the two Brunels.

He was a model teacher. In his youth he allotted a portion of his day to elocution. In his lecturing he set before himself a list of "Dont's":

Never to repeat a phrase.
Never to go back to amend.
If at a loss for a word, not to Eh! Eh! Eh! but to stop and wait for it.
Never to botch an experiment.

How often have we, on the Arts side, writhed under lecturers who "mean to say" and "sort of," and jeered at slides which come in the wrong way up or are undecipherable even by the lecturer! And because he was a supreme teacher, he had a philosophy of education which could not only stand up to cross-examination but even carry his examiners with him, as his evidence of 1862 before the Public Schools Royal Commission shows.

And now for what he was not. He was not a John Tyndall. He writes to Lady Lovelace:

Religious conversation is generally in vain. There is no philosophy in my religion. I am of a very small and despised set of Christians known, if known at all, as Sandemanians and our hope is founded on the faith that is in Christ. But though the natural words of God can never by any probability come at contradiction with the higher things that belong to our future existence—and must with everything concerning Him ever glorify Him, still I do not think it at all necessary to tie the natural ends of religion together, and in my intercourse with my fellow creatures that which is religious and that which is philosophical have ever been two distinct things.

To Tyndall the physicist and Huxley the biologist this was to surrender the field to the bishops—to surrender it also to the "saintly Keble," who, when Oxford gave to Faraday, Dalton, and others a D.C.L. at the British Association of 1832, sneered at this "hodge-podge" of philosophers.

He was not an Oliver Lodge. I have only one letter from Faraday, and that was a polite refusal. We were operating then at 326 Regent Street and sent him an invitation to our seance. "The Honour of Dr. Faraday's company is requested at a private seance to be given by the Bros. Davenport and Mr. Fay." To which the veteran replied, October 8, 1864: "I leave those [manifestations] to which you refer in the hands of the Professors of Legerdemain. If spirit communications not entirely worthless should happen to start into activity I shall trust the spirits to find out for themselves how they can move my attention. I am tired of them." But in a later existence I had my revenge, in the person of my son, F. S. Fay, an electrical engineer in the service of A. Reyrolle and Company, Hebburn-on-Tyne, who pays tribute to the discoveries of Faraday in these words:

Towards the close of the 18th century there was a great renaissance in scientific observation and investigation. It was occurring not only in England but in many other European countries and, despite the times, there was a reasonable interchange of knowledge. The outlook of the scientist in those days was however different from that of his modern counterpart. In the first place the sciences were completely isolated from one another and no vital connection was looked for between the laws governing even allied sciences and secondly notwithstanding the separation of the sciences the same men studied them all.

Michael Faraday was no exception and experimented in a number of fields, as for example chemistry, electricity and light. His work, which was characterised by thoroughness and attention to detail, resulted amongst other things in his remarkable discoveries in the field of electricity and magnetism.

When Faraday first became interested in electricity Oersted had already shown that an electric current affected a magnetic needle and made it take up a position relative to the direction of the current. Faraday repeated this experiment but went further: and from the position the needle took up concluded that there was a tendency for the separate poles of the magnetic needle to move in circles around the wire. This he proceeded to show but was not satisfied completely, for he was a believer in the law that "to every action there is an equal and opposite reaction." Accordingly he made up a device which showed that a wire carrying current would revolve around the pole of a magnet.

It was in 1831 that Faraday made two of his most important experiments which followed logically from this early work. He knew at that time that a body carrying a static charge could induce a similar charge in a conductor brought into its field of influence and so he set out to prove that a dynamic charge, that is an electric current, would have a similar effect and induce a current in another conductor. To do this he wound two separate coils around an iron ring. The two ends of one coil were led away, connected together and passed over a magnetic needle. The ends of the other coil he connected to a battery. Deflection of the magnetic needle was shown to occur at the moment of connection and disconnection of the battery, showing that a momentary current was induced in the second coil. This was on August 29.

Two months later, on October 17, Faraday made the second important experiment. He plunged a cylindrical magnet into a coil of wire wound on a hollow former [bobbin] and found two things, first that an electric current could be induced in a wire by the movement of a magnet, and second that the current reversed its direction when the magnet was withdrawn.

Shortly after this Faraday rotated the outer edge of a copper disc between the two poles of a strong magnet and found that a current was induced in the disc which could be led away in wires and its effect demonstrated by a magnetic needle or galvanometer.

There is one other experiment in this first series, the result of which should be mentioned. In his own words "This evening at Woolwich experimented with magnet and for the first time got the Mag. Spark myself." By this he meant that he succeeded in obtaining a spark from a current induced by a permanent magnet.

It has been found that for the economical transmission of electrical power over large areas high voltages are necessary. Unfortunately, generating voltages are relatively low and a device for increasing the voltage for transmission becomes imperative. A transformer is such a device and since it was a simple transformer that Faraday made and used in his first important experiment of 1831, it may be claimed that thereby he opened the way to high voltage transmission of electrical power.

In the next experiment Faraday pointed the way to the evolution of the electrical generator, for he showed that by the movement of a wire relative to a magnet a current could be induced in the wire. In the electrical generator a number of conductors are made to revolve in the field of strong magnets and in addition it has been found that by suitable connection of the conductors the resultant current can be made to rise and fall continuously, which is precisely the condition Faraday found necessary for transformation. Thus to these two experiments can be traced the birth of the heavy electrical industry.

The copper disc and the magnet experiments have been mentioned because they illustrate the wide field Faraday covered during his work on induction. The copper disc experiment was the first example of a continuous or direct current machine, whereby mechanical work done in rotating the disc was converted by the use of magnets into electrical energy. And in the magnet experiment Faraday demonstrated that a spark could be obtained from an induced current which laid the foundation for the development of the spark plug used with petrol engines.[2]

Although the experiments of 1831 are the high lights of Faraday's work, they alone are not responsible for his eminence in the World of Science. Each of Faraday's experiments was a logical step from the one before and, rather than a particular step, it was the cumulative effect of all steps which made possible the practical application of electrical phenomena and gave to him his lasting fame.

It is to Faraday and his like who proved and postulated the fundamental principles of science, correlating and knitting together diverse and hitherto unconnected facts, that the World owes the almost unbe-

[2]Hence magneto, a magnetico dynamo used to generate the current for the electrical ignition in some internal combustion engines, being operated by the engine itself.

lievable advance of scientific achievement of the nineteenth century.

As a Cambridge don who has enjoyed the privilege of social intercourse with the great mathematicians and physicists of yesterday, I will make bold to add this for myself. Just as Clerk Maxwell (who wrote the notice of Faraday in the *Encyclopædia Britannica*) paid the most generous of tributes to Faraday when he said elsewhere,

Faraday's original statement remains to this day the only one which asserts no more than can be verified, and the only one by which the theory of the phenomena can be expressed in a manner which is exactly and numerically accurate, and at the same time within the range of elementary methods of exposition,

so the successors of Clerk Maxwell, in celebrating the centenary of *his* birth, show how greatly by the aid of mathematical agencies Maxwell advanced beyond Faraday along the path which Faraday blazed.

Thus Sir James Jeans:

Faraday was above all things an experimenter. . . . By contrast Maxwell began his career by studying the geometry of the regular solids . . . when he crossed the bridge from astronomy to physics, he left behind him forever the prospect of becoming a great mathematical astronomer—but only to become the greatest mathematical physicist the world has seen since Newton.

Sir Joseph Larmor:

If modern development rests on the mental activity of Maxwell, as of W. Thomson and Helmholtz and the other giants, in their turn Maxwell and Thomson had interacted with Faraday and were his interpreters, just as he for long years studied and improved upon Ampère according to his lights. . . . The rapidity with which there had followed, after the preliminary very subtle exploration by Ampère, the presumed electronic state of the intervening medium, its presumed state of stress, to be developed later into arresting mathematical precision by Maxwell, with culmination in 1831 in the law of induction, is surely the proof of Faraday's penetrating familiarity during all those ten years [1821–31] with his relevant ideas of physical interaction to which the want of mathematics perhaps fortunately had drawn him.

Sir J. J. Thomson:

The discovery of electrical waves [through Maxwell, Helmholtz, Hertz] has not merely scientific interest though it was this alone which inspired it. Like Faraday's discovery of electromagnetic induction, it has had a profound influence on civilization; it has been instrumental in providing methods which may bring all the inhabitants of the world within hearing distance of each other and has potentialities, social, educational and political, which we are only beginning to realize.

Sir Oliver Lodge:

. . . And so gradually, by many inventions, a world-wide system of wireless transmission was inaugurated, until to-day a wireless set is a domestic apparatus in nearly every household.

Thus, the whole system of wireless telegraphy is a development of the original and surprising theory of Clerk Maxwell, embodying in mathematical form the experimental researches of Faraday.

(Sir Oliver had explained how in 1901 Marconi found that the waves would curve round the earth to America and beyond.)

We pass from High Physics to the classrooms of the young— to Faraday House, 62-70 Southampton Row (a continuation of Kingsway), W.C. 1, with its syllabus and *Jubilee Year Journal, 1889-1939* before us.

GNOSIS KAI PRAXIS

The College has an unusual history, having been founded as an adjunct to a commercial company for supplying towns with electricity. It covers the whole electrical field, at a level less theoretical than, for example, the City and Guilds Institute at South Kensington, and leads to a diploma (D.F.H.). It is a four-year course: first year at Faraday House, eight months at a mechanical engineering works, five terms at Faraday House, final period as a graduate apprentice at an electrical engineering works; fees £75 p.a.

The examinations are supervised by the Institution of Electrical Engineers (which, incidentally, is at the bottom of the Kingsway tram subway, facing the Embankment, and houses a number of Faraday treasures, including Faraday's journal of his tour in Europe with Humphrey Davy, 1813-15, on a permit from Napoleon). Its two senior scholarships are the Faraday, £75 p.a. and the Maxwell, 40 guineas p.a. Dr. Alexander Russell, the senior lecturer of the college at its foundation, observed with pride at the Jubilee: "Though the average was only about 80 students per annum, one in five of the Presidents of the I.E.E. were Faradians, while of the I.E.E. members who came from all parts of the world, one in 25 was a Faradian."

Never has the health of England, at all ages: never has the education of England at all levels: been as high as it is today in 1950. I have lived and taught in two continents, and making no invidious comparisons, I assert that the youth of England today, mentally and bodily, stand level with their fellows anywhere in the English-speaking world. Such is our final thought on Britain past and present; and as the past gives ground for pride, not unmixed with criticism, so the present is full of hope, apart from war's grim shadow.

Appendix

The evidence of Michael Faraday, F.R.S., November 18, 1862, before the Royal Commission on the Revenues and Management of Certain Colleges and Schools* runs to approximately 12,000 words, and merits reprinting in full as a pamphlet by the physics department of some University. I must be content here with reproducing the official analysis of it.

"FARADAY, MICHAEL, Esq., F.R.S.

Was for 20 years lecturer on chemistry at Woolwich for the Government; is one of the originally nominated senate of the London University; has been in the habit of lecturing at the Royal Institution for many years; also of giving juvenile lectures. Not being an educated man, according to the usual phraseology, and therefore not being able to make a comparison between languages and natural knowledge, but regarding it only as a means of conveying thought, thinks that the fact of conveying knowledge of the physical sciences which has been so abundantly given to the world during the last 50 years should not be conveyed to the young in public schools, a matter so strange that he finds it difficult to understand it. Habit and prejudice arising from pre-existing

*Royal Commission on the Revenues and Management of Certain Colleges and Schools, and the Studies Pursued and Instruction Given Therein, *Report* (1864, XXI).

conditions are the causes. The opposition, however, is breaking away; there are good, strong-minded, willing men at work to promote education in these things; they are knocking, there is a prospect of the door being opened, and it must be opened, or England will stand behind other nations in the mode of education. Gives instances, in connection with the lighthouses of England and France, of the superiority of the French common man over the English; the ordinary intelligent workman so common in France can hardly be found in England; Hands in a lecture delivered at the Royal Institution before Prince Albert, in 1855, on the subject. Mathematical and classical attainments spoken of. 'Training the mind' is an indefinite phrase; the highly educated men are those who are continually asking simple questions in chemistry or mechanics, and showing themselves as far from the power of judging of these things as if their minds had never been trained; they require to learn the A B C of science as much as or more than children; exclusive attention to literary studies seems to create a tendency to regard other things as nonsense, or belonging exclusively to the artisan, so that the mind gets to run in a particular groove, from which it does not easily extricate itself, and is really injured for the reception of real knowledge. Who are the men whose powers are really developed, who made the electric telegraph, the steam engine, and the railroad? Not the men who had been taught Latin and Greek; the Stephensons had that knowledge which has been habitually neglected in the public schools, and been pushed down below. Asked how he would effect the changes he considers desirable in our system of education, says he finds it difficult to reply; it requires a good man of business, a man educated up to method, and with a knowledge of all things needful in a good education, so to arrange, as in the University of London, that a large knowledge of things in general being required on matriculation, the literary man, the physical man, the medical man, and other classes should, as soon as possible, separate and go to their own special kinds of education. Boys might begin to learn physical science very early if there were competent teachers, a class to be yet created, but might be done without difficulty by encouraging natural knowledge and gradually introducing it into education. Unable, from want of knowledge to compare the training power of classical with physical instruction, he yet thinks that nothing can be so competent to make a young mind think, and logically too, as the action of natural laws. Supposing physical science were introduced, say at Eton, he would teach all boys of ordinary intelligence, and 11 years of age, all those things that come before classics at the London University, namely, mechanics, hydrostatics, hydraulics, pneumatics, acoustics, and optics. Mode of teaching natural science. Time he would devote to it, speaking very generally, would be about one-fifth of the whole time devoted to the studies of the school. In half a century probably more time still will be given to natural science. Reverting to the subject of classical training and its effect, the witness states that men of high education come to him and talk about mesmerism, table turning, flying through the air, and so on, notwithstanding their classical training; the system of education that can leave the mental condition of the public body in this state must have been greatly deficient in some important principle; and nothing, he believes, but a knowledge of natural laws and natural science will ever clear their minds from those most absurd inconsistencies. The study of the physical sciences would not only last through the period of school years, but, like education generally, would never be exhausted; proficiency could be tested by examinations. The classics as connected with scientific nomenclature."

CHAPTER TEN

Tasks Ahead

THE FUTURE into which I seek to peer is that of economic history in the English-writing world. How is it to be synthesized? How can we get team results?

The first and most obvious method is by analogies. I have taken selected towns in Britain for the period *circa* 1830–60. What can Canadians do for Toronto, Montreal, Halifax, Winnipeg over the same space of years? Should it be the selfsame years, in which case in addition to analogue there will be cross-currents: think of Liverpool and Halifax; Glasgow and Montreal; Whitehall and the colonial governors in pre-Ottawa days, wherever they might be? Or should you set out from a corresponding vantage point— 1830, the opening of the Railway Age in England, and therefore say 1850 for the opening of the Canadian Railway Age—in which case you will end with the building of the C.P.R., which raised Montreal to full metropolitan status, to a Glasgow and Liverpool in one, for the summer months only at first: and now, with Montreal air port, for the whole year round?

During the late war I had occasion to compile a report on the economic development of India and Burma, in so far as that was achieved by British enterprise and capital. As I wrote the history of Bombay I was reminded constantly and *fruitfully* (I underline this) of Merseyside. As I wrote the history of Rangoon I was at a loss for an analogue in Britain, which has no Irrawaddy. I needed a continent with a river economy—a Mississippi, a St. Lawrence, a Nile. Mississippi yields this thought: great wealth from the hinterland brought little profit to the fever-ridden denizens of Eden. So too the rice growers of the Irrawaddy delta endured an economy of exploitation, from which traders and overseas consumers benefited, but they hardly at all. Nile yields another thought: the composite value of a river system, yielding transport, irrigation, power, and beauty. This holds for all river systems large or small, witness the water-power stage of the English cotton industry, or the Falls of Clyde at New Lanark. St. Lawrence yields yet a third. In Burma for reasons of geography the line of communication for all traffic, rail, road, and water, is north-south; it is a country of high parallel ranges, running north-south. In Canada for reasons of geography, history, and trends of trade, it is west-east. On the Mississippi, however, it was north-south, while the general line of expansion was from east to west and no insurmountable barriers opposed an overland route. The railroads, therefore, smashed the steam-boat life of the Mississippi, but on the Great Lakes, as on the Irrawaddy, the rival methods are only rival in part. For certain types of traffic the water route is still better, and the two can be made to tie in with one another and with the air. So much for analogue.

The second method, equally obvious, but requiring more detailed research, concerns the chains of business interests which span the ocean. These under the general title of Anglo-American trade relations have for some time interested Americans, and now the study is in full spate in Britain too: at Birmingham under Sargent Florence who is of American ancestry, and in certain coastal universities on either side of the Atlantic. I think of Albion at Columbia and Gras at Harvard, of MacInnes (of Canada) at Bristol and Hyde at Liverpool. I have had occasion recently to run through the MS minutes of the American Chamber of Commerce in Liverpool preserved in the Liverpool Public Reference Library. They are full of good matter for Huskisson's period. American Chamber, I may explain, meant merchants, either British or domiciled American, engaged in the American trade.

In the front rank of this class of study comes the research on which Mr. Hidy is engaged, which I had the honour of reviewing for a recent number of the *Canadian Historical Review*. What Mr. Hidy has done in *The House of Baring in American Trade and Finance* (Harvard, 1949) we must do for the Barings in Canada and in London; and your contribution may be the greater, if, as I believe, there is at Ottawa a unique collection of Baring papers, assembled by the late Adam Shortt. I have heard enough to know that I dare not write "Economic Policy from Huskisson to Peel" without seeing them. But here is a warning. We shall get the background of our own country right unless we are unusually stupid. Let us not crash on the background of the other. To stimulate a highest common factor of background is not the least of my purposes in this course of lectures.

The third method is more formidable, but it must be done one day if we are to make anything of that elusive concept, general economic history. We must ride high over the centuries, and even though our eye is on the Western world, we must have regard to other continents in the past, present, and future.

We in England are almost compelled to a wide view, because we have been the mother country of a chameleon empire. To take a simple case of economic policy: what Britain in the mid-nineteenth century did or did not do for Canada was conditioned by what she had to do (or not to do) for other parts of the world in which Canada then had no obvious interest. The Montrealers forgot this in 1848. Nay more. We in Britain dared not look at the United States only through the spectacles of Canada. In those periodic negotiations with Washington which so exasperated Canadians, we appear as poltroons, giving Canada's case away. But that was because, while Canadians won the 1776–83 war at their end, we lost it dismally at ours; and the sober sense of Britain told her there must be no third American War, however intransigent the United States might be; and I believe that our sacrifice of Canadian claims was worth while if, as was probably the case, it averted war. For the Americans were not bluffing: they were then too buoyant for that.

But economic policy is only a cross-section, or, I should rather say, a longitudinal thread in economic life. The bigger thing is economic civilization, with emphasis on *civis*. I could have made no sense of these lectures if I had presented to you a sextet of our rural countries, and invited you to parallel them! County history is the history of *minutiae—vide* the *Victoria County History*. General history is at the opposite pole. But the history of great towns, as they grow to metropolitan stature, is local enough for variety, and broad enough for generalization. God forbid that I should offer you yet another *Study of History*.

If one starts with fixed ideas, one ends with fixed ideas, whether one is a Toynbee, or a Marx, or an H. G. Wells. We must hold back our generalizations till by argument and illustration they are projected of themselves on the screen.

Sometimes in my academic life, now officially over, I have wondered whether the time spent on lectures is worth while. I think that it is, because constructive lecturing is a two-way thing. Questions asked and answered, paper work done for the lecturer bring him new ideas, as well as, now and then, an introduction to new material: that is one side of it. The other is its part in the economic snowball. There is for the pupil only one right frame of mind in the lecture room. How can I pass it on to others, formally if teaching is my profession, informally if I am only that more valuable entity, an educated human being?

Broadcasting I reject as a vehicle of education except by way of recreation. It is active on one side, passive on the other, unless accompanied by a mass of correspondence which, in order to save its speakers from premature death, the B.B.C. has to deny in advance.

Furthermore, reading, speech, and creative thought are a subtle trinity. Certain of the greatest scientists—Davy, Faraday, William Bragg—have been brilliant lecturers, but they have been assisted by experiments before the class, which Faraday for one rehearsed, as meticulously as Charles Dickens rehearsed his readings. We cannot experiment. We can do something with films and lantern slides, but it is remarkable how often a good scholar spoils his spoken word by slides which do not synchronize or which are unreadable from the back of the room, and at which he himself glances from time to time with as little profit as his class.

There is among the reading public a rather general feeling that historians (however much they may have helped others, under A. L. Rowse's guidance, to "teach themselves history") have not kept level with politicians or scientists in group technique—level with the working parties of the one, or the laboratory teams of the other. We have our Cambridge Histories, Modern, Medieval, Ancient, of India, of the British Empire. Specialists write to an editorial plan and a ruthless rule forbidding footnotes. There is a bulk of bibliography which, however, is *démodé* almost before the volume has been reviewed—at least for recent centuries, since every worth-while new book in that field presents hitherto unknown material. And these defects apart, their great weakness is that in such a specialists' compilation one can so rarely see the wood for the trees. Is there any escape?

Before I make my suggestions let me say most distinctly that when I speak of myself or Professor Alexander Brady or Sir Alexander Gray or Professor Vincent Bladen doing this or that, I do not mean myself or themselves in person, but me for my part, speaking for someone of my choosing, and them for their part speaking for someone of their choosing. And by choosing I mean giving a welcoming hand to those who come forward with a view to a higher degree, when they hear of the tasks we have in mind. The adumbration of these is our share in the business. I envisage these young men starting in their own country, doing much of their work in their own country, coming over at some stage to the country of the other for the enlargement or completion of their work, and presenting their final results to the home base.[1] I can see no disadvantage in a man undertaking a task which is presented to him as part of a larger plan. One fear, I am convinced, is imaginary, namely that more than one may choose the same subject. If it is reasonably broad it will bear several treatments; for, in defining the subject for himself, an intelligent man will individualize it to his own abilities and taste. A secretive or proprietary instinct at the outset of research is merely ludicrous.

In imperial history there is much scope for this kind of team work. I would undertake, in some form or other, "The Place of Canada in the British Economy, 1783 to 1867," if Professor Brady (whom I have not consulted in advance!) would write the complementary volume, "The Place of Britain in the Canadian Economy, 1867 to date." It is essential that both writers should know both Canada and Britain. But it is impossible for me ever

[1]It is almost a law of our trade that in seeking for A we come across B. Let us suppose that B are *Canadiana* in the Public Record Office, Chancery Lane, or a private collection in some country house. These could be earmarked for transcription, if the necessary organization were in being. A senior could tell fairly quickly whether a document is important, and set the transcription in motion, leaving it to juniors, under organization at the Canadian end, to make a fruitful use of it.

to know Canada as well as Britain, or for Professor Brady to know Britain as well as he knows Canada. The switch point is not haphazard, for it stresses what I conceive to be a cardinal point in the evolution of the two economies. And what could be done for Canada could be done, I think, for India, South Africa, Australia, and New Zealand with, perhaps, a different dividing date.

I doubt if any two men could manage this for Anglo-American history. But as England has visiting professors of American history, and America visiting professors of English history, they might prepare the ground and entrust the detail to an English-writing Union which really does write English. Only in one respect should the Old Country be obdurate: no relegation of footnotes, with back chat, to the end of the book. That has been America's greatest disservice to Clio.

Here, were I modest, I should end—but your missionary knows no modesty. I can suggest a duet harder than that which I have composed for Professor Brady and myself. It is for Professor Bladen and Sir Alexander Gray of Edinburgh (I speak in possessive anticipation of my Scottish domicile!). Sir Alexander could unfold to you the evolution of economic thought, beginning where he thinks best and ending where Professor Bladen proposes to step in. To the latter is left the formidable task of showing us how imported theory gradually forgets its origin: how history tries to take its place, but being only history cannot: how a new corpus of economic theory, post Marshall and post Keynes, must arise in our lifetime on this continent, unless theory is to declare itself bankrupt (and the first person to endorse this would have been Lord Keynes himself).[2]

I believe in social, as in academic, planning; and I loathe the laudation of the Industrial Revolution on its evil side, where upstarts were free to swindle and sweat. Institutional planning, regional planning, central planning: these are the hope of society. As one grows older, one thinks of the tasks which (if the grey

[2]It has been urged that Canada should be content for the present to delineate her distinctive economy and give it statistical precision. But you should not confine the success of your plural economy to the national saga, nor the success of Hydro to local admiration, loud or reluctant, as the case may be. It is for you now to place them in general theory: in the theory of sovereignty and the theory of free enterprise.

matter holds out) one would like to perform. I desire to write just one monograph on money, and that monograph on just one episode—I think the most intriguing episode in the history of international currency. The date is September 1838: the scene the Atlantic. On it rides the clipper *Mediator* laden with 104,960 gold sovereigns (exchange value, *tempora mutantur*, $508,318.46) for the Philadelphia mint. It was the bequest of James Smithson, chemist and mineralogist of Pembroke College, Oxford, to the people of the United States for the foundation of the Smithsonian Institution, formally established by Act of Congress August 10,

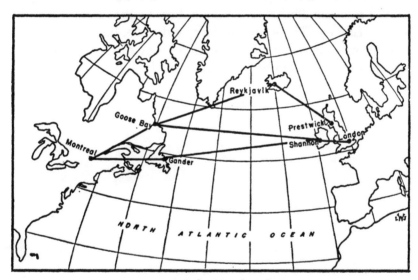

Air map of the North Atlantic

1846. The key note of its policy is the international exchange of knowledge "For the Increase and Diffusion of Knowledge among Men," as its motto runs; and its special study has been meteorology, leading to aerophysics and aerodynamics.

I have before me the guide to the National Aircraft Collection exhibited by the National Air Museum under administration of the Smithsonian Institution. The frontispiece is a giant plane, and beneath it a clipper in full sail. The illustrations within picture the evolution from Icarus and medieval flying demons through Leonardo da Vinci's flying kite and the ballon of the Mongolfier brothers to Orville and Wilbur Wright, December 17, 1903, and beyond them to Charles Lindbergh, World War II, and the jet plane. "On December 17, 1948, the forty-fifth anniversary of the first flight, this famous aeroplane, popularly known as the 'Kitty Hawk' and which had been loaned to the South Kensington Museum in London, England, was returned to America and deposited in the United States National Museum by the heirs and executors of Orville Wright who had died on January 30 of that year." South Kensington retains a model.

Gift and counter-gift. From James Smithson to Washington, D.C. From the Rockefeller Foundation to the Cambridge University Library. These are on the grand scale, but to me not less moving was the return of the manuscript of *Alice in Wonderland*, which American admirers had purchased for a goodly sum, having donated first the glorious Lewis Carroll window with the Tenniel panels in Daresbury Parish Church. And so may it continue to the end!

Index

Lightning Source UK Ltd.
Milton Keynes UK
UKHW010002210722
406167UK00001B/187